A New Pathway
to World Peace

A New Pathway to World Peace

From American Empire to First Global Nation

BY Ted Becker
AND Brian Polkinghorn

RESOURCE *Publications* · Eugene, Oregon

A NEW PATHWAY TO WORLD PEACE
From American Empire to First Global Nation

Resource Publications
An Imprint of Wipf and Stock Publishers
199 W. 8th Ave., Suite 3
Eugene, OR 97401

www.wipfandstock.com

PAPERBACK ISBN: 978-1-5326-1819-2
HARDCOVER ISBN: 978-1-4982-4355-1
EBOOK ISBN: 978-1-4982-4354-4

Manufactured in the U.S.A.

Uses, Directions and Side Effects
of the New State Solution

Uses: This remedy can relieve stress and despair due to long-term American and Israeli policies in the Middle East. Fully digested, it can relieve high anxiety over the increasing threat of wars with Iran, Russia and/or China. Properly taken, it may even lessen regrets over past American foreign policies and worry over the future of the American economy.

Use in place of the "Two State Solution" which has been removed from the market. Use in place of the "One State Solution", to which many Jewish Israelis are allergic.

The New State Solution will lead to much better outcomes than the "No solution," which will create a severe vacuum which will worsen the present conditions and their symptoms.

Directions for Use: Do not take this remedy all at once. It needs to be taken steadily, but slowly, so that it all seeps in. You must take all of it or else aggravated symptoms of "the two state solution", "one state solution," or "no solution" may reoccur.

Side Effects: This remedy may overstimulate the brain into discarding comfortable but debilitating political thoughts and habits. Digesting too much new knowledge creates discomfort. Rethinking dogmatic beliefs and prejudices hurts even more and might even cause nausea or symptoms of Tourette's Syndrome (e.g., eye rolling, throwing the book across the room, outbursts of profanity).

If any of these occur, you need to finish the book.

The Authors

Ted Becker (B.A., J.D., Rutgers; M.A., University of Maryland; Ph.D., Northwestern University.) Becker is the author of 14 books in the fields of Law and Politics, American Government, Global Geo-Politics, and Conflict Resolution. He is the former chairman of the Department of Political Science at the University of Hawai'i and also at Auburn University. He has also been the Distinguished Visiting Professor at California State at Los Angeles and Victoria University of Wellington (NZ), as well as The Walter Meyer Professor of Law at NYU School of Law and the Alma Holladay Professor of Civic and Community Engagement Emeritus at Auburn University where he presently teaches. Dr. Becker is also a professional mediator who was co-founder of the first university based community mediation center in Hawai'i. He also was the Executive Coordinator of Honolulu Neighborhood Mediation Network for the City and County of Honolulu and was Vice President of the Asia-Pacific Organization of Mediators (APOM), of which he was a co-founder.

Brian Polkinghorn (B.A., University of Maryland; M.S., George Mason University; M.A. Ph.D., Syracuse University). The coauthor of several books and many articles on conflict resolution, Dr. Polkinghorn is a Distinguished Professor and Program Director in the Department of Conflict Analysis and Dispute Resolution and the Executive Director of the Bosserman Center for Conflict Resolution at Salisbury University. In 2009–10, he was a Senior American Fulbright Scholar to Israel, at the Evens Program on International Conflict Resolution and Mediation at Tel Aviv University helping launch the M.A. degree there, where he continues to teach regularly. For many years he has worked as a mediator in that region in particular with Israeli, Palestinian and Jordanian scientists, scholars and policy makers to help plan and manage major water project issues. Dr. Polkinghorn has also helped establish graduate conflict resolution programs in Central America, throughout Africa and parts of Asia and was a third party neutral at the end of the war in Nepal. Currently, he is a Fulbright Ambassador and working with UNESCO.

Contents

Acknowledgments

THERE IS A SMALL core of dedicated people whose technical assistance and comments have contributed a great deal to seeing this unusual idea come to print. Patricia Lantz is not only a patient and superb copyeditor but first class reality checker. Over the course of several drafts her attention to details and keen insights helped take a slightly organized idea and shape it into what is now the focus of the book. Matthew Correia also copyedited the book and his fresh eyes fixed mistakes and along the way also detected thoughts and ideas that were in need to clarification. Sara Cukier read the last draft of the book and proceeded to construct the index. Sarah, Patricia and Matthew have made the book easier to read and, we think, enhanced the core focus which is to ask the reader to imagine a lot of unusual "what if" scenarios designed to take an old and vexing problem and to think about it in a new and perhaps creative way.

CHAPTER I

Introducing Ourselves: How Two Americans Became Interested in Israel, Conflict Resolution and This Practical Solution.

CAUTION!!!

N EITHER OF THE AUTHORS of this short book are considered experts on The Middle East and its politics or its ugly spasms of wars over great spans of time. On the other hand, thank God for that. We see our relative ignorance on all the ancient minutiae of the internecine hatreds and regular massacres in that pocket of the world as an advantage we have. After all, look what all the American, European and Middle East "experts" from all cultures, nations and sects hath wrought: a colossal geo-political accident that keeps on exploding and spewing wreckage all over the world.

Sorry to say, but they have certainly helped to create the yawning abyss of pain, deprivation, degradation, suffering and plagues of death throughout that entire region . . . whether they be of Western or Islamic expertise. Worse still, there is the myriad of American experts and American "special interests" who have prodded American government to voluntarily plunge deeper into this whirling maelstrom and who seem, to us laymen, to be totally bewitched and bewildered as to how to conceive an honorable and peaceful solution.

We believe that most Americans are just as weary, as are we, of all these formal and informal, official and unofficial wars in that part of the world in which the United States is a heavy-duty participant, if not principal instigator . . . no matter how many spokesmen and spin-masters reassure everyone that the U.S. military are really there to protect us. Just this century, wars started in that region by the U.S.A. have cost us in the many trillions of dollars, and as far as can be seen at this moment, and as the world is told by the Pentagon, there is no light at the end of a lengthening tunnel. And there is always a new and more deadly enemy.

Thinking that any politicians anywhere in this world today, with the counsel of their colorful array of wizards and solons, will solve this persistent, pressing problem is just wishful. We try to keep drunk drivers off the road. We should try to keep politicians of all stripes and national identities, along with their trusted mini-Rasputins, from making any more bad decisions about America's future role in the Middle East, Central Asia and North Africa. They are drunk with power, are careening wildly off the road, and need to be arrested, not shot, justly arrested.

Our expertise is in conflict resolution. We are both well-trained mediators with many decades of experience in resolving tons of very complicated domestic, interpersonal, labor and international cases. We have many decades of experience in teaching about this at the undergraduate and graduate level and in training a veritable brigade of students and volunteers in the art and science of peacemaking.

Thus, we understand very well how warring parties get locked into bombastic, unrealistic and counter-productive positions, neither seriously nor thoughtfully considering the other party or parties' interests, nor pondering all the negative unintended consequences of what they are claiming or demanding.

When they hit the proverbial wall, and the anger-meter has reached a new high and is beeping: "Danger! Danger! Danger!" one tactic a good mediator needs to deploy is "brainstorming." In other words, it is high time to recommend some imaginative, well-researched options for the killing parties to consider seriously, over time, without dismissing them out-of-hand.

That is the single, solitary goal of this book. Does anyone on Planet Earth have the foggiest notion of how to alleviate or palliate, much less terminate, this tragic vertigo of vengeance and violence in that part of the world or modify Israel's or America's continuing angst about what to do next?

True, some excellent, high-minded and super-qualified peacemakers have spent an inordinate amount of time in gestating a bevy of seemingly sound and workable resolutions over the past half a century. They have constuctured ingenious ways to end the Israeli-Palestine problem, which is at the root of many other Middle East conflicts as well, but all to naught. In fact, the most universally respected of these proposals has been "The Two-State" solution, which almost everyone in the world has thought to be, by far, the best way to go.

However, thanks to Prime Minister Benjamin Netanyahu's campaign promise in March 2015, "The Two State Solution" has now been burned to the ground by the present Israeli ruling elite. Of course, no one knows the full consequences of this maneuver in the near, intermediate or distant future. As we write this, the dominos have hardly begun to fall, but fall they will in the Middle East and North Africa, with ripple effects that are bound to be felt worldwide.

From the title of this book, the reader knows that we think that the United States and Israel need a total rethink of their core interests in order to generate an entirely new way to end this long smoldering international hot-spot ASAP. We hope this book precipitates an in-depth discussion in Israel, the United States, Europe, the entire Middle East and the rest of the world as well. If our idea does not pan out, but produces one or more open, political and peaceful roads to reach a more halcyon destination, then our effort will have been more than worthwhile.

Obviously, there are other serious, global war threatening, conflicts in which the United States is currently involved (Ukraine, Korea, Iran, Syria, South China Sea, and more sure to come). If this one can be successfully resolved in the full manner in which we recommend, then others can follow a similar or more appropriate paths of innovation to heal the other bleeding wounds as well. If peace and prosperity can be brought to the former "Palestine" and its neighboring nations, this would go a long way to calming that entire region and show the world that the United States is more than a one-trick pony.

In this first chapter, we will present a short introduction to each of the authors so the reader can judge for her or himself whether to read on. We do this in the hope of developing a bond between ourselves and each reader, because as any successful mediator can tell you, the key to coming to a mutual understanding in any interpersonal interaction is: trust. What we think each of these abbreviated biographies will show the reader is that each of us has deep ties to the state of Israel, to a love of our own country, the United States of America, and has a long and personal commitment to the innermost values and most pragmatic practices of the field of conflict resolution.

From Newark, N.J. to Hawaii to Alabama to the Indefinite Future

Dr. Ted Becker was born into a professional family during the first years of the Great Depression in 1932. His father was a well-known, upper middle class (for the time) attorney, living in the southern district of Newark, New Jersey. It was named after the local Native American tribe who resided there before the white man intruded: The Weequahic section.

That part of Newark was overwhelmingly Jewish, up to the late 1960s. Weequahic High School was, when he attended it, at least 95% or more Jewish. Though a public high school, it closed on "the high holidays" because the faculty did not want to teach a class with 1 or 2 students in it, that is, if the faculty even showed up.

Newark during the 1940s was the 11th largest city in America and was pretty much divided into highly concentrated ethnic enclaves. So, there was an Italian precinct, an Irish enclave, a Polish district, and a large black section. They all had at least one significant thing in common: Anti-Semitism.

When Weequahic High School would play a football game at Newark's Municipal Stadium, some diehard students who went to see their team lose again (The Weequahic Indians were 0-26-1 in the three years Becker was there), they dared not wear the school colors for fear of being mugged. When its band, one of the best in the state, marched in any holiday parades, people booed and a few threw rotten tomatoes and eggs at the bandsmen and twirlers. Of course, Newark was hardly unique in this regard at this period in American history.

In the 1930s, there was a large German-American Bund movement that supported Adolf Hitler and his Nazi Party and many famous Americans were very public about their hatred of Jews. For example, there were very strict quotas for the number of Jewish students who were allowed at Ivy League and other high prestige private schools, colleges and universities. What is more, an ominous sign could be found here and there in hotels and motels in America that said: "No Jews, blacks or dogs allowed."

In other words, Becker grew up in an America where being Jewish was somewhat intimidating . . . and events in the world only made many American Jews, including him, feel queasy and uneasy about what was to come. In 2005, Philip Roth, who graduated six months before Becker from Weequahic H.S., wrote a novel: *The Plot Against America*, (2004) about what might have happened to Jews in America if aviation hero Charles Lindbergh (a notorious Anti-Semite) had won the presidency of the United States. This was the kind of high anxiety Becker felt at the time. It was a conflict of which he wanted no part and wished, with all his heart, could be amicably resolved.

Undoubtedly, this is part of the reason he wondered whether it was a good idea to create a political entity of Jews in the Middle East smack dab in the midst of all those Islamic people whom he knew were not particularly fond of having Jewish neighbors, much less dealing with them as overlords. Yes, yes, he was well aware of the lengthy and quarrelsome history between the Jewish people in that area and non-Jews and of the Roman rout of them in the first century after Christ.

He was and remains quite aware of the sacred ground that Israel/Palestine is to most Jewish souls around the world. Still, he thought a Jewish nation-state in the midst of hundreds of millions of Muslims could easily become a serious problem for Jews in America and all over the world. A Jewish nation state, THERE, really?

One thing he did like about Israel at that time were the "kibbutzim." Those Jewish agrarian settlers, men and women equally, were portrayed as very sturdy farmers and brave soldiers who shared everything. They were also not the least bit reluctant to defend themselves with force against mean and hostile Arabs who fervently wanted to drive them into the sea as well as perdition.

To him, the "kibbutzniks" were something akin to how the early American pioneers were depicted in the American movies, defending themselves against "savage Indian" attacks. After watching all the newsreel footage of *Kristallnacht,* images of Jews being herded into freight cars and actual motion picture footage of the Atrocity of Auschwitz, it was heartening to see and hear about Jewish people standing their ground and fighting back. So that part of "Israel" sounded pretty good to him. But a "Jewish National State"—THERE—did not.

It was not until Becker became a history major at the Newark Colleges of Rutgers University that he began to get some broader perspective on American history and the two World Wars in which America fought. His father fought in the trenches of the First World War I and his brother was in the first wave of two Pacific island invasions in World War II. He came to realize that, no matter what their personal motivations, both were imperial warriors. That is when he came to grips with the intricacies of and contradictions in American history. That was quite a revelation to him, and some of what he learned there and then became the seeds of much of what is in this book.

He also minored in Psychology, which has had a major impact on his thinking ever since. His father, though, was determined that his son should become an attorney and take over his practice, and so young Becker dutifully went to and graduated from the Rutgers Law School in 1956, loved Constitutional Law, and served for a year on the staff of the Office of the Attorney General of the State of New Jersey.

It was there, in the state capital of Trenton, N.J., that he was dunked into the "real world" of lawyers and judges and legislators. What Ted Becker saw and heard was hardly what he learned in law school. It was just all about politics. As his mother used to say all the time: "It's not what you know, it's who you know." He still hears her words ricocheting in his psyche, and she's still right.

As fate would have it, an opportunity arose for him to bolt from the practice of law and head for a Ph.D. and the life of the exalted Ivory Tower instead. His good luck continued and brought him to the Ph.D. program at Northwestern University, which completely changed his head and life.

It was under the tutelage of a brilliant, kind and wise man, Victor G. Rosenblum (who was a lawyer and a political scientist), that he learned that courts and law and the adversarial system were only one of a number of ways in which human beings resolved conflicts all over the world. One of his Ph.D. committee members taught anthropology at Northwestern Law School, and it was through him that Becker first heard about and came to understand the process and value of mediation as a human way of peacemaking that had been around forever. His brain put that in the "Save for Later" file.

Another member of his Ph.D. committee was a sociologist of the law who had just arrived at Northwestern from Yale. He had conducted a study in Israel of various kibbutzim and how the denizens thereof collaborated so well together and prospered. What Becker learned from him only increased his admiration for these people. They were altruists and idealists to his taste. So, his estimation of Israel climbed a bit more.

A few years later, when Becker was an assistant professor of political science at the University of Hawaii, he accepted an invitation to teach summer school at NYU in Washington Square. He flew to San Francisco, spent the night at the Hilton, picked up his car at the Alameda docks, and began to drive cross country to New York City.

Coincidentally, that day was June 5, 1967. Becker had been aware of growing tensions between Israel and Egypt, Jordan and Syria over the Palestinian-Israeli problem, but that was not in his field of study at the time and was marginal to his life in Hawaii, so far, far away. "Pray for surf" was his mantra. The Middle East was a gazillion miles and four constellations away.

So, when he began his drive toward Sacramento, he was more or less pro-Israel—as the American media had cast the Arabs as drooling aggressors who were an overwhelming and over-the-top military force ready and able to exterminate Israel and its rough and tough but diminutive army. During that first day of the "Six Day War," the American press corps pretty much agreed that the Israelis were provoked and cornered and that the Israeli assault was definitely a well-timed, well executed and well deserved "pre-emptive" attack. There is no doubt that the several allied Arab nations did want Israel destroyed, were planning to do that, but that they overestimated their own strength and underestimated the Israeli resolve and its strategic and technical superiority.

Ted Becker had his car radio on all the way, every day, listening and reading every newspaper he could find from Lake Tahoe to the East Coast. However, by the time he hit New York City, he was convinced that the Arabs actually never stood a chance. If they were such a mortal threat, how come so many more of them died for every Israeli? Being a World War II buff, and looking at Pearl Harbor every time he returned from the North Shore of Oahu to Honolulu, he kept wondering why the Japanese sudden strike was universally called a "sneak attack," but the Israeli's wasn't.

This kind of 1967 media bias reminded him of the 1964 Gulf of Tonkin pretense behind the American escalation of the Vietnam War . . . and that was something he knew a lot about and vehemently opposed. Two plus two equaled three and a half: close but not exactly.

The Israeli and the American military appeared to Becker to be first cousins in Southeast Asia and the Middle East Each was spoiling for a fight with an enemy that looked formidable (the North Vietnamese had crushed the French army), but which intelligence had shown to be weak. The American media was prejudiced and misleading (then and now). By the time Becker reached NYU, Israeli General Moshe Dayan had become General William Westmoreland, but he wore an eye patch and was bald.

Because of those events and since that time, Becker decided to exit the emerging political science field of "Judicial Politics"—which he had helped invent (Becker 1970)— and come to grips with the up and down relationship between American imperialism and Israeli expansionism. Up until 2015, from his point of view, these two countries were like wrangling twins, albeit joined at the hip. The way he has come to see it at this point in time, Israel was, is and will remain as America's largest and most permanent military base in the Middle East, but one which is not nearly controllable under present arrangements.

That's where he stands on Israel. But what about conflict resolution?

As some ethereal force would have it, in 1979-80, Ted Becker and Christa Daryl Slaton founded the first university-based community mediation center anywhere. They called it the *Community Mediation Service (CMS)* and it was created and operated out of the University of Hawaii Department of Political Science curriculum. In other words, students were the heart of the Center—they were the Board of Directors, the mediators, the PR staff, the intake workers, the outreach team, everything. They were paid in credit hours, sort of like internships or directed studies.

CMS was trained in the practice of mediation by one of the top mediation programs in the U.S.A. at the time, the *Center for Conflict Resolution* of New York City. About 15 people were trained at the University of Hawaii in the 3-mediator panel method and practiced it to near-perfection.

Thus, the center was a huge success, but ran into overwhelming external political problems and infernal, internal university politics which in concert snuffed it out. But that is not "The rest of the story."

Despite a string of setbacks mostly at the hands of the legal community in Hawaii (up front and personal "judicial politics"), Becker continued to train students in mediation at the U of Hawaii and continues to do that at Auburn University to this day. He is a great fan of the mediation process as being good for him, good for his students, and good for the communities and professions in which they choose to spend their lives.

Even though Becker has never actually mediated an international dispute, he has been organizing and conducting lengthy simulations for many years at Auburn on what he calls "A Comprehensive Middle East Peace Conference." In this exercise, students play the roles of various nations that are party to the conflict . . . including the U.S., Russia, Iran, Saudi Arabia and China.

His students focus pretty well on it, but the main goal of the role plays is to teach them how to distinguish between "positions" and "interests," since they read Roger Fisher and William Ury's classic book *Getting to Yes* (1980) and thus learn the 4 steps to obtaining a win/win solution through a process called "Principled Negotiation."

In part, through his extensive involvement in teaching conflict resolution and mediation, right up to this minute, Becker has kept in close touch with developments in the Muddle (not a misprint) East, particularly those involving American, Israeli, and Palestinian positions and interests. He insists that he has heard Auburn undergraduate students come up with more novel and practical ways of resolving this ever growing crisis than he has ever heard from any political leader or lead negotiators anywhere—whether American, Israeli, Arab, Russian, Chinese, Norwegian or Saudi. This view is reinforced by his knowledge that his student and volunteer citizen mediators in Hawaii were as good as, or better than, the lawyers and ex-judges he witnessed in various conflict resolutions then and there.

The truth of the matter is that the Middle East, Central Asia, and North Africa are expendable pawns in the "Great Chessboard." This phrase was re-coined by Dr. Zbigniew Brzezinski, the former Columbia University international relations professor/Director of the Trilateral Commission/ National Security Advisor and *Eminence Gris* behind much of American geo-politics (Brzezinski 1999; 2012). Of course there are elites in some of these quasi-countries with their own interests, which are local, economic and sectarian, but they are really being backed and manipulated by huge military/economic imperial powers not in their neighborhood.

What this "game" has led to in the second decade of the 21st century is widespread and ever-growing violence, bloodshed and nonsensical reasons given for why America, the EU, NATO and some Arab Sunni countries work more or less together against others backed by Russia and China and other powers against them. The ever-shifting local coalitions and antagonists on the ground there are highly resistant to peaceful settlement due to long-standing hate and distrust. Western and Eurasian powers seem utterly clueless about what to do about it other than goad, train and feed the dogs of war more and more—in part because they are also the makers and sellers of armaments that most Islamic people use to kill other Islamic people.

In the central part of this gory chaos sits the solitary nuclear power in that entire region, Israel, which itself remains totally outside of international law and numerous resolutions of the United Nations due to its unending occupation of and widely condemned treatment of the Palestinian people—both on the West Bank and in the Gaza Strip. The Zionist Dream has become a global horror movie and the Zionist state a nearly universal pariah that is far more viewed with distaste worldwide, than savored. After all, there are roughly 15 million Jews in the whole world, but nearly 1.5 billion Muslims.

BBC World Service conducts a worldwide poll annually—in collaboration with the University of Maryland's *Program on International Policy Attitudes (PIPA)*—of tens of thousands of people in over 20 countries about whether people view various other nations as negative or positive influences in world affairs. In 2012, Israel ranked near the bottom of the list—tied with North Korea and only slightly ahead of Iran and Pakistan, the two lowest in world favor.

Over 50% of the respondents globally saw Israel in an unfavorable light. Worse yet, Israel's ratings in NATO nations was extremely poor, with over 2/3s of citizens of Spain, Great Britain, France, Canada and Germany giving Israel a big thumbs down. The same 2013 *BBC* poll showed similar results, although North Korea fell a tad behind Israel in the negative ratings, which is hardly something to brag about. (BBC World Service, Global Poll, 2013)

Further bad news is that the trend of unkind thoughts by this sample of global public opinion about Israel was even worse than years before. In other words, Israel is sinking its own ship. The only good news in this poll is that American public opinion about Israel has gone up, in 2012, with 65% of Americans saying that Israel's influence in the world is "positive." (*Jerusalem Post*, 2012).

That is pretty much why Dr. Ted Becker has come to the conclusion that one as yet unimaginable, but eminently doable, way to get a resolution of the Palestinian problem—a clogged artery in the heart of the geopolitics of the region that seems incurable without drastic and novel surgery—would be if Israel were to become a U.S. state. As the reader will find out, when there is a prolonged stalemate in heated disputes, mediators resort to the process of "brainstorming" completely out-of-the-box solutions. So this "wild", "fantastic," "impractical" idea will be thoroughly discussed through-out the rest of this book from many different angles and perspectives.

His colleague on this book has quite a different story, but there are many synchronicities that have cohered to make them co-authors.

From Washington D.C. to Syracuse to a World of Conflict Zones

Brian Polkinghorn was born in 1963 into a decidedly middle class fam-ily. His parents were just starting their careers, with one still in graduate school. The place was Washington D.C. and President Kennedy was in the process of trying to warm the frigid relationship with the late Soviet Union. Soon, his father became a physicist with the Naval Research Laboratory in Washington while his mother was a maternity nurse at a local DC hospital a few miles away.

1960s Washington D.C. was unlike today. Institutional as well as oth-ers social forms of discrimination and exclusion were common-place but the clash of the generations had made for a more tumultuous time. As a child, Brian thought most cities held monthly marches and demonstrations and that all local news should be filled with political intrigue, espionage, protests, riots and other unsettling events that were routine in the District of Columbia, the nation's capital.

The day Dr. Martin Luther King was assassinated Brian remembers his parents talking in the kitchen about the need for medical personnel to come to the hospital fast. Yet getting there was akin to traversing a minefield of pent up unrest that was in the process of flaring. In fact, some parts of the hospital where his mother worked were set ablaze. This was one of his first firm memories of heated social conflict which left him greatly alarmed . . . and deeply wanting it to end.

The early 1970s brought mandatory busing of black children to mostly white schools which was designed, in part, to deliberately reengineer social institutions and, in particular, educational institutions. The general idea was to increase exposure to and integration of diversity and, thus, to mitigate conflict among various racial and ethnic groups using the classroom as the experimental laboratory.

Forced busing was also meant to make corrections to the uneven dis-tribution of resources within education systems and thus provide something of a boost for underprivileged and minority students so that they too might gain access to enhanced educational opportunities that would ultimately ameliorate social conflict. Brian experienced busing beginning in the third grade and all the way up through high school. This elite imposed solution was met with great opposition, and instead produced long term social unrest which continues to this day.

From his perspective, though, busing itself wasn't so much a source of conflict as it was kids learning to figure things out amongst themselves and, frankly, after a decade of trying— things seemed to work . . . at least among those who were most directly involved, the students. In fact, some of Brian's closest friends who originally came to school by bus later moved into his neighborhood and then walked to school with him.

Still Oxon Hill High School had invisible lines. Few white guys went out for football and virtually no black guys ran cross country and yet the cross country guys worked out with the track sprinters who often were black. So the high school melting pot contained not so much a chef-planned soup but more of a potluck stew. Brian learned early that imposed conflict resolution—social engineering by experts—has lots of unintended consequences, positive and negative. Becker learned a similar lesson in Hawaii, where the pros (the bar and judiciary) did not take well to students and community activists resolving local conflicts before they even got to the legal system.

In a large school there is plenty of room for exclusion. By that we mean there were the usual suspects: the jocks, exquisite girls in sororities, burn outs, red necks, thugs, kids who hung together because of where they lived, clusters of common interests (clubs). Then there were the rest of us who constituted what was most likely the majority. For the record, Brian never stood out as anyone special, nor did he achieve anything remarkable. He managed to survive high school as an anonymous face in the crowd. This is something he and Ted Becker also had in common before they met, neither was cliquish, elitist, or a groupie: good traits for mediators.

There were some other indicators, even back then, that DC was a high profile Mecca for both the generation of and hopefully the resolution to some pressing national or international conflict. After all, it is a mass media hub. In addition to many radio and TV stations, it had two major, independent local newspapers and Brian got into the newspaper business at an early age. Like many young boys, including his brothers, he was a newspaper delivery guy for both papers. But unlike many of them, he actually read both.

So in the morning Brian read the liberal *Washington Post's* take on the news and events and in the afternoon read the *Washington Times* conservative version of the same phenomenon. While not a political animal he couldn't help but notice subtle differences in how stories were covered and how certain homes read certain papers. It is here that he developed a mediator's perspective when it came to typical political discourse: There's one side, there's another side. There are many sides.

Reading both or several versions of what was going on and what "leaders" were saying led to a greater appreciation of the true complexity of important, or at least newsworthy, political events. This is how he also learned the subtle, nuanced ways to present stories about political conflict to different audiences and how catch phrases, what we now typically call code words, operate at a subliminal level.

Like Becker, Brian Polkinghorn's little world suddenly expanded when he graduated high school and became a college student. It was at the University of Maryland where he realized that his high school experiences—due to forced integration—were much the same even on a much bigger stage. Even at the humongous U of Maryland, everyone seemed to have a rabid sense of exclusivity based on any form of identity one could muster or invent. What was it that when a conflict arose on campus there was this tendency for people to almost automatically gravitate to one group or another or frame the dispute in terms of race, ethnicity or gender instead of zeroing in on the problem? Why didn't they think about how to negotiate a settlement in which all would find some relief or comfort?

As luck would have it, he took some classes that, in isolation, were excellent but when combined made for a powerful "wait a minute" epiphany. One prof was George Ritzer, who taught Sociology in the area of work, conflict and change. Another was Dr. Kenywn Smith, a social psychologist, who taught about groups in conflict. These courses stimulated his already budding interest in the dynamics of conflict, especially as an form of human interaction and socialization that can lead to functional change, and Brian began to look around campus and see who else was studying (not making) conflict.

Luckily again, there were two giants in the newly emerging field of conflict resolution teaching at UM and Brian took courses from both. Given that he had already learned to read across a political spectrum as a paperboy, Polkinghorn liked the idea that conflict analysts like Professors Burton and Azar were, in essence, data junkies and didn't get their news and information from any one source. They knew well enough that it took 20 other references to get a much clearer idea of what was going on and modeled that for him.

Moreover, they were not into the blame game and didn't personalize issues like politicians are wont to do, but rather kept their focus on the problem almost as if it were a puzzle. This seemed like a brilliant idea – side-step the tendency to get sucked into a nasty dispute, but get close enough to accurately appraise it.

Thus, Brian came to think of all conflicts as being a puzzle, but with many moving parts. That fit his trajectory because when he was a kid, his mother would periodically come to him and ask if he would untangle a piece or two of her costume jewelry. Being tapped to untangle a necklace and presenting it back in all its beauty was a source of great satisfaction to him.

He feels the same way today when he helps very difficult parties, with radically differing viewpoints and changing positions, reach a creative, self-sustaining agreement. And what feeling is that? Great!!! He and Becker share that sense of accomplishment as well.

Then, another turn of events: Dr. Burton had gone to George Mason University in Northern Virginia where he was helping to launch one of the first Master's programs in . . . .Conflict Resolution. What an idea! Let's face it: we learn a great deal from conflict. It is a great change agent as it indicates when institutions and systems are in need of a tune up, are failing, or are so dysfunctional that they have to be dumped into the trash heap of misguided historical experiments.

So college-grad Polkinghorn was off to George Mason where he sopped up a lot more about this emerging field and earned his Masters degree. One day, during a guest lecture, he was totally "blown away" by a visiting professor's description of a project at Syracuse University's Maxwell School called the *Program for the Advancement of Research on Conflict and Collaboration (PARCC)*. Thus, Brian Polkinghorn, D.C. born and bred, went to the snowy climes of Syracuse University to get his Ph.D. in this new field that he had come to really love.

But at Syracuse, something new was added. *PARCC* had a core faculty who were well known for their theoretical work but, better yet, they treated their program as a place for collaborative research where students were treated like young colleagues who were free to explore areas of actual practice and applied research. That environment forged the values and style that would guide him as a professor and practitioner of the wonderful art and science of mediation, particularly with the university as a base and students as equals—something else he and Becker share as values and experiences.

But Israel? A 51st state? How could that ever become a blip on any Conflict Resolution radar in Brian Polkinghorn's life? He's not even Jewish!

It was through gaining several plum fellowships that he lucked into his first solid connections to Israel. There seemed to be a steady flow of Israeli professors coming and going in one of the programs in which he worked. It became very clear to him that many of these Israelis were personally involved in their research and practices, unlike any he'd met before.

He sensed that these Israeli conflict resolution specialists knew they were in the midst of a protracted, deadly dispute that could go either way and which had existential import. So they had a dedication to trying to find ways to co-exist by meeting the needs of the parties. This was not a field of study to them, it was a matter of life and death.

These folks were struggling to create a mutual-gains approach to problem solving that was meant to be carried on to the next generation. These Israelis were not as interested in the identity aspect of conflict as they were in the massive suffering that resulted. They knew darn well what had happened in several Middle East wars since Israeli independence because most of them were soldiers in any number of them.

Unlike their American counterparts, who seemed hell bent on pointing fingers of accusation and guilt, or focusing on theoretical causes of conflict itself, the Israeli contingent was intent on finding pathways to peaceful outcomes. All that study at Maryland, George Mason and Syracuse began to coalesce in the context of Israel and its neighbors. Brian was drawn into the practicality and meaningfulness of their research because of the severity and universality of their conflict.

The way Polkinghorn has come to see it, there is something unique about Israelis. They know they aren't likely to readily get any life-saving help in solving their dilemmas, even from a close ally like the U.S.A., so they push on through and figure things out for themselves. There is a self-sufficiency and recognition of the precarious nature of life that allows for unusual, even "crazy" ideas to be aired that wouldn't be welcome in less threatening situations.

The other thing Dr. Polkinghorn learned from Israelis is that—at this point in time—they have nowhere to go so they have to either fight or really solve their problems, or perhaps a little of both. This exposure stoked his desire to make it his life's work to assist other people-in-deadly-conflict resolve seemingly intractable international conflicts, Israel being just one, albeit of primary importance.

So, Brian began to undertake field work and research in several conflict zones in South Africa, Bosnia, Northern Ireland, Colombia and a few other locales. In the 2000s, he branched out even further, to Asia, working on the peace process in Nepal, participating in Gandhian experiments in India, and in indigenous leadership development in Myanmar. He also had a rewarding gig with the University for Peace in Costa Rica where he taught and was able to work on a large program designed to launch graduate programs in conflict, peace and development in 16 countries.

If you like to travel and are good as a peacemaker, the whole world is your oyster.

Israel, however, still held that special place in Polkinghorn's mind and heart. So, in 2010 he applied for and received a senior American Fulbright award to Tel Aviv University in order to help launch a Masters program in international conflict resolution and mediation. That led to more program developments in several other Israeli universities and from this he started some serious practical mediation on several cross border cooperative projects.

One of those involved working with Jordanian, Palestinian and Israeli scientists on water conservation, waste to energy, and alternative energy projects in the Jordan River valley from The Sea of Galilea to the Red Sea. This was the epitome of what it was he now believes he was meant to do.

But it wasn't Israel that brought Becker and Polkinghorn together. Brian, like Ted Becker before him, had started to run a university-based community mediation program. Unlike Becker, though, Brian's has been a long running project at Salisbury University in Maryland, one which has a well-developed Master's program which emphasizes cutting edge research. One of these futuristic endeavors involved how to utilize new Internet technologies as an enhancement to successful dispute resolution processes. As fate would have it, that was exactly what Becker was doing at the same time and within the same extended group.

So Becker and Polkinghorn got on speaking terms, and as the reader must know, one thing leads to another and then on to another and Presto!: *Israel, the 51st State* was born. Talk about innovative ways of conflict resolution! From here to the end, that's exactly what we intend to do.

Toward a More Perfect Union: How Adding Israel as a U.S. State Would Make America Even More Exceptional

Actually, this idea of Israeli statehood fits mysteriously well into the historical development of the United States of America—as an ever-expanding nation and not an empire—and is also reasonably consistent with Theodore Herzl's (the founder of Zionism) deepest yearning for why Jews needed a "Jewish state". Before we discuss how various states have come to be included as part of the present U.S.A. under analogous circumstances, and how the core interests of the U.S., Israel and all its neighbors would be served well by this merger, we need to explain to the readers of this book something else, i.e., the subtext and subtitle of this book.

We are talking about a concept in wide use today to justify global American hegemony that is now used in certain U.S.A. circles as a compliment, but in certain other capitals and political movements around the world, as a source of outrage. After all, it is because of a strongly held belief by some powerful cliques in the United States about "American exceptionalism" that the U.S. is currently mired in different stages of warfare throughout the Middle East and Central Asia.

To our way of thought, the first thing that needs be done is to rethink and restore this concept of "American Exceptionalism" to what it meant at its birth and through at least a century of its development and the nation's very reason for being. What we are experiencing in contemporary times is its misconception, misdirection and faulty applications, plus a burgeoning global blowback to and anger towards the loud proclamations of it from American leadership of all stripes and the entire U.S. mass media.

Think about it, how would the reader feel about anyone he or she knows, or works with, or encounters, who constantly refers to themselves as being an "exceptional person?" What would the reader think of anyone at work calling themselves the "indispensable" one? If they clearly are not, they are just bombastic fools. If they are what they say, they are irritating snobs and completely insensitive to the feelings of those who must deal with them, to say the least.

All empires think that they are exceptional, above the rest. Imperialism connotes superior—if not divinely gifted— powers. Thus, they explicitly, brazenly, and proudly use force to get their way. They kill. They plunder. They pillage. They exploit the labor of "lesser" people. They imprison, exile, torture, or execute those in conquered or compliant lands who resist them, particularly if the resistance uses countervailing force.

Moreover, empires are prone to laud the virtues of their culture or their religion to justify these acts to their own people as well as the vanquished. They set up governments run by acolytes and compliant local elites who do their bidding for money, status and power. Local resisters to this skewed and lewd arrangement—particularly if they are organized and/or use violence—are tagged with names like "rebels," "insurgents," "terrorists," "savages," "outlaws," "extremists," and on and on.

So, although Americans are never taught to believe that the United States is an empire or has any imperial ambitions, which is not the way most of the rest of humanity perceives the U.S.A. in the 21st Century. What most of the world today sees is a uniquely American-style globe-straddling, chest-beating imperialism.

Americans are taught and psychologically conditioned otherwise. To the vast majority of modern day Americans, the United States is a "force for good" in the world. Of course, there are many truly bad guys out there throughout this world. Some of them are friendly to American commercial and strategic interests. They are called "allies"—as long as they comply with U.S. dictates. Foreign leaders who are not, or become turncoats to American "interests", become spurious "Hitlers"—diabolical Nazi clones who seem to spring up regularly in the contemporary American political lexicon like mushrooms after a rain.

America spends more on military equipment and deployments than the rest of the world combined. Why? Well, someone has to be "the world's policeman." Someone has to maintain global "stability". Someone has to exterminate or exorcize Hitler XIII and Hitler XIV wherever he pops up in this world. It's America's God-given mandate to do all this because, yes, America is "the exceptional one." How many times has the reader heard it?

Unfortunately, that is not what "The City on the Hill"—the core value of original and traditional American "exceptionalism"—was all about. World dominion is not why America was founded or the Declaration of Independence was written. That was not why the American Revolution was fought. Clear words enabling and authorizing extremely warlike federal government interventions everywhere on the world scene are not anywhere to be found in the U.S. Constitution and have nothing to do with the true spiritual-governmental content of original and traditional "American exceptionalism."

In fact, The U.S. Constitution, written for "We the people of the United States," makes it abundantly clear at the outset in its Preamble that the reason for forming a United States of America federal national government is: "in Order to form a more perfect Union, establish Justice, insure domestic Tranquility, provide for the common defence, promote the general Welfare, and secure the Blessings of Liberty to ourselves and our Posterity." It is about preserving, inspiring and improving The United States of America as a nation, not about saving the world from itself or patrolling it or about "regime change" elsewhere.

Actually, according to *Wikipedia*, the very first use of that particular word "exceptional" to describe America was Alexis De Tocqueville in describing its public affairs, democracy and economic practicality. It had zero to do with "global empire." But it had a lot to do with the early American Protestant religion.

According to him: "*they brought with them into the New World a form of Christianity which I cannot better describe than by styling it a democratic and republican religion. This contributed powerfully to the establishment of a republic and a democracy in public affairs; and from the beginning, politics and religion contracted an alliance which has never been dissolved.*"[1] So the very person who coined the phrase linked it inextricably to purely American spiritual values and its inextricable relationship to American local democracy and general civic mindedness.

In Chapter 3, we will show the reader how the laudable purely American goals of being "the city on the hill" have become distorted beyond all

1. De Tocqueville, *Democracy in America*, 1835, Chapter 17.

recognition and the limited continental and/or hemispheric "American empire" that was dimly perceived by a few American visionaries and great men
in the 17th and 18th centuries has become a hindrance towards achieving the
more explicit objectives of the founding of America and the writing and
ratification of the U.S. Constitution in this, the 21st century.

Yes, the United States of America may well be "exceptional" among
nations given its material resources, geographical positioning and unique
political and national development. But it is not as some Godly-endowed,
Heavenly-driven, earthly dominant, militarily imposed imperial super-
power. It is exceptional in its unique form of government and a sense
of divinely destined purpose to make the nation inspirational for—not
dominant over—other peoples on this Earth. What needs be done is to
reset what its exceptionality best means for America (as a nation) and how
it can continue in its quest of "perfecting the union" under present and
future circumstances.

To our way of thinking, one excellent way to do that under the geo-
political realities of the 21st Century, would be to jettison the muscular,
nuclear-tipped empire currently in place and transform into the world's
First (and probably only) Global Nation. One big leap in that direction, a
direction which began with the incorporation of Hawai'i and Alaska into
the Union in 1959, would be to welcome Israel into America's fold.

That step, plus some others which must necessarily compliment it,
would go a long way towards forming "a more perfect union" within 21st
century parameters. It would also eliminate the stigma and self-damaging
aspects of present-day American extra-territorial political and economic
malicious and aberrant behaviors erroneously and/or deviously couched in
terms of "American Exceptionalism."

In Chapter 3, we will also detail how the idea of a new kind of Ameri-
can empire came to be from the first centuries of the settlement of North
America and how that grew into the purely American concept of "Manifest
Destiny"—which drove both the pioneers westward and gave them the
spiritual strength to persist in their quest against incredibly great odds.
It was the drowning of that religious ideal in the vastness of the Pacific
Ocean, and subsequent disfigurements and disguises of it, that have led
America astray to become the "Global American Empire" that bedevils the
present-day American nation, and many parts of this world, to this very
moment in human history.

If the reader is satisfied with the *status quo,* or present day American
so-called "conservative" or "liberal" ways of thinking about present-day
realities and the future of the world and the United States' role in it, then
there is no reason to read on. If the reader is fretful and fearful about the

future of this world and is open to unconventional, novel, thoughtful solutions, then keep going.

Consider the rest of this book to be our attempt to practice—in addition to our devotion to the fundamental principles and ideals of conflict resolution—one of the most singular and best traditions in American philosophy, that of "pragmatism." It finds its motivation in the American desire to break free of mindless tradition, destructive mores, or aggressive behavior that impede material and spiritual growth in the face of new challenges and threats. What we propose might sound weird and undoable, but so did President Jefferson's wild idea of dispatching the Lewis and Clark Expedition into unknown and treacherous terrain, Secretary of State Seward buying Alaska in the midst of the American Civil War or President Kennedy promising to put an American on the moon.

Thus, our proposal, as the reader will see, is not to disparage America as an "exceptional" nation. Instead, we wish to revive and reinvent it while adhering to its best and most noble mission as a revered "City on the Hill" as preached by Jesus in his Sermon on the Mount. We abhor its use as a euphemism for being the overwhelming armed force and fiscal masters of the world—an illusory chimera of all failed imperialistic ambitions.

As for the two authors, we have trod different, but closely parallel, paths towards the same calling. We would like to help bring peace and comfort and God's bounty to The Promised Lands—The Old and New Zions— where humans of all faiths can live in peace and mutual respect, particularly for another's religion.

Sad to say, though, it will take a long time to exit the present yawning morass in the Middle East and elsewhere in which the United States finds itself in the presidential election year of 2016. As the reader will see, this didn't just happen to the United States overnight, it has been a long time coming and is the result of misguided decisions made by a small group of Washington insiders over a century ago and against the contrary advice given and actions taken by other great Americans at the time. It was the latter group who saw exactly the wild and raging flood of negative consequences that were sure to come. Sadly, Americans are living out their tragic forecasts right now.

CHAPTER 2

How We Got Into this Mess: Making Lemonade from Lemons in Geopolitical Terms

S O, EXACTLY WHAT KIND of irresponsible detour was taken and by whom? Something new and shiny was gained, but at the same time, something important to America as an exception to the rule of international power games was lost. And here we are, as the year 2016 begins, on the rim of unfathomable catastrophes for a nation that showed such rare promise and potential.

Global Hegemony and Plutocracy as the Engines of the American Devolution

Let us start our explanation by using the thoughts and warnings of a great American—albeit a person whose name, much less what he said and did, will likely not register with the reader. His name was William Graham Sumner. Like this book's two authors, he was an American university professor who gave a lot of thought to the unique history, and somewhat distant dismal future, of the country he loved.

Sumner was the first political science/social science/ sociology professor at Yale University in the waning years of the 19th century (he graduated from Yale and during his undergraduate days was a member of the super-secret society still known as Skull and Bones). In terms of present day political and economic ideologies, he'd probably best be described as a Libertarian and as a devotee of pretty pure "lassez-faire" economics. He had made a name for himself as a proponent of the emerging philosophy of the time known as "social Darwinism" (a term actually coined by the British which meant "survival of the fittest") —although there is a lot in his later writings which could be read as disputing that.

Actually, Sumner was extremely sympathetic to the common laborer, farmer and entrepreneur whose toil, labor, frugality and devotion to family he thought was the basis for the singular economic and industrial development and national prosperity of the first century of the United States. He called each of these people "The Forgotten Man." (*"Now who is the Forgotten Man? He is the simple, honest laborer, ready to earn his living by productive work. We pass him by because he is independent, self-supporting, and asks no favors."* Sumner 1883)

The people of whom he thought much less were the "plutocrats" (men with wealth who bought political power with money—legally and illegally), who were America's first classic "imperialists." These were not the humble people who made America the great continental democracy he cherished— a self-governing nation of independent small farmers and entrepreneurial merchants and artisans, so well described and admired by Alexis de Tocqueville in his all-time classic *Democracy in America* (1835). They were, instead, the ones who caused, directly and indirectly, the country's most pressing and increasing domestic social, economic and political problems due to their insensitivity and callousness to those who created via hard labor, their own great fortunes.

When elites drive their own citizenry into revolutionary conditions, they often try to stir up trouble abroad. Thus, at the end of the 19th century, as industrialization in America created horrendously squalid and deadly conditions for millions of workers and ordinary citizens, Sumner saw something occur that was novel and portended to be pernicious to that America he knew and loved: an American world-spanning Imperialism being born and nurtured by some American "plutocrats". Being at Yale, he was in the middle of the traditional corridor of banking and political power that runs from Boston and Cambridge to Washington, D.C. and he heard what the "learned", vain, powerful braggarts were thinking, saying and doing.

He was also quite aware of the conquest of that small monarchy way out in the Pacific (Hawai'i) and he was attuned to the plan simmering in Washington, D.C., New York City and Boston to absorb the rotting cadaver of the Spanish Empire in Puerto Rico, Cuba and the Philippines into an American sphere of naval bases and worldly prominence. To Sumner's way of thinking about the quintessential values and history of the United States, this was a drastic departure that would amount to the undeniable extinction of The American Way.

In Sumner's view, if America was to become an "empire" in the British, French, Portuguese, Dutch and Spanish mode of that day and age and competed as such on the world stage with those other world-spanning empires, this would spell doom for the core American values of national and local democracy, small capitalism and free enterprise. He already saw the diminution of those traditional local American ways of life via the development of large banks, corporate monopolies and the emergence of an unapologetic and greedy industrial and banker class. Adding a global imperialist urge and surge to this new wave of centralized and monopolized economic and political power would greatly imperil the America he savored and wished to preserve.

Thus, in 1899 he wrote his most compelling essay, which was the printed version of a speech he gave to the Yale Chapter of *Phi Beta Kappa*. It was published in the *Yale Law Journal* (still considered among the most prestigious of that literary genre) and was titled—sardonically and prophetically—"The Conquest of the United States by Spain." In other words, this new American Empire would, like all before it, including the decrepit Spanish one at its doorstep, be fated to create foreign and domestic wars that would bring the classic and enviable American small capitalist, decentralized democracy down with it. In Sumner's own words:

> "*Now what will hasten the day when our present advantages will wear out and when we shall come down to the conditions of the older and densely populated nations? The answer is: war, debt, taxation, diplomacy, a grand governmental system, pomp, glory, a big army and navy, lavish expenditures, political jobbery — in a word, imperialism . . .* "
>
> "*The point which I have tried to make in this lecture is that expansion and imperialism are at war with the best traditions, principles, and interests of the American people, and that they will plunge us into a network of difficult problems and political perils, which we might have avoided, while they offer us no corresponding advantage in return.*" (1899)

He continued in his prophecy that has become all too true:

> "*The great foe of democracy now and in the near future is plutocracy. Every year that passes brings out this antagonism more distinctly. It is to be the social war of the twentieth century. In that war militarism, expansion and imperialism will all favor plutocracy.*"
>
> "*In the first place, war and expansion will favor jobbery, both in the dependencies and at home. In the second place, they will take away the attention of the people from what the plutocrats are doing. In the third place, they will cause large expenditures of the people's money, the return for which will not go into the treasury, but into the hands of a few schemers. In the fourth place, they will call for a large public debt and taxes, and these things especially*

tend to make men unequal, because any social burdens bear more heavily on the weak than on the strong, and so make the weak weaker and the strong stronger. Therefore expansion and imperialism are a grand onslaught on democracy." (Sumner 1899)

Does this not sound like a lamenting of the very same evils bedeviling America that one can find spewing forth in countless newspaper articles, political speeches, and online blogs in 2016?

True, America had many wars that were fought in North America in the 1600s, the 1700s and the 1800s, but they were all meant to create a great and unique vast "empire" that was set within expanding national boundaries . . . one blessed with a novel set of political and economic values and way of social life. It is also true, as the reader will see later in this book, that there were a number of "visionaries" who thought of and used the word "empire" in their view of America's expansion westward past the Appalachians. However, they had no sense of becoming the same kind of corrupt and rotten imperial system against which they had revolted: effete and brutal aristocracies and monarchies who amassed mountains of wealth to the detriment and demise of peoples in faraway lands.

Not only did Sumner see that America's adventure into foreign-style imperialism would bring about the kind of huge, arrogant, and corrupted government that would rob the American people—"the forgotten men"—of the fruits of their labor and education and personal betterment, but he also realized that it would make America into the world's biggest hypocrite.

Wasn't America all about "individual liberty" and freedom from empire? Are the values of egalitarianism and individual political liberty and those of world imperialism compatible? No, they are not.

All empires consider themselves to be superior civilizations to those they conquer, colonize, oppress and drain. Any people in those remote places who resist are robbed of their "liberty" forthwith. So how can the United States of America—go beyond its national boundaries— become The American Empire and be true to its original, deep national spiritual, economic and political values? It can't.

Sumner saw that such was impossible, a blatant and inexcusable hypocrisy.

*"We know what is good for you better than you know yourself and we are going to make you do it. (*The reason these words are*) false and wrong is that they violate liberty; or, to turn the statement into other words, the reason why liberty, of which we Americans talk so much, is a good thing is that it means leaving people to live out their own lives in their own way, while we do the same. If we*

believe in liberty, as an American principle, why do we not stand by it?" (Sumner 1899).

Worse yet, those words used by any traditional imperial entity are just cants and chants to obscure their real goal: to suck the lives and lands of faraway places dry for the benefit of a few "special interests" in the imperial homeland. According to one of America's all-time greatest war heroes, U.S. Marine Major General Smedley Butler (one of only two Americans who won the Congressional Medal of Honor in two different wars): These imperial wars are just a "racket"—exactly like organized crime—except the hit men wear uniforms and convince themselves that they are idealists doing a tough job. Here is how General Butler put it in a speech he gave to the national convention of the *Veterans of Foreign Wars (VFW)* in 1933:

> "*I helped make Mexico, especially Tampico, safe for American oil interests in 1914. I helped make Haiti and Cuba a decent place for the National City Bank boys to collect revenues in. I helped in the raping of half a dozen Central American republics for the benefits of Wall Street. The record of racketeering is long. I helped purify Nicaragua for the international banking house of Brown Brothers in 1909-1912. I brought light to the Dominican Republic for American sugar interests in 1916. In China I helped to see to it that Standard Oil went its way unmolested."*
>
> "*During those years, I had, as the boys in the back room would say, a swell racket. Looking back on it, I feel that I could have given Al Capone a few hints. The best he could do was to operate his racket in three districts. I operated on three continents."*(Butler 1935).

There is also an excellent 10 minute re-enactment of his speech to the *VFW* on YouTube called "War is a Racket")

What General Butler did in the juvenile days of the new international American Empire pales in comparison to what the American Imperial Forces of 2015-16 are doing today and plan on doing tomorrow and, absurdly, forever after. President Eisenhower in his Farewell speech of 1959 warned America how the new modern equivalent, which he called the "military-industrial complex," was taking over America to the detriment of American democracy and the American people. Even he, as the Supreme Allied Commander in World War II, could not have imagined what kind of Frankenstein Monster he helped create.

The American Empire, as we will show, has become analogous to a widespread bacterial infection on the world body politic. But the world's immune system is reacting organically and mechanistically to purge it and the parasite is killing its own political body host, the U.S.A.

The Only Unified Global Political Ideology in the Early 21st Century is: Anti-American Imperialism

This two-faced aspect of America's identity on the world scene in 2015 (and surely into and through 2016) does not go unnoticed by many nations and political leaders in this world and, worse yet, it makes people distrust and even despise the U.S.A. as never before. The United States is no longer widely believed to be a staunch defender of great political principles like liberty, justice, freedom, free enterprise and democracy, it is now much more widely perceived as a gigantic financial hustler using strong armed—even science fiction-like—tactics to "rule the world." "The Leader of the Free World" now has no clothes.

As we will show later in this book, the principal reason they think this way is because today's version of American imperialists and militarists explicitly and often boast that such is precisely their goal, i.e., to be The Global Dominator. They mince no words. They even think they are eloquent. We will quote liberally from a book written by their chief thinker and architect in the Epilogue from a book he and a colleague wrote in 2015 updating their goals into the indefinite future and use it to show how ruinous a path this would be to America and the rest of the world.

But people all over the world read about or experience (directly or vicariously via TV and the Internet) this incessant American obsession with violence, controlling the world and global loan sharking. Only the general American public is relatively clueless about these sobering truths, which is the harsh reality to so many humans alive today everywhere but in America. Even of those Americans who are either vaguely or keenly aware of this situation, and what a negative image the U.S.A. has earned internationally, few question how antithetical this imperial theory and activity is to the best values of what this country has traditionally had to offer.

Rule the world? Isn't that what 500,000 Americans died fighting against in World War II? Weren't the Nazis and the Japanese Empire all about "ruling the world"? Wasn't America the great defender of "liberty" and "freedom" and "democracy" against Soviet Communism who proclaimed it was the vanguard of the world's proletariat and was destined to overthrow global capitalism and rule the world? When did the American people ever say they wanted to rule the world? No poll or survey or politician ever asked that question. That is because it would have been voted down by huge majorities. It is, in Sumner's words, the plutocrats of America, together with their allied corporate, military and financial plutocrats worldwide, who entertain such hallucinations of grandeur.

Does the rising behemoth China, four times the population of the United States, believe in American democracy? No way. In fact, the Communist Party of China routinely mocks American democracy—and is seriously challenging America globally with its oxymoronic model of what Karl Marx would wince at: "State Capitalism". And what is that exactly? It is precisely what its founder, Deng Xiao Ping, said it was: "It doesn't matter if a cat is black or white, so long as it catches mice." Well, this cat was and remains Red, is very large and the American mouse owes it an awful lot of money, which to the Chinese Communist Party is pungent cheese to bait the voracious rodent.

Does Russia believe in America's "democracy" and its claims to be a generous and fair arbiter of world affairs? Of course not. President Vladimir Putin—whose popularity soared once he annexed the Crimea— detests the goals of the American geo-political "game", one into which we will delve later.

In the meantime, Russia is heavily involved in several alliances with small and huge countries all around the world in order to outflank and outwit what they see through their own historical prism as American economic and military aggression. That is the reason for their military build-up in Syria; for their wanting the Eastern Ukraine to become "autonomous states"; for their war games with China in the Mediterranean Sea and the North China Sea. There is more to come from Russia, which will not roll over and play dead for The American Empire. Both are playing a zero-sum game in which everyone loses.

What about Islam? The U.S.A. is loathed by large majorities of Muslim populations, with more than enough evidence to interpret American attacks throughout the region as a modern "crusade" against Islam. President George W. Bush personally gave them enough ammunition to feed the belief that America was not fighting "terrorism" and for "liberty" and "democracy"—but against Islam itself: "Alia Toukan, a Jordanian journalist and media consultant who has lived in both the United States and Canada, said her suspicions and other Muslims' suspicions about American motives are personified in President Bush, a born-again Christian who used the word "crusade" five days after the terrorist attacks of Sept. 11. 'This crusade, this war on terrorism is going to take a while,' the president said.'" (*ABC News*, Harris and Walters).

Using that word "crusade" may not have caught many American ears, but it certainly registered loud and clear throughout the world—even outside Islam. According to the *Christian Science Monitor*: "President Bush's reference to a "crusade" against terrorism, which passed almost unnoticed by Americans, rang alarm bells in Europe. It raised fears that the terrorist attacks could spark a 'clash of civilizations' between Christians and Muslims, sowing fresh winds of hatred and mistrust (Ford, 2001).

All of this killing, war-making and militarization of American society is sapping the moral, entrepreneurial, democratic and economic energy of the United States—as Sumner brilliantly predicted—just as it is destroying its natural resources and geographically secure position in the world. All sorts of previously unthinkable political-economic alliances are cropping up with only one shared goal: to topple this outrageous "American hegemony" reinforced daily by threats, doctrines, drone attacks, air attacks and secret missions to topple American-unfriendly regimes.

Sad to say, but the U.S.A.—and its former imperial allies in Europe— are in the midst of some aggravating and aggregated "imperial blowback": some economic, some military, and some "terroristic." If this comes as a shock to the reader, who, a few decades ago, could have imagined such an alliance as the *BRICS*? What conceivable interests could nations as huge and different in their political and cultural systems as Brazil, Russia, India, China and South Africa have in common so as to form a loose, but very real, "alliance"? Obviously, given the tremendous spatial and cultural distance between them as well, one might say "absolutely none."

Unfortunately, though, they are unified in only one way: To counter American Imperialism politically, economically and culturally. Even in the Western hemisphere, there is a new and growing alliance between many Latin American countries along with others in the Caribbean to stand up to and reverse a century plus of "Yankee imperialism." They recently established one organization called *UNASUR*. They have others.

One of them, called the *Summit of the Americas,* told President Obama in no uncertain terms in 2014 that Cuba would be part of them in 2015 whether the U.S. liked it or not. So, now Cuba and the U.S. have re-established "diplomatic relations" with commercial and societal thawing on the way. However, the way we interpret it, all this is simply changing tactics, with the ultimate goal of regime change in Cuba still the Holy Grail in the Caribbean for American strategic believers.

Sad to say, the American plutocrats with "special interests" throughout Latin America are trying to roll back "The Pink Tide" in many ways, mostly political and economic (and we hope not militarily). These folks don't like to be shown the door and want to prolong their dominance over their Latin neighbors to the south forever, if at all possible.

Nonetheless, The Global Anti-American Imperialist movement continues to gain traction just as the United States of America is falling deeper and deeper into national debt with an economy that is getting worse for most Americans. This resistance is sprinkling a number of "hot spots" hither, thither and yon, each being unto itself a potential powder keg to set off a truly global holocaust. American Imperialism, particularly with its intimate interaction with carbon energy industries (coal, gas and oil), continues to increase exponentially the unprecedented natural disasters that are inherent in what more and more climatologists fear: Rapid Climate Change. Time is not on humanity's side, much less America's. A lot needs to change, and fast.

Like what? America needs to get truly conservative, that is to conserve our most traditional and positive value systems, literally, not figuratively! And what would that entail? First and foremost, it would mean that Americans need to regain control over their government and get it to abandon "The American Empire" and maintain zero foreign bases—instead of the many hundreds it sustains and needs to pay for in many ways. The U.S.A. is well in excess of the military power it needs to defend itself against any foreign aggression, all of which is deployed right now on its own national turf and coasts, not to mention America's nuclear submarine and cyberwar capacities.

The people of the United States need to make the Department of Defense live up to its name and not be, what it used to be called, The Department of War. When this is done, there will be no more enemies to fight abroad . . . and the global Anti-American Imperialist movement will start to fade into history and the "military-industrial complex will shrivel back to a more reasonable size and dwindle its influence on American society.

But what about the Islamic State (IS or ISIL or ISIS) and the Arab hatred of Israel? What about China's expansionism in Asia, Central Asia and globally? What about the new Russian-Chinese strategic alliance? What about Iran's nuclear program? What about "The Pink Tide" in Latin America? To our way of thinking, the most probable scenario for the near future is the "Multi Polar World."

We realize that there is a historical pattern, as Franz Fanon astutely observed in his famous book *The Wretched of the Earth* (1961, 1963), where the formerly oppressed morph into the oppressor (Fanon 1961, 1063). But we do not think—given America's unimaginable capabilities of mass destruction, extraordinary ingenuity for economic growth, plus the international interdependence for survival that will be necessary in the future—that such a negative reaction is the direction the world will take after an American imperial drawdown.

Of course, the political and military expansion of The American Empire has wreaked some terrible hardships on many people on Planet Earth which cry out for rectification. Thus, there needs to be some leaps taken by the U.S.A. that could significantly ameliorate their problems which, in turn, would help the United States grow into an even more formidable power that performs good deeds for all, as was intended from America's insemination.

America does not need more land to settle as in earlier centuries. It does need to re-establish its well-deserved reputation as a leader in personal liberties, religious freedom and tolerance, and technological innovation, all of which are necessary to make this world a better place for all. And it can show the world that it still has political skills and will to make good things happen.

Incorporating Israel into the First Global Nation

Israel is a unique and powerful state in the Middle East which would not exist but for America's empathy with and recognition of this Jewish state in the first place, plus the generous amount of fiscal and military support it has given to Israel since 1948 both from government and private sources. If and when the United States is compelled by political, economic and natural causes to withdraw all its military from the Middle East, what would happen to Israel then?

Israel is probably the best armed nation in that region, including being the only country there that just about everyone believes to have a hidden cache of nuclear weapons, with the military hard and software to deliver them. But the last thing the world needs now or in the immediate future is an all-out slugfest in the Middle East with nuclear missiles and bombs flying around and creating tens of millions of casualties and a tidal wave of refugees that would make the one from Syria to Europe in 2015 look like a creek.

The deal brokered by the UN Security Council + Germany with Iran in mid-late 2015 to block Iran's alleged path towards nuclear missiles has lessened the chance that such a miscalculation will ever occur. However, given the jumble of global politics in that region, one never knows if and/or when the present or future Israeli leadership might decide on a preemptive attack, since it presently remains a sovereign nation in charge of its own foreign policy.

Given the self-perceived perilous position of Israel right now, it would become even more so if the U.S. removed all of its bases in Qatar, Kuwait, Afghanistan, Diego Garcia, and throughout the Mediterranean Sea. Israel cavalierly continues to defy UN resolutions and international law by expanding settlements into Palestinian land and thus increases pushback and enmity from neighboring Islamic countries—particularly Iran.

If the United States withdrew all of its forces from the region, Israelis, feeling even more isolated and insecure, might try to expand their borders at an even greater pace than at present. This would surely provide even more cause for war against them, and, in return, give Israel greater motivation for military retribution—some of which could drag the U.S., Russia, and China into nuclear or other serious and violent confrontations.

That is why we think that the best solution to the already precarious Israeli situation—before the eventuality of a nearly total American military drawdown on the ground in the Middle East, Central Asia, North Africa and Europe occurs—would be for Israel to become an American state. Whoa, you say, that could never happen. America having a state in the Middle East with all those Jewish and American hating Arabs on its borders? Israel giving up its national sovereignty? No way, Jose.

Yes, we realize it sounds improbable if not completely impossible given present day perceptions. But as we will soon show, there have been similarly unlikely conditions for various political entities to become American states. Yet all have turned out well for those states and America as well. As we proceed we will demonstrate:

- How it can be done in terms of the unique political process of gaining American statehood;

- How it would conform to the primary goals of Jewish Zionism;

- How such a political move can transform the Middle East from a powder keg into a major American-led supplier of global sustainable energy, inter-denominational collaboration, and producer of food for all.

Thus, the re-formed United States of America would stand very tall in the emerging Multi-Polar World as the world's first and only Global Nation, one dedicated to peace in The Middle East and to global ecologically sustainable growth—if not prosperity. Doesn't this sound more "practical" than an endless set of wars in that region? Joining hands with a peaceful and neighborly Israel would also demonstrate to one and all that America has reinvigorated its spiritual self, an identity which was such an important factor in the development of the American nation to the end of the 19th century.

That is the essence of what has been called "American Exceptionalism" and that will be treated at length in the next chapter.

CHAPTER 3

Rethinking American Imperialism and Exceptionalism in the 21ˢᵗ Century

D REAMERS OF AN ENDLESS expansion of American values and power have been with us from way before the American Revolution. In fact, arguably it was the British Proclamation Line of 1763 that forbade American colonists from going any further west than the Appalachian Mountain range that was an even more incendiary cause of the American Revolution than the-then extremely perplexing and vexing issue of "taxation without representation."

It was clear that this new law or "proclamation" was intended to cage American colonists within an arbitrary geographical boundary imposed by a Royal Court in far, far away London. However, many strong willed and highly capable Americans were inner driven to develop this "exceptional" country and explore far beyond that line on some Brit-centric map and for a wide array of reasons: trapping, the fur trade and tariffs being the least of them. Both secular and religious missionary zealousness were at least as important, if not more so. So let's look back to America's founding.

An American Empire and American Exceptionalism Are Traditional American Ideas and Ideals

It can safely be said that some great Americans of the early days of Colonial America and the American Republic were convinced that the new America being formed in the eastern part of what is now called the United States of America would someday be the predominant country influencing huge swaths of the planet earth, i.e., being an exceptional country. Yes, a few dared call it "empire" even back then, as that word was known in English at the time, that is, a political and military expanse on Earth upon which "the sun never set."

This very early sense of American exceptionalism and imperiousness in the future, however, mostly had its primitive compass pointed due West and due South, for the most part of its first two centuries, but to some day-dreamers, it was an infinite and yet unimagined horizon in every direction. Two of the most vocal and inspirational of these men were Congregational-ist ministers by the names of John Winthrop in the early 17th century and Jedidiah Morse in the late 18th century . . . each whose combined religious and political concepts are greatly unappreciated by Americans to this day.

In fact, we see that Christian missionary zeal, combined with a steady growth of democratic ideals in the spirit and behavior of other American colonists, as being two major strands in the DNA of the United States from its birth in 1789. They combine to make an "innermost core interest" of America, the conflict resolution implications of which we will discuss later in this book.

So for all American citizens who, to this very day, are squeamish with the idea that America is, indeed, an "imperial power", if not "THE imperial power" at this very instant, this is to prove once and for all that it has always been so in the minds of some of the greatest of Americans who founded, trampled and hacked trails and gave birth to this country. It is not just some claptrap conjured by modern left wing intellectuals who are anti-American, or by some "liberal intellectuals" who chafe about some sick clique of glo-balist power sharks swimming at the pinnacle of the American food chain in the 21st Century.

And it surely is not simply a propaganda ploy by the Supreme Leader of Iran (who calls America "The Great Satan"), Putin (Hitler, the Fifteenth) and the Chinese Communist Party who both refer to the U.S. as the "global hegemon." No, it is an Original American Inspiration come to, if not well past, its fruition.

Recognizing that the idea of an "American Empire" has been with us for a long time, for the purposes of this book, is a "reality check" in the extremely complex history of the United States. In other words, the concept of The Great American Empire is neither something new nor un-American. Instead, it actually has deep Biblical and tangled historical and political roots.

Indeed, the viewpoint that there is a widening space under an ever-swelling American dome lit by a Heavenly devotion to God is at the heart and soul of American expansionism to this minute in time even though it has been well camouflaged by a more material, self-absorbed rhetoric in recent and present times. So, whether it be called "The City on the Hill" or "The American Empire", these ideas and beliefs are both fundamental to

American political and moral thinking and have been through its nationalist infancy to its current globalist senility.

Its threads run as through a mural that actually began long before the Declaration of Independence, endured through the American Revolution, and kicked into over-drive upon the ratification of the U.S. Constitution (in 1789). We will show how it came to be known as America's 'Manifest Destiny,' and eventually deform itself into what a Secretary of State called the modern United States: "the indispensable nation." (Albright 1998)

The Growth and Development of the God-Blessed and Ordained American Empire: Manifest Destiny from Sea to Shining Sea

Most Americans do discover in their high school history books that there was actually an American theory of western expansionism that was called, rather early in its maturation, "Manifest Destiny." What they take this to mean is pretty much accurate. Manifest Destiny is a narrative about the irresistible lure of the seemingly boundless American western frontier granted to America, and to all who came to America's shores to find "liberty," by God's grace.

There were two basic parts to it: (1) a challenge to conquer a gorgeous, precarious, already populated terrain upon which they could squat and build the ever growing American nation and (2) as a glorious gift from The Good Lord that should be transmogrified into His purposes—social, economic, political and spiritual—for the good of all humanity.

"God Bless America" is not just a song. It is a popular musical testament about the deep and strongly held early belief that America was bequeathed "The Word" and a huge fertile land, and this was to be spread further than the early American eye could see or its infantile psyche could possibly fathom.

The third English colony on mainland America, founded by those whom many Americans refer to as the "Pilgrims", settled in Massachusetts in 1620, were avowedly on a religious mission—and they were fleeing from heavy handed Anglican persecution in England. Ironically, though, they had their own unique, vertical, rigid authoritarian system of church and secular governance, which many refer to as a "theocracy."

The fourth major English settlement, the Massachusetts Bay Colony, was a slightly different breed of Calvinism from their brotherly Pilgrims . . . and it is this "Puritan" movement that put the American spirit on a strong missionary quest to live the Godly life, combined with a primitive and/or confederate structure, which its leader and his followers believed were entirely consistent with The Scriptures. Pure, simple, strict Christianity in the spiritual realm, but a somewhat more democratic way of selecting the ministry and some local leeway in interpreting the Bible, were the "Congregational" way that has played a key role in America's history up to the 20th Century.

So, exactly what was that "Word" in the "Scriptures" that has been worshipped, believed, embraced, acted upon, and kept sacred from the very germination of the New America, or as it was actually called by its founders, The New Zion? It is that passage from Jesus' "Sermon on the Mount", the one that proclaims this as THE Christian mission:

"You are the light of the world. A city set on a hill cannot be hid. Nor do men light a lamp and put it under a bushel, but on a stand, and it gives light to all in the house. Let your light so shine before men, that they may see your good works and give glory to your Father who is in heaven."—Jesus, from the Sermon on the Mount, Matthew 5:14-16.

Thus began a departure from England of a group of anti-Anglicans (who believed ardently in the separation of church and state) under the tutelage of the aforementioned *John Winthrop*. In a sermon on board one of the boats, which was given in a question and answer format, he laid out some basic premises upon which their colony would prosper if they heeded the message correctly. It is in this *Sermon on the Arabella* that the idea of "American Exceptionalism" was born.

He proclaimed that God had chosen these people to go to America and excel in creating a prosperous Christian community, working individually but together towards God's purpose, so that it would become "The city on the hill" that the whole world would notice and learn from. By pulling together—rich and poor, young and old, men and women, as a community—and not as individuals, this could be done. There would be no central church, only separate congregations who elected their ministers, smaller religious communes which, at first, even met in homes without erecting any edifices devoted only to prayer and religious discussion.

One American historian called this "The New England Way," and this is part of how he explains it: "First, they believed in both personal and collective autonomy within each village or settlement. Their faith, which survives to this day, was known as Congregationalism. That gave them local control over both religious and political matters. The well-known New England town meeting was the secular spin-off from their idea of church self-government." (Sage 2010)

The history of the Congregationalists is far more complex and divisive than we need to go into here. Suffice it to say that heated dissent within the church involving things like the extent of tolerance of divergent opinions about Calvinist predestination; individual conscience; and fair compensation for land taken from the Native Americans. Perhaps most of all, though, there was the deep tension between the more theocratic and aristocratic leadership of men like Winthrop and Cotton Mather and the more democratic principles of Roger Williams and his colony-in-exile at Providence, Rhode Island.

The latter's disagreement with the theocrats was about who should be admitted to the church and allowed to vote. Williams' view was that all the members of the congregations, not just those who passed a religious bar exam given by a self-appointed already-anointed elite, should have an equal say in secular, and even spiritual, matters.

The ascendant theocrats, however, ultimately went "a bridge too far" in their anti-witchcraft frenzy in 1692, when they executed a number of people for being witches and warlocks in Salem, including a rather popular male minister. The repercussions of this repression from the top reverberated deeply through the Puritan communities to the detriment of the Mathers, who had become in their way the high priests of this relatively humble religious society. The chief witch hunter, Cotton Mather, confided to those close to him, after the executions he championed, that people had begun to let their true feelings against these injustices be known, but behind his back. It was the beginning of the end for this distortion in Congregationalist secular theory. (Schiff, 2015)

Looking at the whole patch-quilt, the emphasis laid upon individual participation in governing local community matters intertwined with their religiosity, was a key part of "The New England Way" –which spilled over into the development of The New England Town Meeting. This latter institution is particularly important to understanding American—and thus modern world—history.

Perhaps the greatest minister who advocated the democratic aspects of Congregationalism against the more hierarchical minded, "divinely selected" leadership was Rev. John Wise, who published two volumes espousing the true Biblical nature and superiority of democracy over both monarchy and aristocracy. In fact, he vilified monarchy as being a "monster" of Biblical proportions and ridiculed the idea that learned and so-called virtuous men could rule in the interest of all the members of the church and villages.

His most persuasive, permanent and productive work was called *A Vindication of the Government of New England Churches* which was first published in 1717 but republished and became most famous well after his departure from Earth in 1772—when it served as some part of the inspiration for the *Declaration of Independence*. The importance of John Wise is not in his person, his speeches, his sermons or his books.

His significance is that he was able to state clearly for all the common Congregational Americans what the vast majority of them really thought, believed in and actually did. This was despite the overbearing self-righteousness of most of those who called themselves the leaders of their theoretical anti-hierarchical church, but who harbored hidden agendas for personal and communal elite power.

Here is how one of America's greatest historians, Professor Vernon Parrington, describes the transformation of Congregationalism due to the excesses of the punitive, hierarchical theocracy in his classic treatise *Main Currents in American Thought* (1927):

> "*After a spirited contest lasting three-quarters of a century, theocratic Puritanism yielded to ecclesiastical democracy. For two generations it had remained doubtful which way the church would incline. Dominated by gentlemen* (sic), *it was warped towards Presbyterianism* (Author's note: centralized hierarchy); *but as interpreted by commoners, it leaned towards Congregationalism* (Authors note: decentralized, democratically organized congregations)."
>
> "*The son of a plebeian, Wise inclined to sympathize with the . . . facts of the New England village world. The struggle for ecclesiastical democracy was a forerunner of the struggle for political democracy which was to be the business of the next century.*"(*Parrington 1927, Vol I., Ch. 3.*)

So, it is this Congregationalist/individual community/democratic dynamic—paired with that of the "City of God" mission—that laid a fair part of the foundation for the westward growth of America from its narrow confines on the Atlantic Coast, to and through the Appalachians, clear out to the Pacific. Together they became a strong underpinning of the twin aspirations for Independence and Revolution against the centralized, mercantilist, hierarchical, aristocratic, theocratic British system and the development of a whole new kind of continental empire.

Paul Frymer, a Professor of Politics at Princeton University, started off a recent scholarly paper—titled "Building an American Empire"— with a series of quotes from some highly revered American folk heroes and patriots way back to demonstrate how deeply ingrained the idea of a new kind of American Empire is in yore and lore (Frymer 2010). Here are three of them:

> "*Where wretched wigwams stood, the miserable abodes of savages . . . we beheld the foundations of cities laid, that in all probability, will rival the greatest upon earth.* —Daniel Boone, 1784 (emphasis ours)

"*The [Constitution] speaks its own importance; comprehending in its consequences, nothing less than the existence of the UNION— the safety and welfare of the parts of which it is composed—the fate of an empire, in many respects, the most interesting in the world.*" —Alexander Hamilton, 1787 (emphasis ours)

"*[I]t is impossible not to look forward to distant times, when our rapid multiplication will expand itself beyond those limits, and cover the whole northern, if not the southern continent, with a people speaking the same language, governed in similar forms, and by similar laws; nor can we contemplate with satisfaction either blot or mixture on that surface.*" —Thomas Jefferson, 1809 (emphasis ours)

One of the first clear indications of this strong urge to actualize the American expansionist dream throughout this continent (or hemisphere) was President Jefferson's paying a few million dollars to France for an enormous tract of land west of the Mississippi called the Louisiana Purchase in 1803. After all, Jefferson, himself, was a fervent devotee of Jesus Christ's teachings and even cut and pasted his own bible of Jesus's teachings (*The Jefferson Bible*, see References for online links).

It almost goes without saying that Thomas Jefferson was also among the greatest of American pro-democratic philosophers and a major intellectual and political force behind *The Bill of Rights*. Put them altogether and "The New Chosen People" now had an incredible trove of land open for them to fulfill God's mission and spread this unique American Christian Democracy light years beyond what even Jefferson's futuristic eye could see.

Although the specific concept of "Manifest Destiny" did not really gain momentum until many decades later in the Westward expansion, Jefferson himself had already laid one of the theoretical cornerstones of it through his unique concept of an "empire of liberty" during the Revolutionary War. It was then that he told a famed frontier Indian and Revolutionary War fighter, George Rogers Clark, that: " *. . . in the event of peace [ending the American Revolution]...we shall . . . add to the Empire of liberty an extensive and fertile Country thereby converting dangerous Enemies into valuable friends.* " (*Wikipedia*, "Empire of Liberty", emphasis ours). As President, he added a third more land upon which to plant his avidly held American ideals of separation of church and state, decentralized democracy, entrepreneurial fueled commerce and what he believed to be the pure teachings of Jesus.

This original and emerging public theory of a divinely inspired cultural, territorial and political expansion of U.S. political and moral values was emblazoned in print cleanly, clearly and emphatically by a writer named John O'Sullivan in an 1839 journal called *The United States Demo-cratic Review*. Here is the phrase that captured it so well in the author's original words:

> *"The far-reaching, the boundless future will be the era of American greatness. In its magnificent domain of space and time, the nation of many nations is destined to manifest to mankind the excellence of divine principles; to establish on earth the noblest temple ever dedicated to the worship of the Most High — the Sacred and the True. Its floor shall be a hemisphere — its roof the firmament of the star-studded heavens . . ."* (O'Sullivan, 1839. Emphasis ours)

He goes on to elaborate on America as the "Great Nation of Futurity" in a way that has in the eyes of many, if not most of today's Americans, is a prophecy come true . . . even well beyond America's initial continental turf. O'Sullivan continued:

> *"This is our high destiny, and in nature's eternal, inevitable decree of cause and effect we must accomplish it. All this will be our future history, to establish on earth the moral dignity and salvation of man — the immutable truth and beneficence of God. For this blessed mission to the nations of the world, which are shut out from the life-giving light of truth, has America been chosen; and her high example shall smite unto death the tyranny of kings, hier-archs, and oligarchs, and carry the glad tidings of peace and good will where myriads now endure an existence scarcely more envi-able than that of beasts of the field. Who, then, can doubt that our country is destined to be the great nation of futurity."* (O'Sullivan 1839 emphasis ours).

Notice that he states that it will be the American "example" that will inspire the permanent removal "kings, hierarchs, and oligarchs." America's role is to inspire, not to make empire, but to be that great nation in the future.

The phrase "Manifest Destiny" became famous and was embraced emphatically by many Americans of the time since it resonated so well with all that had gone before and which was deeply believed in the heart of hearts of the American DNA. Obviously, then, those pesky natives in their "wretched" tepees and putrid mounds had to be pushed aside, forcibly if need be to defend the advance of the American Way. Then those Catholic Mexicans needed to be sent packing southward . . . or bought at flea market rates (The Gadsden Purchase). Then a lot more land needed to be purchased from foreign empires who were stretched way too thin, through some hard Yankee bargaining (The Oregon Territory, Alaska).

The foot soldiers of this long march westward, southward, and north-ward were an ever increasing surge of mostly European immigrants. These were ordinary folks who had nothing but bleak prospects to look forward to in their homelands. Thus they were willing to gamble their lives and the lives of their families on acquiring their piece of this "empty" land America was willing to give to them, if they got there (particularly after the Home-stead Act was passed in the 1860s). Forests, hills and prairies that they could convert into "their property" equaled freedom, liberty and democracy, three major American political concepts deeply rooted in the spirit of this novel and ever burgeoning national empire.

But this next wave of newcomers was also imbued, once it reached American shores and before it embarked upon their harrowing travels into the yawning Wild West expanses, with the ideal of the political-religious spirit of the Manifest Destiny of their new homeland. These were the trap-pers, traders, mountain men and scouts. And if some of these more ad-venturous types didn't carry "The New England Way" with them, the next waves of development westward contained the settlers, shepherds and farm-ers who did. And, given the American way, it was a certainty that alongside them were sure to be religious "circuit riders", who would help erect small churches wherever crossroads appeared.

The History Channel's program on "Westward Expansion" noted that Sullivan: "put a name to the idea that helped pull many pioneers toward the western frontier." Westward migration was an essential part of the repub-lican project, he argued, and it was America's "manifest destiny," to carry the "great experiment of liberty" to the edge of the continent: to "over-spread and to possess the whole of the [land] which Providence has given us," (*History Channel*, "Westward Expansion," emphasis ours). Property + Freedom + Democracy + God's Providence was a powerful formula to steel many human beings to take such a huge risk to their lives, limbs and the fates of their families.

Yes, commerce, religion and particularly voluntary associations, the latter which the aforementioned French political philosopher Alexis de Tocqueville saw as the essence of American democracy, were intricate parts to the success of the Westward movement. The rugged will to survive could not turn to any "government" to help out other than occasional support from the nearest frontier fort. Individuals mostly turned to others in their "wagon trains," and small cooperative communities sprung up ever west-ward, which comprised most of any "authority" that would help them sur-vive, much less prosper. "The law" was carried out mostly by local citizens as vigilantes and posses, both collaborative private groups bent on punishing "outlaws." The frontier was settled by these kinds of people, not gunslingers.

As this process accelerated into the plains and plateaus of the West, the "civilized" religious Eastern part of the nation, knew that it could not divorce its own interpretation of morality and sense of divine purpose from these ever growing collectives of trappers, traders and settlers . . . who were easy prey to false prophets and spiritual snake-oil salesmen. Thus, they sent duly ordained, proper missionaries of the New England Way, carrying The Word westward, also in ever growing numbers. The great American historian of the Westward expansion, Henry Jackson Turner, put it like this:

> "The New England preacher and school-teacher left their mark on the West. The dread of Western emancipation from New England's political and economic control was paralleled by her fears lest the West cut loose from her religion. Commenting in 1850 on reports that settlement was rapidly extending northward in Wisconsin, the editor of the Home Missionary writes: 'We scarcely know whether to rejoice or mourn over this extension of our settlements. While we sympathize in whatever tends to increase the physical resources and prosperity of our country, we cannot forget that with all these dispersions into remote and still remoter corners of the land the supply of the means of grace is becoming relatively less and less.'
>
> Acting in accordance with such ideas, home missions were established and Western colleges were erected. As seaboard cities like Philadelphia, New York, and Baltimore strove for the mastery of Western trade, so the various denominations strove for the possession of the West. Thus an intellectual stream from New England sources fertilized the West."(Turner 1893)

Masquerading naked, violent and intolerant imperial land expansionism by a technologically superior civilization into a moral belief system and a sense of divine guidance was not a unique phenomenon in human history for sure. Alexander the Great had Aristotle himself as his philosopher-in-chief. Thus, he spread his Macedonian "civilization" all the way to the Hindu Kush via a combination of ethical conviction, a huge mass of well-armed, disciplined warriors, and fancy words and beliefs about their bringing light to the unenlightened, a parody of Socrates' *Allegory of the Cave*. (There are some brief but excellent videos on YouTube that depict and describe *The Allegory* well.)

And so the early American Guardians of the New Light would have been thrilled to see all obstinance to their enlightenment and Godly predestination trampled underfoot and wagon wheels throughout the 19th century. They would have relished all the plains, deserts, mountains and coasts of the Pacific populated with the new Americans carrying that very light they wanted the world to see. Denver and San Francisco would be new cities of "the light", but sited on a mile high mountain and situated on much higher hills.

Just as its ancestors had envisioned, America's Manifest Destiny had become a continent-wide nation—millions of Native Americans, Mexicans, French, British and Spanish be damned. But then a funny thing happened to the Believers in "The City on the Hill", the "Empire of Liberty" and in "Manifest Destiny." They ran out of land to settle upon and exploit for their material and spiritual gain at the astoundingly beautiful beaches and rocky crags of the Pacific Ocean.

The End of the Frontier Perverts Manifest Destiny.

The Prairie Schooners wouldn't float and the pioneer trains couldn't homestead, farm, build churches and communities and tend their herds in The Briny Deep. This was a dramatic jolt to the, by now, hoary and encrusted American expansive and spiritual psyche and it precipitated substantial inner psychic turmoil for the still young United States of America. It also drove a new and challenging theory to the fore, that was advocated by two famed American historians. One was the afore-named Henry Jackson Turner and the other a future president-to-be: Theodore Roosevelt.

Writing at about the same time in the early 1890s, each of them saw an important feature of American history coming to an abrupt end. The Civil War had ended the most glaring Christian and democratic American hypocrisy of its history: Slavery. The "Indian Wars" were won and the uncivilized natives "pacified". There were American outposts, villages, towns and cities sprouting up from coast to coast. "The American Frontier", at least as it was lived and described up to then, was either at a dead-end or perhaps needed an entirely new trail to blaze. (Turner 1893, 1921).

Actually, Turner never did explicitly define "the American frontier" as a specific place, or having a border, or it being any line in the sand and rock. In fact, he thought of it more as a "*process*", as a "*state of mind,*" and as *an ephemeral boundary between old civilizations and ideas and the thrill of the wild, the unknown, new worlds to conquer.* Keep Turner's abstract definition in mind when we get to the discussion of The First Global Nation in a subsequent part of this book.

He also saw that this mind-set, as such, created a somewhat democratic society that was scattered and battered by battles for the land between most white men and Native Americans but also between the white men themselves. Those that lived on were, by and large, those who found ways to collaborate for survival, just as had the early pre-historical hunter-gatherer societies, and just as Winthrop had preached on the Good Ship Arabella. This frontier mentality was a hypothesis, but one that many had come to embrace as their true identity.

Roosevelt was no less enthusiastic about the lure, promise and necessity of the Western frontier experience and mental gyroscope for developing a unique kind of American society for what lay ahead. He prized rugged individuality, however, more than the collaborative communities that actually "won the West". He saw a new American, not of the European industrial worker or the capitalist "robber baron" type. He saw the frontier being a magnificent cauldron which forged a brawling, competitive, persevering Americana . . . which it also was (Roosevelt 1894).

Roosevelt's theory was another take on the importance of the drive westward to America's solitary character. It did not contradict Turner. It was a different side of a multi-faceted phenomenon that was so key to what America has come to be on today's world stage: The Most Self-Righteous, Biggest Bully on the Block.

Teddy Roosevelt did not shy away from being a "bully" either. In fact, he believed that one of the greatest powers of being an American president was the way Americans could be influenced and led from "The Bully Pulpit." In fact, the word "bully" in the early 20th century was more of a compliment than it is in America today, where is more used as an epithet to describe unacceptable, brutish and vulgar interpersonal behavior. In international affairs today, it still well describes America's behavior, but is definitely not meant as a compliment.

Roosevelt, however, was not just an academic like Turner, so he decided to act and remove the physical obstacle to America's previously finite frontier(s). Just about the time that he wrote his book about the end-of-the-frontier problem, *The Winning of the West* (Roosevelt 1894), American adventurers, whalers, missionaries (many of whom were Congregationalists) and U.S. Marines were already overthrowing the monarchy of Hawai'i. That was in 1893.

So, both Turner and Roosevelt were already behind the actual events of the times because that American frontier actually did not come to a screeching halt at the mighty Pacific Ocean. It was already ingesting land further west than the California coastline. Once again, it was due to an alliance between commerce (whalers, planters), American "democracy" (vs. Hawaiian monarchy), and a number of Congregationalist (and other Protestant) missionaries.

As for the whole lot of those pious American missionaries who were shoulder to shoulder with those who held the tools of trade and weapons

of war— as the modern Hawaiians say about those New England prosely-
tizers—"they came to do good, but did well." The Pequot Indians of Massachusetts probably thought the same about the Puritans.

With the acquisition of Hawai'i—the religious and spiritual aspect of
American expansionism to the extent to which it was actually motivational
and acted upon—began to disappear, other than through an occasional reference to it for effect. In its place, a more nationalistic and political theory
came to the fore.

God's will and beneficence and The City on a Hill would fade as a real
credo for settling on other people's sacred ground and naked, raw politics
and geo-politics would become the mainstay of a new brand of American
empire building. The new brand would accept no boundaries whatsoever in
terms of acquisition of territory and had little concern for moral turpitude.

After all, Teddy Roosevelt and a small coteries of new American imperialists operating out of Washington, D.C., were neither Puritans nor of
missionary stock. They were of this materialistic world and thought about
"geo-political" power in terms of where the United States stood at that time
compared with the rest of the world. America may have wondrously spread
from coast to coast, but on the world scene it may have become the world's
largest marketplace, but in geo-political terms, it was minor league. TR (as
he was called) and his buddies—including Senator Henry Cabot Lodge and
Secretary of State Elihu Root—wanted to play major league ball in The International Empire League.

They saw their chance to up their level of play by noticing that one of
the old big time empires was losing its mojo. It was the flailing and failing
Spanish Empire in the Caribbean and much further west than Hawai'i, that
is, in the Philippines. If they could replace Spain in those areas by a short
series of wars, bully for them and America. But with "Manifest Destiny" no
longer a workable theory to galvanize America's need for expansionism of
its glorious political ideals and religiosity, they needed another.

So just in the nick of time, came a little known, but widely admired
(among the powerful) naval captain named Alfred Thayer Mahan. He
taught at the Naval War College and had written a book banally titled *The
Influence of Sea Power upon History: 1660-1783* (1890). That title insured it
would never become a best-seller, but it became a Bible to kings, potentates,
prime ministers, czars, emperors, sultans, admirals, generals and spymas-
ters throughout this world from its publication until well after World War II.

If you just glance at a map of the geo-political world at the end of
the 19th Century and just about up to the present, it is quite easy to see
why Mahan saw the U.S.A. as being in the world's sweet spot to become the
world's most powerful empire ever, but only if it realized and capitalized on

its perfect location as a sea-power. No other country in the world in the late 19th century to the present instant in time has a better set of coastlines than continental America.

It has three long warm water coasts that are on the Atlantic, Pacific, and Gulf of Mexico each of which has lengthy strings of naturally safe harbors, ideal for projecting naval power globally. This was at the heart of his theory: the establishment of "coaling stations" (now naval, army, air force bases and CIA "dark locations") all around the world.

Great Britain was a tiny brace of islands stuck in the North Sea. Japan was a smallish necklace of islands surrounded by the Pacific. Russia was always pining for "warm water ports." China had an enormous coastline hospitable to numerous naval bases . . . but only on the Pacific. No single nation comes close to America's naval good fortune . . . or will again. Other empires had to conquer many lands far, far away to get so many naval bases. America has more opportunities within its own national boundaries.

To Mahan's militaristic way of thinking, this was a new version of "Manifest Destiny." Thanks to God putting America where it was geographically, the world was the U.S. Navy's banquet. What America needed was to embrace naval superiority as the keystone to a future imperial presence through a worldwide matrix of "coaling stations". These would fuel its global projection of power to protect its international commercial trade routes and would provide a foreign presence capable of subduing competitors and local hostility to American overseas "interests."

The New American Imperialism: From "A Splendid Little War" to Global "Containment of the Heartland"

It is at this juncture of American history that the deeply etched and substantial religious sub-text to American expansionism becomes little more than a footnote and/or occasional reference point—to be used when deemed useful to shield various and sundry hidden agendas from the American public. The "religious" aspect of American expansion became little more than a spiritual facade to mobilize the American people's support for strategic war and imperial expansionism, with strictly mundane and political-economic objectives.

From the hand to hand combat of the Spanish-American War, to American "pilots" (jets and drones) simultaneously bombing targets in Afghanistan, Somalia, Yemen, Syria, and Iraq (and who knows where else), to aircraft carrier groups in every ocean and computer stations in Las Vegas, Nevada—this is hardly about spreading "The Word," the "light" and

American-style democracy and religiosity. In fact, it is acting out the never ending revisionism of Admiral Mahan's (he got promoted) "geo-political" theory spelled out in his (to say the least) globally influential book.

To be sure, a whole new batch of catchy, non-religious or quasi-spiritual war-whooping phrases have been coughed up, ever since Mahan's theorizing, to cloak more sinister motives for more and more warfare. One of the first pro-war public relations gambits was proffered by a Kansas Senator to justify the American gulping down the remains of the Spanish Empire in the late 1890s. Sen. John J. Ingalls called it "America's War for Humanity." (1898) Here is the recipe he dreamed up, one that seems as harmoniously tuned to America's far flung militancy today as it must have to Americans of that time:

> *"We enter upon this war, therefore, with no ignoble or selfish purpose, but moved rather by that lofty moral impulse which has inspired the heroes of every history and the martyrs of every religion. We are ministers of that eternal justice . . . we draw the sword to avenge the helpless . . . Our victory will be the triumph of democracy over absolutism."* (Ingalls 1898; Gibson 1971, p. 177 emphases ours) Amen.

So Americans were persuaded by a small number of powerful and cleverly insidious politicians and media moguls that the Spanish were European barbarians who oppressed poor natives in Cuba and the Philippines, and when an American battleship (the U.S.S. Maine) exploded and sank in Havana harbor (the cause of which, strangely enough, has never been scientifically determined), they were heavily conditioned to back the Spanish-American conflict as bearers of The Lord's lightning bolts. The stage was set for what Secretary of State John Hay had to say about it afterwards—considering the relatively meager American losses and huge American gains in "coaling stations":

> *"It has been a splendid little war, begun with the highest motives, carried on with magnificent intelligence and spirit, favored by that Fortune which loves the brave."* (Gable 1991)

When the smoke had cleared, a new American 'empire' spanned the world from the Philippines to Puerto Rico and Cuba, with "The Panama Canal Zone" soon to be added. There was a minor mixing of a religious and business interests in America's part to help suppress "The Boxer Rebellion" in China in 1900, but this was more of a hang-over or aberration than a continuation of the personally embraced, albeit well rationalized, missionary zeal that was at the heart and soul of "Manifest Destiny."

We mentioned in Chapter 2 what William Graham Sumner thought of this unnecessary and reckless adventurism. He was joined by many other great Americans of the time who joined in the noble, historically correct, but long-forgotten *Anti-Imperialist League*. For example, none was as flummoxed and goaded by this turn from the religious spirit of the continental expansion of the United States to become as bad as any of the other evil empires in the world at the time than one of the most famed Americans of his time: Mark Twain. Though Twain had joined a Missouri Confederate militia for two weeks during the early days of the Civil War, he saw no good in killing other men and was also an arch enemy of racism and elitism. Thus, he saw this "splendid little war" and new-fangled imperialism as the crass and wicked plotting of cynical and jaded men.

As a notorious member of the *Anti-Imperialist League*, he spoke out frequently against the war with Spain and the Philippines. However, his most barbed poetry in opposition to this new, utterly hypocritical kind of American imperialism came in the way he rewrote "*The Battle Hymn of the Republic*," the most religiously-based anthem of the Union Army in the Civil War. No longer was God a motivating force behind the growth of this so-called "republic." So Twain revamped that stirring religious war song to reflect the swapping of spiritual motives for an un-American colonial-style expansionism. It went like this:

Mine eyes have seen the orgy of the launching of the Sword;
He is searching out the hoardings where the stranger's wealth is stored;
He hath loosed his fateful lightnings, and with woe and death has scored;
His lust is marching on.

I have seen him in the watch-fires of a hundred circling camps;
They have builded him an altar in the Eastern dews and damps;
I have read his doomful mission by the dim and flaring lamps—
His night is marching on.

I have read his bandit gospel writ in burnished rows of steel:
"As ye deal with my pretensions, so with you my wrath shall deal;
Let the faithless son of Freedom crush the patriot with his heel;
Lo, Greed is marching on!"

We have legalized the strumpet and are guarding her retreat;
Greed is seeking out commercial souls before his judgement seat;
O, be swift, ye clods, to answer him! Be jubilant my feet!
Our god is marching on!

In a sordid slime harmonious Greed was born in yonder ditch,
With a longing in his bosom—and for others' goods an itch.
As Christ died to make men holy, let men die to make us rich—
Our god is marching on.

Twain was a wise man though. He had this published only after he died.

A better example of how lofty, non-religious, archetypes became the driving force of what has become the Latter-Day, or New American Imperialism, was a slogan coined by President Woodrow Wilson. Wilson had been re-elected in the campaign of 1916 largely on the catchphrase that he "Kept Us out of War", that is, World War I that was on the rampage in Europe and the Middle East. So, in order to once again shape American public opinion to back yet another morally questionable overseas war, Wilson did an about face and convinced America to send hundreds of thousands of Americans to France and Belgium to "Keep the World Safe for Democracy."

Of course, God was invoked as being on "our side" in churches throughout the country (Twain made mincemeat of them in his also posthumous "War Prayer," which has many dramatizations on YouTube). Army chaplains reinforced this belief as best they could despite unrelenting chants of "hypocrisy" from remnants of *the Anti-Imperialist League.* They were joined by truly conservative Americans still mindful of President Thomas Jefferson's Inaugural address warning about and promising not to get America trapped into "entangling alliances" in foreign affairs.

The staggering loss of U.S. troops in about a year with little to show for it, coupled with the aforementioned internal resistance and domestic economic turmoil, was enough to keep American war-makers at bay for more than two decades after World War I. Combining these conditions with a booming internal economy in the 1920s and a Great Depression in the 1930s led to 20 plus years of a new American "isolationism" that became a hallmark of the Republican Party which held the presidency for that time. A host of dramatic events throughout the world in the 1930s, well outside of America's still extant empire, conspired to whet the American public's desire to re-entangle the United States in extravagant military endeavors.

The sight and sounds of Nazi rallies and the rants of Hitler scared many Americans quite a bit, particularly listening to the London Blitz live over that relatively new invention: the radio. Within a few short years, from 1939-41, the German army and air force had smothered almost all of Europe, blasted London to smithereens, laid siege to Leningrad for over 800 days causing millions of deaths there, charged to the gates of Moscow and the Caucasus oil fields, and smashed across all of North Africa to Egypt. Things did not look good from this side of the Atlantic, but what could America do?

Moreover, German submarines were sinking American merchant vessels all along its Atlantic coastline trying to reinforce the British—with oil slicks and debris washing up on the shores from Maine to Florida. But this still did not seem like a good time for a maritime power like America to try to take back France, Belgium, the Netherlands, Czechoslovakia and Poland and to invade Africa. There was no stomach for more war. God was never invoked as a reason to come to the aid of a German-vanquished Europe.

Worse still, during that same period of time, the Japanese had marauded through and occupied Korea and Manchuria on the Asian mainland and were penetrating deeply into China. "The Rape of Nanking" was heavily covered by the American press, but few in the U.S.A. clamored for war against Japan either . . . even if the Japanese were capturing and torturing every Christian missionary or ravaging every Catholic nun they could find.

There were those in Washington, D.C. who knew about Japan's plan for its "Co-Prosperity Sphere" in Asia which, if you could read fine print, was actually baying: "U.S. and Europe Leave Asia and the Pacific!!" That meant that once they had fed upon and digested all of China, Southeast Asia would be next, then the Dutch East Indies (now Indonesia) and Australia, New Zealand . . . and . . . of course, The Philippines—with its hosting the most distant bases of The American Empire.

It was just a matter of time. Japan was out to diminish—if not oust— The Pacific Ocean part of the American Empire and turn all of Asia and the Pacific into the "Empire of the Rising Sun." And for dessert? Hawai'i. The Japanese adore Hawai'i. The Americans just got there first. It was time to add it to The Emperor's plate.

After all, the Emperor was, what else— a deity! God seems to be on everyone's side in imperial wars. According to a distinguished American historian at the Louisiana State University, Dr. William Pederson: " . . . the Emperor was not only Japan's ruler, but also a god in human guise, his people were not even allowed to look upon him." (Pederson 2006, p.119)

Thus, with God on their side as well, this eventuated in Japan suddenly attacking and destroying almost the entire U.S. Pacific fleet at Pearl Harbor,

Hawaii in December of 1941 and Hitler and Germany declaring war on the U.S. shortly thereafter. President Franklin D. Roosevelt did not need any sloganeering about moral imperatives and nothing was said about Christianity vs. Satanic forces. Entering into World War II was about national survival and revenge . . . as well as about the survival of two long-standing European empires with which the United States had a long history and very deep economic ties: Great Britain and France.

World War II was also, by far, the most destructive and global war ever fought by humanity (at least up to World War III). Hundreds of millions of people were killed or wounded or maimed or displaced. Major industrial nations were turned into heaps of smoking rubble. Centuries old empires imploded in a few years.

When it ended, only one empire remained physically intact, albeit with half a million men dead: The United States. The only other remaining empire was the Communist regime called The Soviet Union, but the Russians alone had suffered 20-30 million dead and many of its cities were dunes of ash and trash. However it had recovered sufficiently to have the large, victorious and well-equipped Red Army occupying all of Eastern Europe and half of Germany to boot.

It had something else, too, an ideology entirely opposed to the peculiarly unique American system of political economy. The political system of The Union of Soviet Socialist Republics (the U.S.S.R.) was 100% owned and controlled by The Soviet Communist Party—one dedicated to the abolition of all religion in the entire world.

Karl Marx, who had written the guide books for world Communism (*The Communist Manifesto* (1848)and Das Kapital (4 volumes from 1867-1883), made it an article of Communist orthodoxy that organized religion was an "opiate" injected into the working classes of the world. According to Marx, religion was created by the ruling class to produce a fantasy of a magnificent afterlife for the working class, one which made their economic enslavement tolerable during their physically miserable time on Earth.

These words and ideas about the government owning the entire economy and the abolition of organized religion were not music to the ears and minds of American religious leaders and the giant industries and financial institutions that had come to dominate life in the United States. It was clear that another potential world war might be in the offing, but this time a new weapon made that seem like an extremely bad idea. World War II had ended in 1945 with the United States dropping two "atomic bombs" on Japan and by 1949, the USSR had atomic weaponry as well.

The stage was again set for perhaps an even more horrific World War III, one in which America's formerly isolated, continent-wide homeland would be at great risk of massive destruction. Except for perhaps a few psychopathic jingoists on either side, no one wanted a nuclear conflagration. So, there was a clear option of pitting American Christianity vs. Communistic Atheism for the war hawks to rally that "old time religion" as well as to revive America's heavenly mission to spread its wondrous form of "democracy" to the rest of humanity.

But common sense, a continued desire for national existence, and great domestic economic growth prevailed. Thus, Cold War 1.0 broke out between the U.S.A. and the U.S.S.R., ensuing for 45 years.

By the time the Cold War began in earnest, though, Mahan and Teddy Roosevelt's dream of having American bases all around the world had come True x 1000. Neither of those two naval strategists could have dreamed of all the diabolical new weapons systems that would include strategic bombers, nuclear submarines, intercontinental ballistic missiles, satellite systems, electro-magnetic weapons, climate engineering and who knows what.

Even during the apogee of the Soviet Union's power, it could never come close to the vast spread of America's military might throughout the world, which remains true today. Even so, the U.S.S.R. was a formidable enough foe to wreak incredible damage upon the American homeland, so the Cold War stalemate was a good enough reason to develop the American military-industrial complex to gargantuan disproportions.

As for ideologies, the American and Western European political economic philosophy that can barely and inadequately be summed up as "liberal democracy and capitalism" was more than a match for the Stalinist Soviet and Maoist Chinese brands of what they (not Karl Marx) called Communism. The U.S.A. led the world in all the indicators of personal wealth, national health, individual freedom, industrial heft, middle class consumerism, and cultural innovation compared with Communism's rigid ideological hierarchy, social conformity, political repression and material austerity that bordered on mass poverty.

So the ever expanding American Empire of the 20th century—that was accurately labeled by Republican President and former top U.S. general of World War II, Dwight D. Eisenhower as "the military-industrial complex"— was sold lock, stock and barrel to the American people as: "The Leader of the Free World", with neither God nor spirituality invoked to justify this mission creep. This goal of global "liberty" would be accomplished by bringing threadbare American "democracy" to the world on a platter of gaudy munitions or in the guise of some of the world's worst tyrants siding with America's actual economic and strategic power interests.

The reality was, and is still the case to this day, that the American Empire is simply the final stage of "The Splendid Big War" that was fought to establish, protect and enhance the financial and property interests of American corporate and financial titans at the expense of rival empires. The only religion involved is that of the creation of enough money to purchase endless stores of consumer goods and to worship the status that all those goodies confer and the wealth they imply.

What actually has guided the American power elite from the end of World War II to its multiple warlike misadventures throughout the world today in its quest for global domination was a new quasi-scientific polit-ical-geography based theory that had evolved from post-World War I to Post-World War II. This conceptual scheme was far more sophisticated and malleable than Mahan's—since it did not rely exclusively on sea-power—and was derived from the minds of several like-minded geo-strategists in the U.K. and the U.S.A.

Through this dark looking glass, the entire globe is seen as a land and seascape to be won in what had come to be seriously dubbed by men of extraordinary power the world over as: "The Grand Game." This is pretty much a zero-sum contest with mastery of the world as its aim. Actually, it is what is beneath the soil that is much more important to them than any people who live on and off it, i.e., in the industrial era we are talking about minerals (oil, gas, uranium, gems, gold, etc.).

The key geographic area—incredibly rich in all minerals, but particu-larly oil and natural gas—that has been in play now for about a century, is what is now being called what it really is: Eurasia, e.g., from the English Channel to Vladivostok. On its North-South axis, it runs from The Baltic Sea to Singapore. In classic geo-political terms it is dubbed *"The World Is-land."* The biggest mass of it, however, is that comprising large portions of Russia and a sizable chunk of what is now China, altogether as one central core. This gigantic swath of *Terra Firma* was termed and conceived as "The Pivot Area" or as *"The Heartland"* by one of its foremost theorists, Sir Hal-ford Mackinder, who was a professor of (what else?) Geography in England.

In his oft-cited book *Democratic Ideals and Reality* (1919) he coined a phrase that might just as well be at the center of NATO thinking in 2016 as he wrote a century before: "He who controls the Heartland, controls the World Island. And he who controls the World Island, controls the world." Here are two versions of his mind's map as it evolved over 15 years and World War I . . . and please notice how it evolved to include a vast expanse of what we now call East Europe and all the countries now inside NATO or on the verge of being incorporated into it.

This map is included in an article on the great relevance of Mackinder's theory in modern times for understanding the strategies involved in "Central Asian international relations." The researchers, two Ph. Ds who teach at Sidney Sussex College (UK) and Tashkent State Institute for Oriental Studies, are of the opinion that Western scholars pay much too little attention to how strongly Mackinder's thinking plays out in Central Asia to this very day. (Megoran and Sharpova, 2005)

Regardless, Mackinder's work has been amply reworked—perhaps just updated—by Western geo-strategists since his later version, and particularly by the American school of thought during and after World War II. One of the major theorists was the Sterling Professor of International Relations at Yale University, Dr. Nicholas Spykman, whose revision of Mahan and Mackinder—when seen in its map form below—helps explain Cold War 1.0 and 2.0 more than hundreds of books.

But first, a description of how and why Dr. Spykman saw the world of geopolitics as he saw it and how he carved it up so that America could become what it has become: The Global American Empire, dominating the world via sea, air and boots on every patch of ground upon which it could gain even a toehold. Like Mahan, though, Dr. Spykman saw the requirement for a totally dominating American sea power. Like Mackinder, he recognized the threat of that giant land mass, and he too saw large parts of Russia and China at the heart(land) of it all. However, he never could see how that gigantic land mass, with so many diverse peoples and so much mileage between its east and west poles, could ever cohere in any way that could realistically menace the military and economic interests of a dominant United States as the ruler of the waves—both sea and air.

Spykman's major contribution to American geopolitics was to theorize that the World Island's coastal regions were the key to "containing" the Heartland. That is why he is sometimes referred to as "The Godfather of Containment Theory."

Containment theory? Yes, if he who controls the Heartland is contained by whomever controls what Mackinder called "The Inner or Marginal Crescent"—but which Spykman reconfigured and renamed "The Rimland"—then the lions of The Heartland are penned. Keep that abstraction in mind: The Rimland. That academic notion is pretty much what the last century of massive manslaughters, woman-slaughters and children-slaughters have been and are still all about. For the Rimland includes all of what we today know as Southeast Asia, South Asia, Central Asia, the Middle East, and Eastern Europe.

Essentially, Spykman reworded Mackinder's famous dictum to read: "Who controls the Rimland rules Eurasia; who rules Eurasia controls the destinies of the world." In one simple equation: Containment = Checkmate!

We are not going to delve much deeper into the respective geographic boundaries, definitions, and specifications of the many geo-political strategists that have come and gone since Spykman's death in 1944. If anyone should be singled out in the post-World War II era, it would be an American diplomat, stationed in Moscow in 1946, by the name of George F. Kennan. It was he who coined the term "Containment Theory" in an article in the *Council of Foreign Relations'* (referred to among insiders by its acronym, *CFR*) premier journal *Foreign Affairs* in 1947 under the pseudonym "X."

In point of fact, this became the ironclad rationale of the entire Cold War 1.0. We think we show that it has resurfaced as the pretense for the currently brewing Cold War 2.0 (i.e., the current gambits in East Europe and The Middle East are all "Rimland Wars") which mindlessly could spark World War III and end the human experiment on Mother Earth.

Our point is simply that this kind of "strategic thinking" has long replaced any guiding and inspirational spiritual values that at one time may have been the foundation of American territorial expansionism. Geography, geology, physics, engineering, weapons manufacturing and sales, and a philosophy of raw, naked global hegemony have long since left any sense of God's will and God's work in a cloud of double-talk.

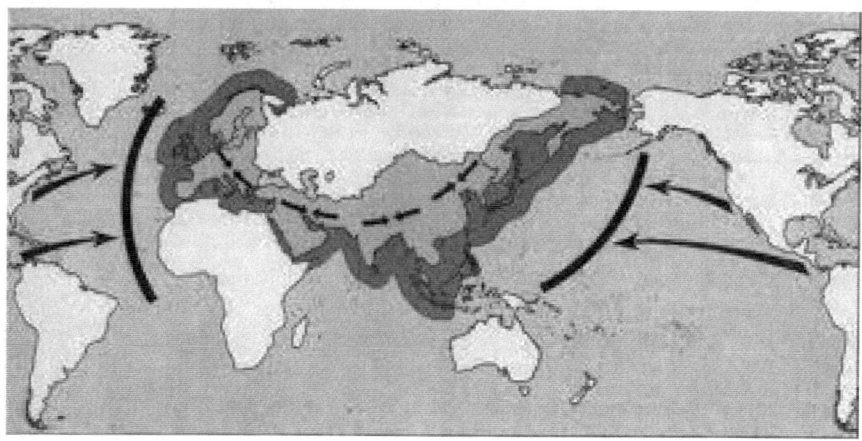

Here is a map from an article of contemporary geopolitics from *the Center on Globalization* in Montreal, Canada. It is part of an article by M.D. Nazemroaya in 2007 and shows rather clearly The Heartland (in white), the Rimland—which is the rest of The World Island and mistakenly includes all of China (in pink or gray)—and the American maritime containment of both in red (or dark gray). The latter includes an inner ring of islands under American military control or economic dominance, i.e., Great Britain, Malta, Sicily, Diego Garcia, Indonesia, the Philippines, Taiwan and Japan. The white area will be discussed as part of the greater geo-strategic aims of the newly minted heirs to Mahan-Spykman-Kennan, that new kid on the imperialist block, The American Neo-Conservative Movement (Neo-Cons) and their grandiloquent theories of *"Full Spectrum Dominance."*

Full Spectrum Dominance? So what is that? Whatever it is, it sounds a bit unobtainable, sort of like searching for "The Holy Grail." So are the Neo-Cons the modern equivalent of The Knights Templar? Let's hope not, but here's a bit of their history and current affairs.

After the Soviet Union collapsed in 1989, the American imperial elite not only proclaimed "victory" and the triumph of "liberal democracy" over "authoritarian communism"—but vaingloriously proclaimed the historic moment as *The End of History* (Fukuyama 1992). We think we can safely conclude that he was, and they were, astonishingly wrong.

Indeed, for the never fully satisfied American Imperial Class, there was more of this material world to conquer, not the least of which was every last inch of the world island . . . including the air above and the strategic minerals below. The Soviet Union may have vanished, but there was all of East Europe and the Rimland and The Russian Federation plus that whale of a country, China itself, yet to fall completely under the American veil of dominion. We are not making this up!

It was no longer God's Destiny. It was simply the timeless, borderless desire to be what they themselves came to think of themselves as being— in the inimitable phrasing of a world-class novelist named Thomas Wolfe: "The Masters of the Universe." (Wolfe 1984).

"The New World Order" and "Full Spectrum Dominance" (Plus Cheney and Cheney 2015 Update)

These conceits, risen from vulturing the remains of the collapsed Soviet Union, was first boasted about in 1990 from the lips of an old-wealth Wall Street scion turned President of the United States, George W. H. Bush, when he coined the phrase "The New World Order" in a speech he made to Congress. Flush with victory over the collapse of "The Berlin Wall," he affirmed a never ending struggle that sought "peace", "security," "the rule of law," and "victory over tyranny and savage aggression." (Bush 1990)

We notice the complete omission of any divine inspiration or mission in his oration, which can easily be found in its entirety on YouTube.

But hadn't the nuclear standoff between the U.S.A. and the Soviet Union ended? Who then became the "savage" aggressors in 1990 and the indefinite future? Well, President Bush, the First, found one in the blink of an eye in an Arab socialist leader named Saddam Hussein, a former ally, who had dared to invade and occupy its next door neighbor, Kuwait. This was what allegedly led to the 100-hour Gulf War . . . and a great "Victory" parade up Broadway in New York City celebrating the revived notion of "invincibility" of the American military after its humiliating defeat by a ragtag army of "gooks" in Vietnam in 1975.

But a new global geo-strategic theory was needed, since the old Communist/Aetheist/World Dictatorship of the Proletariat vs. Capitalist/Democracy/Religiosity had become embarrassingly threadbare. The Heartland (now the nations of Russia and China) was alive and kicking like the meanest bull in a rodeo, not yet broken and tamed by brave American bareback riders.

Thus, several of Bush I's close advisors and associates, including Dick Cheney and Donald Rumsfeld, along with a number of Washington, D.C. insiders (including major Neo-Con theorists like William Kristol, Paul Wolfowitz, and Richard Perle) and private, well-funded foundations (Cato Institute, American Enterprise Institute), began to develop a new and even grander geo-strategy stocked full of future American foes to vanquish.

They came up with a doozy, one that had as its endgame: the complete control of the World Island, the Heartland, and the Outer Crescent as well, in other words, total global control by the U.S.A.—with no spiritual context whatsoever.

In other words, this was a re-re-revised, revamped, restyled and re-tooled American expansionist theory that would allow for the Conquest of Everything, forget about "containment" of Russia, China, the Heartland, whatever. Mere "containment" was no longer enough for this new coterie of American imperialists who founded yet another "conservative" think tank in Washington, D.C. called *The Project for the New American Century*, or *PNAC*, in 1997.

PNAC became closely allied with a powerful network of like-minded thinkers, billionaires, and institutions like Rupert Murdoch (and *Fox News*), the Koch Brothers, the aforementioned *American Enterprise Institute, The Cato Institute*, and *The Weekly Standard*. They did not shy away from the phrase "The American Empire" and actually embraced it. Still, they found it useful to peddle it alongside the old bromide about spreading the traditional theoretical values of "democracy," "liberalism," "capitalism"—and when expedient, "American Exceptionalism"—to the rest of the world, by "shock and awe" when necessary, which would be more often than not.

Immediately prior to the George W. Bush (Bush II) Imperial Period, *PNAC* and its associates had infiltrated deeply into the Department of Defense, along with their many military allies therein, and came up with a Department of Defense document called *"Vision 2020"*. This explicitly set forth the goals and strategies for the development of the new American imperialism for the next two decades.

Chief among its aims was that which we mentioned above, i.e., "Full Spectrum Dominance." (Garamone 2000) What this meant, in plain English, was that the United States was committed to spending trillions upon trillions of dollars in the future (which it has done, is doing, and will continue to do) to dominate the world in every imaginable human sphere. Like what? You name it: ground forces, navy, air force, satellite and cyber-warfare, global electronic surveillance, electro-magnetic warfare, psychological and propaganda warfare, economic warfare (sanctions, currency wars) . . . plus ultra-fantastic ways of manipulating and fooling people beyond Hollywood's most high-paid imaginations.

Indeed, President Eisenhower's warning to America in his Farewell speech in 1961, alerting its people about the encroachment of the "military-industrial" complex's effect on all aspects of American lives at all levels of governance and life has now come full cycle for much of the world. It is really difficult to define the presence of America's military might around the world in Mahan's term of "coaling stations" or more recent American military doctrine of a mere containment by a ring of various kinds of military "bases."

Hawai'I, Okinawa, Europe, Central Asia, the Middle East, the Caribbean and South America are host to way too many American garrisons to count (although the maker of the map below counts 737), which probably includes small outposts and "rest and recreation" centers. This 2009 map of this over-the-top, extravagant and ubiquitous network, will give the reader a mind-blowing eyeful of its global pervasiveness in the name of "American national defense." Really. (Melanchthon 2009)

US military presence overseas

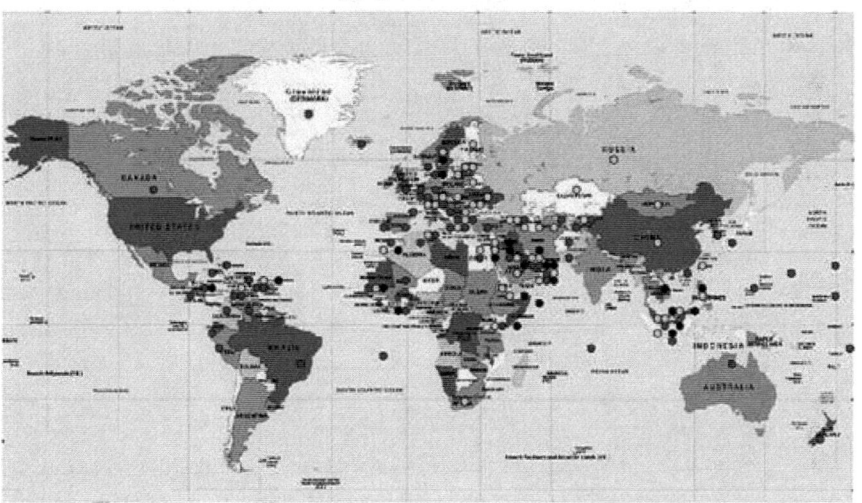

● Country with US
   Military Base

● Country with Access
   Arrangement

◐ Country with other Forms
   of Military Cooperation

So, what has this led to in the first 15 or so years of the 21st century? Is the world pleased with America's military and political clout? Are the American people safer, healthier, richer, and happier today than they were at the turn of the Millennium? Are the World Island and Rimland comfortably within the American sphere of military and political power now that it is surrounded by dozens times dozens of U.S. bases, aircraft carrier groups, and fleets of drones? Does peace and prosperity flourish throughout the globe under America's New World Order and Full Spectrum Dominance? Is America seen as the purveyor of peace, prosperity, freedom and democracy all around the world?

The answer on all counts, to anyone who is still conscious and sane on this planet, must be a resounding NO!

One little example of the level of worldwide discontent with America's overbearing claim to being "The Exceptional Nation" is a recent international Gallup Poll which surveyed 66,000 people in 65 countries. Most worrisome of its findings was that more than half of Russians and Chinese see America as the greatest threat to world peace (Brown 2014). And this percentage is at least as high throughout Islam, including America's fake ally, Pakistan.

The U.S. military (and allied "defense" institutions) budgets eat up more than half of America's national budget annually to date. That would mean that something in the vicinity of $10 trillion dollars have been spent (actually borrowed and added to the unprecedented and unsustainable national debt soon to reach $20 TRILLION dollars) since 2000. This has apparently made America (that shining city on the hill) appear to be the greatest global threat to world peace. Could that have anything to do with the fact that America has been bombing Islamic people on a daily basis ever since Bush the First called it "The New World Order"? Why would any American citizen in her or his right mind vote for anything like that?

Worse yet, much of that money has gone to various civil wars, proxy wars, special operations, and drone strikes throughout the world which continues to wreak special havoc and chaos in countries like Afghanistan, Iraq, Syria, Libya, Pakistan, Somalia, Yemen, and last but not least, the Palestine "political authority." If this is a "New World Order," we'd hate to see what "A New World Disorder" would be like.

We would be remiss in leading the reader to believe that this theory and this global juggernaut is the handiwork of a small syndicate of extreme right wingers in Washington, D.C. who think this way and have in some insidious way twisted the minds of today's "best and brightest" to think so wrongly. The phrase "the best and the brightest" was actually meant sarcastically to describe the high and mighty, "group thinking" intellectuals affiliated with the Democrat Party who inaugurated and executed the astoundingly stupid war crime in Vietnam in the 1960s and 1970s (Halberstam 1972).

Actually, some long-term, "best and brightest" American strategic thinkers of today within the Obama Administration and all wings of the Republican Party (with the exception of true Libertarians), and probably most of the traditionally powerful American strategic think tanks like the CFR, have come to think similarly to the Neo-Con network. Like who?

Well, to name and quote one who has been a highly decorated professor at one of the leading universities in the United States (Columbia University), the founding director of *The Trilateral Commission* in 1974, and a

National Security Advisor to President Jimmy Carter, there is Dr. Zbigniew Brzezinski. His latest contribution to high level strategic thinking in the 21st Century can be found in a very recent book, aptly titled: *Strategic Visions* (2012). In it, he seems to have progressed well beyond any "containment of the World Island" parameter and embraced a fully expansive view of American power in "The Grand Game." Here is an example:

> "*Without a stable geopolitical balance in Eurasia promoted by a renewed America, progress on the issues of central importance to social well-being and ultimately to human survival would stall. America's failure to pursue an ambitious transcontinental geopolitical vision would likely accelerate the decline of the West and prompt more instability in the East . . . (which would contribute to) intensifying the latent hostility between China and America, to the detriment of both.*
>
> "*Alternatively, a successful American effort to enlarge the West . . . extending from North America through Europe into Eurasia and embracing Russia as well as Turkey, would geographically reach Japan.*" (Brzezinski 2012, p.184, all emphases ours)

So, there is his plan. An American Eurasia . . . .devoted to American style "universal democratic culture" and with America at the apex of a world parabola. Key to his scheme is the "democratization of Russia!" Good luck to Dr. Brzezinski and the Neo-Cons—whether Republican, Democrat, or Libertarian. Napoleon and Hitler both thought their hierarchical cultures were superior to the Russian brand of authoritarian governance and Washington, D.C.'s brand of "democracy" is as about as rigidly hierarchical and super-secretive as any other.

So what about China? Well, here the good doctor disagrees with the Full Spectrum Dominance crowd. As one of the pre-eminent global power chess grand-masters, which he demonstrates in his book *The Grand Chessboard* (1999), he displayed a forward looking intuition of the Chinese Communist Party's deeper global ambitions and its keen awareness of the U.S.-NATO encirclement (viz, "containment") that such a successful strategy outlined above would mean to China.

Here is the way he sums up what he believes to be the Chinese Communist Party's long-range strategic goals. He correctly sees China's current multiple short and long-range economic and geo-political tactics as reflecting:

> " . . . *China's historical view of its rightful entitlement to a dominant regional—perhaps eventually global—role . . . they do reflect Chinese pride and presumed desire, disguised for the time*

being, for China to become again—as it once was—the world's preeminent power, even replacing America. Indeed, it is already noticeable that China's intelligently calculated foreign outreach—built around slogans regarding 'a harmonious world'—is beginning to intrigue the political imagination of peoples in the world's less privileged parts. For the many who crave a vision of a more relevant future than offered by the 'waning American Dream,' China is beginning to offer a new option, that of the rising Chinese Dream." (Brzezinski 2012, 173).

Where he differs from the Neo-Cons and the Full Spectrum Dominance clique about China is that he knows the Neo-Con pipe dreams are just that. He knows that the U.S.A. with all its present and future military superiority is doomed to fail at bringing about "regime change" in China (a delusion harbored by the extreme American right wing ever since 1949 when they blamed President Truman for "losing China").

This is not to say that regime change in China is impossible, it is only to say that it will not be a result of American meddling, threats or attacks, which would more likely be counter-productive and produce greater grass-roots national support for the CCP (Chinese Communist Party) among the hyper-nationalistic Chinese people. Regime change in China, that is the overthrow of the CCP, will only be a function of China's in-progress "Ecological Apocalypse" and deep state corruption that is endemic there, despite an ongoing drastic "reform" movement under President Xi, (Smith 2015) which some are calling a ruse and a purge.

Thus, in our view, Dr. Brzezinsky is willing to share global dominance with China—if both regimes escape looming ecological cataclysms—as a new "G-2", with the U.S. as "Rome" and China as its "Byzantium." If that sounds a tad reminiscent of the Nazi-Japan alliance for world rule of the 20th century to you, it does to us as well.

But . . . .what about the downward spiraling, chaotic Middle East and North Africa? What about the emerging Eurasian inter-connectivity that will challenge the 500 year old domination of Western European-American political and economic imperialism and colonialization, i.e., The Eurasian Economic Union or EEU, or the materializing Chinese-backed phenomenon known variously as "The New Silk Road" or "One Belt, One Road" (OBOR)? He is probably trying to cope with these developments in an emerging book. We will deal with these below.

Another "establishment" academic, also with impeccable international relations credentials, is The R. Wendell Harrison Professor of Political Science at the University of Chicago, Dr. John J. Mearsheimer, who also takes a long futuristic look at the rise of China as being a very real threat to The

American-led New World Order that evolved from the British-led Old World Order. What he sees coming down the pike is what he calls in the title of a recent volume he authored: *The Tragedy of Great Power Politics* (2014).

And what kind of a geo-political future does he forecast? Dr. Mearsheimer's theory (which he admits to its fallibility) is that the United States is not a global hegemon, but merely a regional one and the world is not big enough for two. The reason for this is that regional hegemons must make sure that no competing regional hegemons exist, since they will be an existential threat to the solitary hegemon. Thus, with China rising to the status of a regional hegemon (for example, their building of military bases on a string of reefs in the South China Sea), the ultimate conflict between it and America is just about a sure thing. Thus, although he never uses the terminology of Full Spectrum Dominance, given his theory, Mearsheimer and the Neo-Cons are pretty much on the same page.

As he concludes his most recent tome:

> "*The picture I have painted of what is likely to happen if China continues to rise is not a pretty one. Indeed, it is downright depressing. I wish I could tell a more hopeful story about the prospects for peace in Asia. But the fact is that international politics is a dangerous business, and no amount of goodwill can ameliorate the intense security competition that sets in when an aspiring hegemon comes on the scene in either Europe or Asia. And there is good reason to think China will eventually pursue regional hegemony.*" (Mearsheimer 2014, p. 411)

Thus Professor Mearsheimer, like the vast majority of "major" foreign policy pundits of the United States—Neo-Cons as well as those he calls "offensive realists"—are fearful of America losing what they believe to be its past, present and future hegemony which, in effect, is the most powerful national influence in the history of the world. If seriously challenged, military means must be used to curtail threats to American dominance from a nation aspiring to its own "hegemonic" status. That is the "tragedy" Dr. Mearsheimer believes we face. As the U.S. Navy continues to challenge China's growing strand of miniature bases in the South China Sea in 2016 and beyond, Mearsheimer's fears are apparently growing more realistic.

To embellish this nerve wracking potentiality—as it will persist and probably intensify through 2016—the pre-eminent American Neo-Conservative strategist, former Vice-President of the United States, Dick Cheney, published an update of that strategic vision, in book form, in the Summer of 2015. His co-author is his daughter, an attorney whose career has mostly been as a mid-level State Department operative in the Middle East and

North Africa. This book reveals she is also a devoted adherent to the Neo-Conservative political philosophy of Full Spectrum Dominance.

In addition to the projection of this durable Neo-Con strategy into the indefinite future, the Cheneys insist on their blatant mischaracterization of American uniqueness and greatness by naming their book *Exceptional* (Cheney and Cheney 2015). We are doubly grateful to them for: (a) the 2015 updating of Neo-Con strategic thinking and policy recommendations; and (b) reaffirming their misinterpretation of America's political-spiritual genius that we celebrate and project into the future later in this book. So, let us summarize each of these for the reader just to make what we have said in the body of the book even clearer and completely up-to-date.

We decided to count the bolded headings (in their book) of their future objectives and to give our estimate as to what percentage of the items involved military or quasi-military spending and action vs. any other way to move into the future as the world's "exceptional" nation. The ratio we found was close to 90% military-related or oriented. Here are just a few of them to give the reader a firm grasp on where the Cheneys and their American strategic allies wish to spend trillions more of American dollars in order to protect America's "security" and "freedom"—which is their oft repeated goal.

- *"Ensure the Pentagon budget includes a robust program to invest in the technologies necessary to maintain our military superiority" (p. 235)*

- *"Upgrade America's offensive and defensive cyber-capabilities" (p. 235)*

- *"Dedicate the American forces necessary to prevail." (p. 237)*

- *"Halt the withdrawal of American forces from Afghanistan . . . " (p. 240)*

- *"Recognize that Iran is America's enemy . . . " (p. 241)*

- *"Expand our military presence in Asia to counter China's efforts at regional domination" (p. 247)*

- *"Task the Department of Defense with developing a new regional defense strategy for Asia." (p. 248)*

- *"Signal American determination to stand by our NATO allies through periodic deployment of forces to the territory of NATO members bordering Russia." (p. 250)*

- *"Provide additional military assistance to the Ukraine." (p. 251)*

- *"Re-establish the primacy of America's nuclear arsenal." (p. 252)*

- *"Recognize that the realistic and credible threat of military force gives substance and meaning to our diplomacy." (p. 254).*

Add them up and the sum total of their view is: "The Long War;" "The Endless War;" "Force others to do America's bidding and call it diplomacy"—or in other words "Full Spectrum Dominance Continued ad Infinitum." To the Cheneys and their colleagues and cohorts in this brand of American imperial Alice in Wonderland, this is what makes America "Exceptional." It is, in the words of their own subtitle: "Why the World Needs America to be Powerful."

So, according to those presently at the apogee of U.S. national strategic power circles (Yes, even inside the Obama Administration), America must continue on its present track even if it leads to more and more, ever more dangerous, complex and uncertain consequences around the world. What the crimped, cramped and claustrophobic minds of all these geo-strategic wizards and warriors cannot come to grips with whatsoever is that staying the course portends a quantum leap of destructiveness that the planet itself cannot absorb. A supercharged increase in these kinds of power games maximizes the chances of unprecedented world spanning self-destruction for all humankind due either to a "nuclear winter" or some other kind of Gaian vindication.

On the plus side, the "rising hegemon", China, will be very hesitant to present a direct military challenge to the hegemons of the West . . . .unless the U.S. decides to forcibly and systematically attack what the Chinese consider to be China proper. It seems to us that the CCP is more likely to use Muhammad Ali's "Rope-a-Dope" tactic to tire the U.S. out and to keep the Pentagon guessing about how well-armed and destructive their counterpunch may be. In other words, those fortified reefs in the South China Sea might as easily be "tripwires" as "stepping stones."

In the meantime, military stalemates, reversals of fortune, and new "hot spots" for the old Western powers continue to pile up, putting extreme pressure on their national and transnational economies (like the EU and the USA) and on all of their domestic tranquility. This is manifesting itself in the forms of imperial backlash from former colonies or exploited "vassal" states plus internal protests, demonstrations, independence movements and random turbulence from uniquely modern disparities of wealth and austerity heaped upon their increasingly restless and diverse publics.

What the present-day American and Western European mindset cannot seem to free itself from is its 17th, 18th, 19th, and 20th century illusions of conquest, plunder, grandeur, and sanctimoniousness about it all. It's over! The 21st century will be about whether Planet Earth can be sustained as a friendly home to all humanity.

The Eventual Retreat of the American Empire and the Dawn of the Multi-Polar Century

So, the 19th Century was known as "Pax Britannica." "The American Century" was the 20th Century. It should be clear by now that the 21st is shaping up to be more like "The Multi-Polar Century," with Eurasia being the largest and most prominent pole. There is no way modern day American imperialism alone, or with a hodge-podge of ephemeral allies, can stop that gestating political economic inexorability short of destroying the entire world, including itself.

The ruling elites in China do not envision today's world and the future one along Western lines of geo-political reality. The contemporary Mandarins in China do not appear to see the maturing China as "the global hegemon." It is not, in their minds, "The Chinese Way," which in their terminology emphasizes "harmony," "diplomacy," and "collaboration." These may be mere words and a smokescreen, but they actually relate to a style of thought and action just as the words "Full Spectrum Dominance" relate to a present-day American mode of thought and behavior. The theories are very different, but they do influence concomitant action.

As we mentioned in discussing Professor Brzezinski's thesis, The Chinese Communist Party's own grand strategy is already well under way. It consists of continued rapid economic and infrastructure growth internally and globally; centralized response to domestic ecological degradation; and cultural expansion globally. This package has already hurdled over the past century's American wall of "containment" in every way imaginable other than militarily.

True, the Chinese Communist Party and much of the Chinese population of today may see China as the #1 nation, soon to become the #1 economy in the world, but the way we see it, they project China itself as being a part of a future in which it is the single most powerful, but not dominant, nation. They are fully cognizant of the fact that any massive armed conflict would bring unprecedented catastrophe to all of China and the rest of the world too.

Thus the CCP is committed to a historically unusual path of mostly peaceable construction and partner-like interconnectivity with nations in every corner of the world. That is the model it states it is following and thus far seems to be, more or less, hewing to it . . . albeit with some "corrections" already in the works due to some attitudes and attributes unique to China that irk and irritate other cultures along with some of their corrupt and nationalistic "capitalist road" practices.

Still, they are making deep inroads everywhere. Look at the cold, propaganda-free facts that provide a vivid comparison between where the U.S.A. and China are headed.

The United States of America—with its addiction to the ultimate of old fashioned imperialism— is approaching a national debt of $20 trillion dollars and its debt-to-Gross National Product ratio exceeds 100% in 2015!! This an unimaginable, unpayable fiscal obligation and an alarming debt-to-GNP relationship. Simultaneously, China, in 2015, has been hoarding a foreign exchange reserve surplus of nearly +$3.5 trillion dollars. (Wong 2015) . . . and has among the lowest of national debt to GNP ratios in the world.

In addition to this, China has been at the top of the heap in both gold production and importation for several years now and is in the process of amassing a gold stash the likes of which the world has not experienced before. Of course, no one but the boys cashiered in the innermost niches of The Forbidden City in Beijing know for sure the true size of their cache, or what they have in mind to do with it, but we'll hazard a guess below, one shared by many economists and international business experts.

Au contraire: what does the ruling elite in America today plan on spending more trillions upon trillions of dollars on in the near future? The answer is: More "long wars" that are incredibly costly to America as well as torturous to people in foreign lands. This approach is certain drive America into probably lethal debt and swelling global abhorrence. All of the currently known military absurdities which have been in progress since the turn of the 21st Century are primarily in the oil zone known as The Middle East: the one in Afghanistan, the one in Iraq, the one in Libya, and the most recent one in Syria—each of which, according to plan, will be "endless" and will suck more American wealth down the military-industrial drain.

According to the Watson Institute of International Relations at Brown University, in a study released in 2011, at that time just two of those wars (Iraq and Afghanistan) had cost the United States—$3.7 trillion dollars— and that did not include the amounts needed to be spent indefinitely for wounded veterans and interest payments on the extra debt caused by those wars. (Trotta 2011) This does not even begin to factor in the incalculable costs of trying to eliminate by force the new Terminator of the area: The Islamic State, which is like a Muslim GMO seed that wafts far afield and pollutes natural Islam wherever it lands and germinates.

Meanwhile, the *American Society of Civil Engineers* currently estimates that it would take at least that Chinese stack of close to $4 trillion dollars by 2020 to repair and restore the U.S.A's aging capitalist infrastructure (particularly transit, aviation, roads, schools and inland waterways, all of which they give the grade of D, for poor). (ASCE 2013) This does not include what it would cost for new, innovative, and necessary 21st century infrastructures. These must include sustainable energy production and distribution; widespread and affordable medical facilities; water purification and desalinization; preparations for coastal city flooding; seriously confronting off-the-charts droughts that are causing desertification of a large part of Western agricultural land and the burning down of large patches of the American West; re-planning and rebuilding desolate urban landscapes filled with many millions of desperate people, and the like.

In stark contrast, China is pursuing a colossal and inter-related series of infrastructure projects called *"The New Silk Road"* (also called *"One Belt, One Road"* or *OBOR*) aimed at establishing a supranational "World Island" grid of telecommunication, travel and trade. In order to help funnel the requisite gobs of cash into this ambitious project, along with Brazil, India, Russia and South Africa (the *BRICS*), China established the brand new *Asia Infrastructure Investment Bank (AIIB)* located in Shanghai in 2015—the first direct competitor to the American built and led Bretton Woods financial empire and two of its key monetary institutions, The IMF and the World Bank.

The U.S., seeing The *AIIB* as an imminent threat to its increasingly porous global financial hegemony, abstained from investing in it and asked many of its allies to refrain from doing so as well. Alas, that was to no avail, as the UK, France, Thailand and Indonesia are now founding members of the *AIIB* along with many other American "allies."

This is a World Island political-economic challenge that is a very loud boom across the American global hegemony bow and a profound rebuke to the classic Western geo-political thought we have been describing above. This is a plan, with many bilateral and multilateral agreements, and there are hundreds of reasons why it might be delayed, changed, or even fail (Rudolf 2015). However, it is so complex and diversified, and is being ramped up exponentially all over the world as we write, that some major parts or phases of it are bound to succeed and interweave eventually into at least a loose global network with China at the center.

We do feel it is relatively safe to say that ten more aircraft carrier groups, countless squadrons of Star Wars-like F-35s, and an ever expanding arsenal of strange new cyber/space/climate/electro-magnetic weaponry will not keep this emerging World Island and quasi-global infrastructure from coagulating. This will more likely transpire, to one degree or another, sooner or later, and become the dominant economic power grid on the planet in the 21st Century.

The United States is attempting at this moment to "contain" this economically by cobbling together—to the exclusion of Russia and China—a patch-quilt alliance of Rimland nations in Asia and Europe. Thus, the U.S.A seeks a possibly unobtainable, and if attained, probably unworkable *Trans Pacific Partnership (TPP)*—a Pacific and Asian counterpart to the much criticized North American Free Trade Agreement (NAFTA).

Its European counterpart, *The Transatlantic Trade and Investment Partnership (TIPP)*, is billed as a US-EU free trade agreement, but is anything but that. After a lengthy series of behind-closed-doors negotiations, it is on the verge of being materialized but there are loud voices against it, particularly coming from a much stronger opposition in the European Union. The major arguments against it are that it has been written undemocratically, its implementation will be undemocratic, and the effects will be disastrous for the public sectors of the EU (and America).

A good summary of these critiques can be found in *The Parliament Magazine* where this statement appears: " . . . *it will deeply impact our environmental, food, social and labour laws through the revision of regulatory frameworks. This will also be done through a strong liberalisation of the services sector, with the risk of undermining the social and environmental mission that many of these services play in European societies, for example, public transport, water management, healthcare and educational services, that traditionally are more protected in Europe than the US."* (Forenza 2014).

These same reservations are voiced on the American side of the Atlantic as well, even though Congress "fast tracked" the president's power to sign "free trade" deals in mid-2015. Both of these trade deals are issues (overt or covert) in the presidential election of 2016 and the American public will more than likely be kept mostly in the dark about what is really at stake.

America needs to think of more collaborative ways to deal with the more likely emerging Multi-Polar world, particularly with that potentially overwhelming Eurasian entity—from Shanghai to Hamburg—as part of it. Innovative international construction and mutual cooperation to solve pressing global problems, not corporate wheeling-and-dealing to find new ways to earn large profits, are the way to go.

Along those lines, the *AIIB* maneuver follows the less widely known Chinese move over the past several years to trade with many nations using its own currency, the yuan or RMB, instead of the dollar. In fact, many countries are now trading in yuan and not in dollars, the fiat (mere paper) currency of the world's all-time leading debtor nation. As expected, *the IMF* decided to include the yuan into its "basket of currencies" in recognition of its true value in December of 2015. This sets the stage for China's projected future economic prominence based on a sound and relatively efficient modernistic economic infrastructure, especially compared to the increasingly decrepit one of the United States.

As we hinted above, there is also a credible scenario, long in the making, where China might have an even more powerful weapon in its opaque arsenal than all the robots, space lasers and climate engineering gizmos in America's. Some crystal ball gazers call it "The Gold Bomb" when (it is only a matter of timing) China issues a "gold backed" yuan (or a complementary currency to the paper yuan). This would give it the role of having one of, if not the most, valuable currencies in the world, just as "The Almighty Dollar" was before President Nixon declared that it would no longer be backed by American gold in the early 1970s.

The effect of this would be to convert the dollar into a less valuable paper currency on the global market. This event could, in turn, cause major economic disruptions worldwide. It would also have some extremely deleterious effects on US-China trade relations, so it may not happen, given China's impressive investment in the American market. We both think "the bomb" will be revealed sooner or later (probably later), and China will unquestionably continue stockpiling its gold reserve and developing other financial instruments before it can seriously compete with the American economy, particularly by way of a currency tussle. All we know for sure is that the boys in The Forbidden City remain mum about their intentions.

Back to the presently unfolding Chinese strategy to miniaturize America the Great on The World Island: The *AIIB* is also aimed to reinforce the growing stature of the *Shanghai Cooperative Organization (SCO)* which includes Russia, Kazakhstan, Uzbekistan, Tajikistan and Kyrgyzstan. Both Pakistan and India (believe it or not)—as well as Iran and Mongolia— have applied for membership. Pakistan was recently accepted in the summer of 2015. India, Iran and Mongolia are expected to be accepted as full members of the *SCO* in the near future.

With Pakistan already in the fold, this affords the Russians and Chinese direct overland trade routes to the Indian Ocean . . . and soon after the UN lifts its economic sanctions as part of the P5+1 nuclear deal with Iran, probably the Persian Gulf as well. Thus more gaping rifts in the wall of "containment" continue to appear with more of them sure to occur.

Actually, the comparison between the Chinese and American strategies is even more pronounced than what we have already described. Allow us to elaborate just a bit more to hammer home our point in this section of the book that the Really New World Order is building up an even greater head of steam, one which has the capability of driving the U.S practically out of the Middle East.

Not only is China well under way in the *One Road, One Belt* plan throughout Eurasia, but they have taken their economic power and philosophy of non-confrontation and constructive partnership to all parts of the globe . . . bursting through containment and becoming an indispensable partner to a wide variety of nations in Africa, Southeast Asia, and Latin America. Their strategy is simple enough to comprehend: build infrastructure for nations everywhere, without regard for its political system or ideology. They do this for a reasonable fee (while employing many Chinese workers and managers in the process) and make friends, allies, money and safe havens for a panorama of natural resources. To add to that, they are investing heavily by purchasing real estate and industries worldwide (including the United States).

Several explicit examples of how they are going about applying this part of their geo-strategy were recently headlined in the CCP's English language foreign affairs online magazine *China Daily*. It outlined a wide assortment of Chinese sponsored and largely financed railroad projects in Africa and Latin America, scattered widely throughout Mackinder's "Outer Crescent."

In Africa, the Chinese have just finished a nation-spanning, 1,000 mile long modern railroad in Angola. China is also funding and helping build "The East African Railway Network" that will connect Uganda, Rwanda, Burundi, and South Sudan. Across the Atlantic, the Chinese government made a deal in 2014 to build a railroad that will connect the Atlantic Coast of Brazil to the Pacific Coast of Peru. (*China Daily*, 2015). Also, as President Christina Kirchner of Argentina stepped down in December 2015, construction had already begun on a mega-hydroelectric project in Patagonia—erecting two gigantic dams—which is in large part funded, engineered and managed by the Chinese. (Watts 2015)

These are astounding plans, all well underway. This is not to mention the huge contract made by Chinese developers with Nicaragua to build a gigantic canal from the Pacific to the Atlantic that would be amenable to much larger ships than even the expanded Panama Canal could handle. The work on that also began in 2015, despite a hotbed of local opposition to it . . . and as suggested above, snags have occurred to delay further work on it until at least 2017. Even if it does not get built, Americans need to be saying their prayers over the death of The Monroe Doctrine.

One way or another, all the above described initiatives will coalesce into a direct challenge to U.S. financial, economic and military supremacy. A perfect juxtaposition of just how China and the U.S. are spending their money with an eye on the future is a good indicator of which will "win" the "long game," occurred in May 2017. Almost within a few days of one another, these two major events occurred.

In Beijing, the Chinese held a meeting of many countries to announce the first grants for major projects throughout Asia amounting to what *Fox*

Business News (and numerous other sources) stated was roughly $900 Billion (approximately over 10 years) for ports, highways, railroads and the like and which invited American companies like Honeywell, Caterpillar, and IT&T to be bidders.(Trentmann 2017) A few day later, Donald Trump let it be known as his entourage left the United States for a 10 day official foreign excursion, that at his first stop in Saudi Arabia, the U.S. would sign a $300 Billion arms deal (also within an approximate 10 year span of time) with that kingdom in the hopes of establishing an "Arab NATO." (Sampathkumar 2017). We doubt that any Chinese arms are part of that deal.

The days of reckoning are not far off and with them will come some sour and distasteful economic repercussions in the U.S.A., the full range of which is impossible to predict. We do foresee very bad times in the United States (a periodic happenstance) when a clear domestic economic constriction adds pressure for a relatively hasty retreat of militaristic American imperialism. Tough decisions will have to be made.

We think that the inimitable convergence of these conditions will probably lead to massive evacuations of long standing military bases (just as happened in Vietnam and Iraq) and withdrawal of financial and weapons support to so-called American "allies" (including the oxymoronic "Arab NATO") against whatever form the New Eurasia takes. Such a retrenchment would also make Israel's quality of living drop precipitously and could well reduce the amount of, or even terminate, American fiscal support that Israel needs to survive as a nation state in such increasingly hostile terrain.

As the world is turning, "Full Spectrum Dominance" could become "Full Spectrum Retreat." In the mid-1960s it was unthinkable that America would be routed by the North Vietnamese. It is not unthinkable right now to consider a total U.S. military drawdown in the Middle East. Thus, Americans seriously need to rethink the wisdom of George Washington's call in his 1796 Farewell Address (which was parsed and edited by James Madison and Alexander Hamilton) to " . . . *avoid the necessity of those overgrown military establishments which, under any form of government, are inauspicious to liberty, and which are to be regarded as particularly hostile to republican liberty*" (Washington 1796) Yes, we think that a genuine "patriot act" would be to end American Empire and restore the republic.

What's needed instead is to resurrect America's original and long practiced idea and ideal of national spiritual and communal "exceptionalism" fostered by its earliest settlers and its Western pioneers. The disingenuous banners of "making the world safe for democracy," "the world's policeman," "The New World Order", "The world's banker", Neo-liberalism, and Neo-Conservatism have diminished America's well-earned and much deserved stature on the world scene due largely to its unique and precious contributions. These include a host of economic, cultural, technological, medical, spiritual and democratic inventions and innovations . . . not military victories (and defeats).

There is a brighter future for the U.S.A., even with a vast new Eurasian Union and a truly Multi-Polar world straight ahead. As Henry Jackson Turner emphasized, "The American Frontier" is a process, not a set of boundaries. The Multi-Polar World is The New Frontier for the United States.

We believe that there needs be an altogether novel vision for a completely new, substantial and useful American political-economic role in this rising Multi-Polar world order, which is neither Eurocentric nor under the sway of American military and corporate "strategic doctrines. As we think we've made clear enough by now, that kind of strategy is about as relevant to modern geo-politics as typewriters are to the modern and future global economy.

Many famous people have foreseen the challenges of this new world ahead and for some time. Journalist and author Elizabeth Dickinson, writing for *Foreign Policy*, affords us a chronological list of famous political leaders, academics, and journals who have been predicting for decades that the New Age of Multi-Polarity will be a reality in the early parts of the 21st Century and that America needs to anticipate it and be pro-active in its response. This list and dates include: Henry Kissinger as National Security Advisor (1969); President of France d'Estaing (1978); famed Yale historian Paul Kennedy (1987); illustrious Harvard political scientist Samuel Huntington ((1991); The *New York Times* (2007); the United States Intelligence Council (2008); and Vice President Joe Biden (2009) (Dickenson, 2009)

As we will show, one exciting and challenging way of moving forward—and demonstrating an authentic revival of genuine American Exceptionalism to the world—would be by using the unique American political system itself to attract Israel into becoming the 51st state. This, in turn, would transform the United States of America into The First Global Nation, a truly exceptional political phenomenon genetically worthy of what that word truly means in American history.

CHAPTER 4

How Joining America and Israel as The First Global Nation Can Help Bring Peace and Transformation to the Middle East and the World.

W HEN WE SAY THAT the United States needs to become a larger and greater "global nation," we are not only speaking in macro geo-political and strictly geographical terms, which is the standard in the social sciences. Given the harsh realities we see coming down the pike for the U.S.A., and the rest of this world, we think that what made America truly "exceptional" as a nation—its inner character as displayed from its beginning and through much of its history—needs to become the most salient part of its national life and global image once again.

That inner drive to succeed materially was greatly propelled by what the world famous sociologist Max Weber called "The Protestant Ethic" in his classic treatise *The Protestant Ethic and the Spirit of Capitalism* (Weber 1905 and 1930). This Christian ethos was surely a major stimulus for the growth of the U.S. through its "Manifest Destiny" phase and led America to become the largest economy in the entire world by the late 19th century—about the same time modern American imperialism got started. So, the U.S.A. had been a truly great nation for a long time before World War II, which established a firm foundation for its most grandiose imperial edifices and military artifacts.

Given the geo-political realities and almost certain seismic changes we can expect in the 21st Century as we just described in Chapter 3, it seems to us that the United States now has an excellent opportunity to reinvent itself; reverse its increasingly negative image; and help restore greater stability to the world. This holds true particularly in the Middle East where it has been a huge contributor to the steadily rising chaos there.

This means that America needs to revivify its original City on Hill doctrine which, like the Declaration of Independence, proclaimed that all humans are equal in the eyes of God, and that they must work together to survive impending threats as an independent nation free of entangling foreign alliances. It must become that again—albeit in a 21ˢᵗ century transformed mode—more like what President Ronald Reagan said in his Farewell Speech in 1988:

"I've spoken of the shining city all my political life . . . . And how stands the city on this winter night? . . . After 200 years, two centuries, she still stands strong and true to the granite ridge, and her glow has held no matter what storm. And she's still a beacon, still a magnet for all who must have freedom, for all the pilgrims from all the lost places who are hurtling through the darkness, toward home." (Reagan 1988, PBS.org, emphasis ours)

As we think we've made clear above, the entire world is about to enter a new kind of perilous global frontier, one in which religious and nationalist fundamentalists will be major players. Thus, America's fundamental religious ideas of "City on the Hill" and "Manifest Destiny" can become extremely useful once again—this time without the excessive "collateral damage" as was inflicted upon Native Americans, Mexicans and other peoples.

As de Tocqueville noticed, it was that combination of religious freedom, economic opportunity and secular self-governance that attracted so many 18ᵗʰ and 19ᵗʰ century Europeans to the shores of the United States. America has expanded its shores before, beyond continental bounds. It needs to and can do it again.

Does that mean that every American needs to become a "fundamentalist Christian"? Hardly. The answer also depends on what kind of "fundamentalist Christianity" is meant. For example, The Quakers adhere quite closely to the fundamental tenets of Jesus' teachings, particularly "The Sermon on the Mount" without having any "churches," cathedrals, sacraments, sacramental ceremonies or ministers at all. They have "meetings" where each individual contemplates his or her spiritual path and shares their thoughts.

They are completely wedded to both non-violence and democratic processes and probably got along better with Native Americans than any other Christian sect. Here is a short statement from a Quaker website that makes explicit their Christian value system, one that every American should embrace, surely as America's foreign policy goals: "Some commonly recognized testimonies include peace, integrity, equality, simplicity, community, and care for the earth."(*Friends General Conference* website, see References for link or Google it).

Due to this, the Quakers are particularly good at peaceful conflict resolution, which the reader will soon find out is exactly the kind of spiritually-based approach we advocate to smother the raging fires stoked by fundamentalist Islamists, particularly those in close proximity to Israel.

Therefore: It is time to change the present day American game and squarely face likely future realities. When the U.S. reaches the point of high-tailing itself out of the Middle East, it would be leaving Israel in the lurch and court a disaster there for which the U.S.A. would bear great responsibility. Thus these two intimate political partners need to think about getting engaged, i.e., that period of time before a wedding, and drafting realistic wedding plans as soon as possible.

This would be demonstrated by being open to and supportive of a statehood movement in Israel (the engagement process) while quickly working out the plans to welcome it into the U.S.A. as a sovereign state (the wedding). Once the nuptials are completed, the U.S.A. would then stretch from the middle reaches of the Pacific to the Middle East and Israel . . . with at least a section of Jerusalem as its 51st state capital, the place where Jesus first spoke of "the city on the hill" as a place of spiritual enlightenment and charity to all.

This matrimony could surely change the contours and pieces of the entire geo-political chessboard as well as the skillfully played CCP's game of "*Weiqi*"—or as it is better known in English as "Go". The U.S. would no longer persist in its futile attempt at "containing" China and Eurasia, and the U.S. would be much too big and global to be surrounded, much less swallowed, by China and Eurasia.

Can this be done? Of course it can. For one thing, it would be strictly an American internal matter. American statehood is a domestic issue between the U.S. Congress and political entities outside the then-current configuration of the United States. No outside political force can keep any such merger from happening.

The people from any polity (whether it be an American territory or an independent state or part of one) interested in joining the United States must seek membership and then it's up to the American people through their Congress to agree or not. The people of Israel could not be kept from developing American statehood movements if they so desired by any people other than in their own nation. And we strongly doubt that any such political movement in Israel could be squelched by any Israeli government, even if it dared to try.

The United States, as First Global Nation, strung through 14 time zones, could turn its attention inward to develop its own "common welfare" (including its newest state, Israel), as was the goal of the original Puritans of the Massachusetts Bay Colony and one of the explicit national goals set forth in the U.S. Constitution. All for one. One for all. It is time to re-revive the liberal, democratic, humanistic aspects of the Congregationalist Dream of Jesus' "Sermon on the Mount" and re-bury the self-glorified and self-selected oligarchy that has stifled true Christian values and self-governance for some time now.

The next two chapters will show (a) how the basic theory and principles of modern conflict resolution can be applied to achieve these goals particularly involving Israel and its contiguous neighbors; (b) how statehood has been accomplished under various analogous circumstances in America's past—all the feared problems of new statehoods have all been overcome over time; (c) how the core interest of all parties involved (the U.S.A., Israel, and all the neighboring Middle East states) will be served in a win/win/win scenario.

The Middle East as the Fulcrum for Positive Global Change: Locating the Mutual, Deepest Interests of All the Neighboring Combatants

If the United States, along with its current "allies", continues on its illogical path in the Middle East, the present maelstrom whipping up there will almost assuredly widen and worsen. At best, it will threaten what is left of stability in that region and at worst it would drag the entire world into its vortex. Certainly, there are other flashpoints which can set off a global inferno, but this is the longest running one, central to the interests all the major powers, and even has Biblical and Crusader roots.

Thus, The Middle East in 2016 qualifies as one of the most inflammable tinder boxes for a potential global nuclear war . . . or the lesser but still severe threat of Samuel Huntington's apocalyptic *Clash of Civilizations* (1996) coming to full fruition. It is also a major area of drilling more and more carbon energy out of the ground thus contributing more than its share towards what the vast consensus of the global scientific community states loudly is already an irreversible trend towards disastrous Climate Change.

Furthermore, the Middle East is the spiritual home to an enormous number of people who are physically homeless, woefully bedraggled and totally desperate. The ongoing wars there in the 21st century have left millions upon millions of people who have no choice but to migrate legally or illegally, with nothing but the ragged clothes on their backs, to other parts of the world. And though they may come with little to no physical possessions, they carry with them great political turmoil—and within the minds of a few, the threat of many acts of random and/or organized "terrorism" in Europe, Asia and North America.

Add to that, the ever-growing millions and millions of unemployable young people residing in the Middle East, Central Asia and North Africa who are easy prey to fanatic and fantastic distortions of Islamic ideas and ideals, and you have plenty of grist for the milling of even more horrendous violence. Isn't it clear enough by now that all this is leading into vicious and widespread sectarian and internecine fighting and massacres in those areas of the world—which is metastasizing worldwide?

This cannot go on in this way and be good for the people of this world in the years to come. Yet there is no one in power anywhere who has anything fresh in mind to de-escalate this situation, much less ameliorate it. The present formula of more bombing and killing by outsiders = peace does not work. We know a new formula that will.

So why not have the U.S.A. as a new resident in that neighborhood?

As professional peacemakers and practitioners of conflict resolution, we are ready for the torrent of abuse we will surely receive for what we advocate, among them the following epithets: "naïve", "crazy", "fools", "madmen", and of course: "it'll never happen." But no one can blame us for not being pretty much original in our thinking or for having the best of intentions. So here we go:

If the people in the United States, Israel, Turkey, Iran, Egypt, Pakistan, Jordan or any Arab state really want to end this seemingly eternal set of wars, uprisings, beheadings and widespread misery: SOLUTIONS ABOUND! Just about every public opinion poll we've seen in recent years show clearly that a large majority of people of the United States do not want permanent war in the Middle East.

It is also just plain common sense that the people of Israel do not want an infinite threat of extermination from their neighbors. It is equally clear that the people of Iraq, Jordan, Syria, Egypt, and Palestine do not want to dwell in abject poverty, be harassed, "check-pointed", bombed, ruled under martial law and live in fear forever!! It is not really in any human being's best interests for this state of affairs to continue on and on and on—not even for most of those who temporarily profit from it!!

It is a truism that what any sane, normal human being wants deep, deep in their emotional, physical, and spiritual selves is to be able to:

- Get along well with their fellow human beings, including neighbors and family. If they can accomplish that on a daily basis, they lay the foundation to achieve the other things they *need* dearly, which include:

- Health, bodily safety and inner peace for themselves and their families;

- Economic opportunity to better their lives and the lives of those they love;

- The chance to learn about life and to gain knowledge and skill to understand the world better and enjoy the gifts of life that have been bestowed upon them;

- Freedom to become the best person they can be, that is "self-actualization";

- Liberty to talk to, pray to and be grateful to the God or spiritual leader of their choice.

These are the elemental, core interests of the overwhelming number of people in all nationalities, regions, and sects, including the United States and Israel. Sadly, though, their deep seated interests and personal well-being does not compute in the minds of those political and religious zealots and economic warlords who want the murderous and torturous fighting to go on forever more. This rather tiny sub-group of tortured souls do their best and worst to gain and hang onto political power at all costs to the detriment of the vast majority of others.

In sum, the escalating tensions in the Middle East and the Western world over increasing Islamic radicalism have plunged the vast masses of the people into a dazed and troubled state of mind. They are told they must let those who have led them into this Hell of a Mess, to continue to do what they have been doing unsuccessfully for decades—if not more and worse.

So, how can two relatively obscure and isolated academic types do anything to change this diabolical equation? Well, we can write this book and rely heavily upon the magnificent democratic capabilities of the Internet to inject these ideas into the world psyche . . . with the hope that it is the right time for it to be planted and fertilized by an ever growing number of people thinking about an entirely new paradigm of world affairs that will work to everyone's benefit.

So, here goes our Intro to Peacemaking 101 as applied to the Middle East, which would greatly assist the growth of the still nascent Multi-Polar World. What we advocate is an entirely new version of proven peace-making processes that enrich and empower all human beings who live on this Earth and who would like to see such exist for their children and their children's children as well. "Peacemaking"? Yes, that is one key tenet of "The Sermon on the Mount", a key component of the "light" needed to illuminate the impending darkness.

So, what follows is a short course on how anyone, anywhere, can become: a Peacemaker, yes even in this Middle East Perpetual War of All against All.

Peacemaking 101: Brainstorming an Option that Breaks Multiple Impasses

Learning to be a peacemaker and having some success at it gives one a rare and ethereal sensation of doing at least a little good in this sorry world. As one gets better at it through repetition and the personal satisfaction one takes in helping others consent to an agreement they were instrumental in crafting. The more one is successful at that, the more the basic values of being a decent mediator-peacemaker take root in one's soul.

Furthermore, the rules and skills of mediation become a part of one's daily life and interactions with one's fellow human beings and the reader can see how well they work for him, her and others. Ask anyone who has done it or still does it. We are sure that almost to a person, all would agree that learning to be and practicing as a mediator has helped them become a better person themselves and has helped them see how those who don't have these values and skills seem to wander into many storms without a compass.

So, what follows are a series of lessons we have learned over the years from being long-time students, teachers, preachers, and practitioners of peaceful conflict resolution and how we know they can be applied to creating a much better world than the one in which we seem to be inexorably headed.

Trash the Past: Don't Make the Same Mistakes

One of the first things you learn about effective conflict resolution of the non-legal, non-violent, non-adversarial sort is that you must get the parties to any dispute, no matter how minor or long-lasting, to block out or discard all or as many of the past grievances as they can and think instead about how to attain a harmonious and peaceful future. This does not mean that past history will or should be forgotten or the losses trivialized. One has to forgive, not forget, and move towards a peaceable, future oriented bargain.

Of course, the past that has led to present iron-clad impasses is important to know so the involved parties don't repeat it, like what we have put forth in Chapters 2 and 3 as the lurid state of human affairs for many centuries past. But if heated and difficult negotiations are bathed in the hates, desolation and selective negative memories of the past, they will bar everyone from good faith negotiating and thinking collaboratively towards potentially workable and amicable solutions.

It is in every party's best interests long-term to do that. Individuals, leaders, and whole nations must learn the hard lesson to back-burner the agonies, desecrations, tears, and sorrow of the dead past and to accept the fact that everyone distorts history to some degree or in some way. They must convince and motivate themselves to conjure a better, more pacific future for all.

This isn't easy to do because of past and present conditioning about one's "rights" or about "getting even", but it is actually done by people on this Earth all the time, every day, around the world. "Get over it." "Move on." Needing a serene center for ourselves, our families, our tribes, our countries is *in every human's DNA—as listed above in this chapter—so it's not counter-intuitive or something that human beings cannot achieve.*

Of course, lawyers, diplomats, and various government and/or religious "leaders" have a particularly hard time doing this. They are stuck with the words in treaties, law books, past political betrayals and criminal wrongs, and in some of them, just pure malice towards certain "others". They also are extremely judgmental about past actions and try to prove their side was either the innocent victim or right in acting as bad as they did.

So these kind of powerful people are extremely comfortable dwelling in the painful past and/or vowing future retributions. They seek "justice" for their cause . . . even if that means raining firestorms on many innocents. They dote on their version of the "truth" or "truths" about what happened in order to feel justified in their quest for vengeance.

But can anyone really know exactly what happened in the past—who said or did what first and then second and who reacted in what way to what and when? Can the reader actually remember exactly what he or she said yesterday to any particular person? Does the reader know what the other heard or saw? The answer to that universally is "no," even if there was a surveillance camera or hidden microphone recording it. How does the video or audio tape know what the other person saw or heard or was thinking or thought they meant?

Scientists and trial lawyers prove over and over that even eye-witnesses are not particularly reliable. Americans tend to believe that the adversarial system as practiced in American courtrooms are an excellent way of recreating the "truth" of past events. However, the rules of evidence, the tactics of the lawyers, and the bias of judges often hide, omit, or tamper with many facts that will make the truth very gray instead of black or white, fuzzy instead of sharply defined. A "verdict" about the truth of the past is expected.

But even a unanimous judgment by a jury of peers doesn't mean it actually happened that way at all.

As mediator-peacemakers, over time, we've found that it isn't easy to keep people from falling into this tempting trap. "This is what happened." "S/he did this and I did that to get even." It seems like a natural human inclination to want to pin the blame for some loathsome act on someone other than themselves and to want to "win" and be compensated for the harm done to them. It's difficult, but not impossible, to get people to forget completely about past wrongs done to them and to not want someone to judge them to be the victims and provide some recompense or atonement for the pain and suffering they had to endure.

As mediators, we have found that this is extremely tough to get people to do even with something as petty as neighbors fighting over parking spaces or divorcing couples fighting over who gets custody of Mr. Pickles, the pet parrot. It is hard to convey how emotional and angry people can get over such relatively minuscule things and how tenaciously they dig themselves into immutable positions over such material trifles.

However, a patient mediator learns, that sooner or later, most humans—individually or collectively—get really tired, emotionally drained, physically sick or psychologically crippled over the fighting and painful discomfort of haggling over their beloved positions for a long time. Lingering conflict is like a disease and slowly but surely begins to seriously harm their financial, physical, or mental health. Ultimately, what we call the "*conflict fatigue" point* (CFP), will be reached.

This then becomes a perfect opportunity for each party to the dispute to come to their senses and co-operate on an entirely new way of resolving it. Professor William Zartman, of the Johns Hopkins' School for Advanced International Studies (SAIS), calls this the "ripe" moment where a "hurtful stalemate" opens the door to look for an amicable way out of the festering impasse. (Zartman 1985, 1989)

Peacemakers have to be very, very patient and empathetic with both or many sides, realizing that "the truth" of the matter is a whimsy and "justice" is truly in the eye of the beholder. Actually time is often on the peacemakers' side since one or both or many of the parties will finally get exhausted or damaged enough by the conflict to listen to the reasonableness of looking for an unforeseen, but practical settlement.

So, are America, Israel, Egypt, Jordan, the Palestinians, Lebanon, and Syria getting to The Conflict Fatigue point yet? What about Turkey, Iran, Saudi Arabia, Britain, France and Russia? We really don't know. It doesn't seem to be the case in 2916 what with the escalation of military violence in the Middle East. But they'd better get to it soon, because they and the entire world need this fight to end due its potential to catalyze ecological, economic and political catastrophes already on the cusp of occurring.

This is a localized dispute in some ways (the Middle East), but one can look at it as a burning fuse that could easily detonate the ultimate nuclear conflagration or climate upheaval to the detriment of the Earthly surviv-ability of all humankind. Do the disputants in the Middle East and intruders from the outside want to perpetrate a global arson and economic morass that destroys them and all humanity? Or would they rather get that part of the world in order so that they can help ward off these anticipatable calami-ties and prosper together?

They all need what we mediators call a good "reality check." What all the political actors there have been doing over and over again is not only not working, it is dangerous to everyone's health and life. All the disputants need to stop making the same deadly mistakes repeatedly. That is the exactly what the English language defines as "stupidity."

Empathizing with the Humanity of the "Enemy":
Distinguishing Positions from Interests

Like it or not, we have all become neighbors on a small planet that is at great risk for all its residents. Past ways, borders, treaties, laws and pronounce-ments are like chains around us. But this world is mostly water and we are drowning with these historical shackles binding our arms and legs and brains so we cannot swim to safety.

Thus, another important lesson in conflict resolution is to help the parties recognize the difference between their "positions" and their "inter-ests". These words are commonly used interchangeably, but actually refer to very different things. For example, after the 1967 War between Israel and all its Arab neighbors, Israel occupied lands previously belonging to various Arabic neighbors and has not only not returned to its original borders, but has greatly expanded "settlements" and militarized outposts into most of the continued-to-be-occupied territories.

Israeli political leaders keep telling their countrymen that expanding these "settlements" is in Israel's "security interests"—its basic right to exist as a nation state in the Middle East—that they need to continue to subjugate these lands infinitely, crush all Palestinian (and their allies') opposition to this ceaseless mission creep, and persist in multiplying these well-armed, walled and fenced communities. This rationale, of course, is met with the derision and wrath of Palestinian, Lebanese, Syrian, and Islamic radicals throughout the Middle East, Central Asia and North Africa, and is interpreted as a blatant falsehood by nations all around the world.

Most Israelis seem to believe what their "leaders" are telling them, that this is the best way to secure "peace" and "security" in the long run. But deep down, do they really feel good about running to air raid shelters and relying on what the Israeli and American politicians and media call the "Iron Dome?" This is an anti-missile system which is supposed to be an impermeable shield against all incoming rockets. However, there is some hard scientific evidence that what the Israeli populace is being told by the government is far from being precise.

An MIT physics professor specializing in ballistics, analyzed numerous photos, images and data of rocket intercepts in the 2012 Gaza War and concluded, in *The Bulletin of Atomic Scientists,* that the Israeli government's claim of 90% effectiveness in destroying or deflecting Hamas's missiles is nowhere near accurate. The evidence he used leads him to say that a much better estimate is 5%. (The actual figure is most likely somewhere in between these calculations.) According to the American professor, the real reason for the low Israeli casualty rate in both 2012 and 2014 from Gaza-fired missiles was their excellent civil defense on the ground—which in our opinion is highly motivated by fear. (Postol 2014)

Do most Israelis really believe that more "settlements" on Arab land, what many people, leaders and analysts globally believe to be a gradual form of "ethnic cleansing", will secure peace and happiness in their babies' futures? Such a negative opinion can even be found in a conservative American university publication like the *Notre Dame Magazine:* "Such Israeli policies . . . threaten Palestinian means for existence and survival. They are enforced depopulation mechanisms that can lead to homelessness, exposure and limited access to medical supplies and treatment. The policies could also be interpreted as a subtle, slow form of ethnic cleansing." And that was written 8+ years before this writing. (Macmillan 2007)

We doubt that the Israeli public's belief that these constant encroachments upon Palestinian land is necessary for Israel's security is little more than a "rationalization" to palliate national fear about what might eventually come to pass: being "pushed into the sea" by hordes of Muslims. Yes, alleviating fear is a core interest of any person or any country. But ordinary Israelis are not provided any solid, alternative positions about how to secure their future existence in peace other than what they've been hearing for decades now either from their leaders or their "allies" in America which is: more settlements = greater security. Just the opposite is true.

On the Western side of the Atlantic, is it really in the interests of the people of the United States of America to be addicted to perpetual violation of International Law and UN resolutions by nearly a half century of Israeli "occupation" of Arab lands and to revel in the penury and destitution of the Palestinian Arabs? In the Eastern Mediterranean, is it really in the interests of the vast majority of Israelis to maintain this hard line position of indefinite occupation and incorporation of these lands that actually (according to International Law) belong to the Arabs? Do they really believe that eternal warfare (a position) is the road to lasting peace (a core interest)?

If national existence, personal and family safety and peace are among the core interests of Americans and Israelis—which they are—then the answer to the above questions is: obviously not. Prolonged and indefinite occupation and perpetual expansion of Israeli settlements into Palestinian land are simply political positions of political and ideological extremists who have gained and retain power in Israel and the United States up to and through 2016.

Back in 2002 and 2007, the late King Abdullah of Saudi Arabia came up with a plan that was endorsed by the Arab League. It was the epitome of the so-called *"Two-State Solution"*—a complex set of mutual positions—*that gave Israel exactly what it said it wanted as its basic interest: the right to exist and to be recognized and treated as a respected fellow nation state in the Middle East.*

The King Abdullah Plan officially "recognized" Israel politically—as a sovereign nation with a right to exist as such—and it included a variety of economic and trade inducements as well. All Israel had to do to secure it national interest was to return to its state borders prior to the 1967 War and give, trade or compensate the "right of return" of Palestinian Arabs to Israel (that is, alter its positions). There were also some suggestions of how to share Jerusalem, a city sacred to both Islam and Judaism (not to mention Christianity).

Naturally, the power managers in Israel rejected it out of hand. Why? Because their personal, political interests were not those of the Israeli people. They were the interests of a radical, power hungry, militaristic, other-hating minority: almost the entire, contemporary political leadership of Israel. They critiqued and nit-picked various parts of King Abdullah's offer to death, and no one has heard much about it since. In January 2015, King Abdullah was 90 years old and finally died. His generous, fair and decent plan actually expired well before him due to the machinations of various and sundry Israeli and American politicians in the interim.

Prior to that another peace plan, one developed by President Clinton along with Prime Minister Menachem Begin and Yasser Arafat in the late 1990s, came razor-thin close in positions to a Peace Plan that traded "land for peace". But this time hate-filled extremists among Hamas in the Gaza

Strip—whose position on Israel was rabidly clear and repeated often, i.e., the extermination of Israel as a nation state—got Yasser Arafat to back out at the last minute. His withdrawal from the agreement as probably because his signing of it would have been equivalent to his authorizing his own death warrant at the hands of Islamic extremists. Does Hamas have any interests? Yes, the same as any theocracy: the power to control the lives and conduct of the people devoted to its brand of religion.

The abject and dismal demise of both of these "two-state solutions have been accompanied by the building of a lengthy, huge and unsightly wall or series of barriers between many more Israeli settlements and Arabic neighborhoods in the occupied lands making any unification of a Palestinian state—between East Jerusalem, the West Bank and Gaza—practically impracticable. Plus there have been several vicious mini-wars between Israel and Hamas in Gaza and Hezbollah in Lebanon.

Again, winning "positional" battles by both sides (Israel keeps building on formerly Arab lands and Hamas and Hezbollah keep trying to inflict greater damage on Israel) is actually more important to these so-called "leaders" than truly securing the interests of the vast majority of the people of Israel, Palestine, Egypt, Jordan, Lebanon and Syria. It's become routine to witness invasions, air strikes, rocket attacks, murders, arrests, stabbings, and secret tunnels galore. Only a horde of violence-prone fanatics on all sides could create a *Quagmire in a Desert*. But that's what we've got.

Despite all of this, there is no doubt in our minds that peace and prosperity can become a reality in that area . . . that quicksand alley can become a fertile valley. Are the authors Pollyanna, playing "The Happy Face Game J"? As grizzled mediators, applying our knowledge as such to such an international catastrophe in progress, we can see what the actual interests of the Palestinian and Israeli people are: a guaranteed national identity with secure borders and peace and prosperity for all the residents of that part of the Middle East.

In addition there are technological fixes that cry for implementation in that neck of the woods, and we don't mean new hi-tech weapons systems. What is needed are new tools to make that entire area into an economic powerhouse that can help the entire world transform into a better place for all to live and even perhaps flourish.

Sad to say, but the major stumbling block to any resolution of this never ending conflict among all the countries who are in that area to stay remains the same: the political leadership of all of them. For reasons, some malignant and some benign, they are stuck in their concretized positions and cannot budge. The interests of all humankind need a radical change in positions consistent with Israel and America's actual national interests at the present time and what they are likely to be in the near future.

This "Endless War" in the Middle East, and particularly around "The Holy Land" must desist as quickly as possible. Every citizen in the Middle East (Jew, Palestinian, Shiite, Sunni, Kurd, Egyptian, Hashemite).—individually and nationally—must face the fact squarely and immediately that their personal and human core interests are the same as those they are fighting—yes that list at the beginning of this chapter!

They must grasp the glaring reality that the longer this goes on, the worse it will be for their descendants. Do they want another 100 Year War, as in the Middle Ages? Do they want another 300 year war, as between the British, the Irish and Northern Ireland? No one alive today—or their offspring—can weather such a conflict, and neither can Planet Earth. They have no rational or reasonable option but to claim their enemies' interests as their own, which in reality they are.

They need a new paradigm which must be consistent with the Multi-Polar World that is rapidly evolving, which we described above in Chapter 2. The United States of America is uniquely positioned to provide that in the context of the Real New World Order of the 21st Century. By doing so, it can regain its own global stature in positive spiritual and governmental values instead of the ersatz ones embraced by the materialistic, geo-strategic ones that came to characterize the past century or so of American history detailed in Chapter 3.

Transformation from Embattled Disputant to a "Good Neighbor"

Once the authentic core interests of all of the parties involved in this Middle East quicksand bog are made clear and widely comprehended, and the absurd positions couched in false "security" language are abandoned, then we come to the next phase of a serious conflict resolution process: conceiving fresh, imaginative, and creative options that would maximize the core interests of all parties to the dispute. This is sometimes referred to as "brainstorming" towards mutually acceptable agreements which can become: win/win/win scenarios.

No, that does not mean a "compromise." It means a whole new and bigger pie to slice which can, in most cases, be made better, particularly with the use of human imagination and, hopefully, new technologies that will make the world a better place for all to live.

Let's face it! Right now, America is the 800 ton Godzilla in the Middle East room. America is in the Middle East to stay, even if only at the fringe of the forthcoming new Eurasia of the 21st Century. If there is to be a peaceful and harmonious resolution, then it there must be a transformation of the American perception of any core interests it may have in that part of the world.

Foreign oil and "winning" geopolitical games are not American core interests. The existence of the state of Israel has come to be an American one and is, of course as we have noted above, is the basic one of Israel's as well. Thus, the only option that can keep the United States as a major and peaceful actor in the Middle East and guarantee Israel's existence as a state, is if Israel becomes the 51st state.

The key prerequisite to this ever happening would be to encourage an American Statehood movement in Israel. If successful, or on the verge of success, only then could a genuine negotiation begin between the United States, as a directly involved party, Israel and all of Israel's neighbors, adjacent and close by. Why the latter? One does not move into a neighborhood where one knows the arrival will be met by acts of violence.

Clearly, the U.S. has been and is presently committed to the existence of, and the nation-state strategies, of the most avid Zionists in Israel and in the United States in the past and at the present. In a sense, the tail has come to wag the dog. Pity President Obama and his successor if he or she continues to see blind adherence to an ever-expansionist Zionist nation state in Israel as being a core interest of the United States.

That was certainly not how the American recognition of Israel began. Israel was a mere blip on the American strategic radar. The United States was, at best, a distant observer of the Israeli-Palestinian contretemps. How America became strategically entangled in Israel's affairs, as it is now, is a long and complicated story. But as we said at the beginning of this chapter, that is the dim, distant past and neither needs be treasured nor forgotten.

However, it is harmful to continue past American positions about Israel as they have evolved when American interests are now quite different and may change again drastically in the near future. Being imprisoned in positions that have been characterized as those of the "American Empire" in that part of the world will only lead to evermore Islamic enmity and vicious, senseless, random and systematic retaliations from an ever more angry and militant Muslim world.

To repeat for emphasis: America and the rest of the world have to admit and accept a present and future geo-strategic reality: The United States of America is going to be a permanent inhabitant in the Eastern Mediterranean region. No matter what the politics of Eurasia becomes, the U.S.A. is no more likely to abandon Israel than it is to abandon Alaska or

Hawai'i. The political and cultural ties are just too tightly bound together at this point in time.

For example, a Jewish American from New Jersey, who became an Israeli and ultimately the Israeli Ambassador to the U.S.A. from 2009-2013 has observed, from his unique vantage point, that sometimes it seems to many people as though Israel is already a state in the United States. (Oren 2015).

Given that empirical truth and come what may, the U.S. will remain a relatively resourceful nation in many ways, why can it not change its pretense that it is a neutral, outside player, either as "fair broker" or "mediator" regarding Israel's various conflicts in the Middle East? That facade has definitely not worked in the past or presently and it will not work in the future. No one is deceived.

So, if one puts together all the past attempts at "peacemaking" between the Zionists and Arabs like the Oslo Accords, Camp David, and Bill Clinton's go at it on the Eastern shore of Maryland . . . the state of affairs between Israel and Islam are as bad or worse in 2016 than ever before. Moreover, they appear headed into even more frequent and regular episodes of violence for America, the EU, and maybe the entire world, a point we will make ever so clear in Chapter 5. "End Times" anyone?

Neither China nor Russia nor Brazil nor India nor NATO are coming to the American-Israel rescue and the United Nations remains as hapless, helpless and hopeless as ever. Plus, as we hope we've made very clear by now, a whole new Eurasia is in the early stages of becoming a major geopolitical reality as a next door neighbor. Where does a tiny, nuclear armed nation state of Israel fit in when none in the Middle East or in Eurasia can be considered tried and true allies, much less friendly, and all that military hardware and troops in the Middle East are no longer sustainable for American national interests?

The downside of having so many military bases and camps and logistic centers throughout the Middle East is that they are properly seen as, and somewhat resented, as what many call and what we emphasized above as being part and parcel of: "The American Empire."

Planting "The American Empire" on Arab soil, with its obvious prejudice towards the "independent nation-state of Israel", and the double standard that this entails, clearly is a major cause of extreme antagonism against both the United States and Israel. Though America and Israel may have issues from time to time, they are inexorably linked in most Muslim eyes as being one and the same. So why not make the United States of America an official resident there?

As we stated at the outset, we think that the best way for the United States to go in that part of the world is for the United States to work out an arrangement with the Israeli people and for the Israeli people (including their 20% resident Arab Israelis) to apply for statehood as the 51ˢᵗ state of the United States of America. Think about the original religious beliefs of the early American settlers being a "New Zion." It would be an amazing spiritual closure to have Israel as a sovereign part of the United States in the Holy Land! The New Zion marries the Old Zion, ironic, but smart.

Of course this still begs the question: Why would Israel, a *bona fide* nation state, recognized as such by numerous nations for many decades, want to become part of the United States and give up its national sovereignty? Why would a Prime Minister of a prominent nation want to become the governor of just another American state?

Given the developments in the world which we have stated before as being inevitable—geo-strategically and climatically—we believe that there are many more benefits to Israel, the United States and the entire region, if this were to transpire. We will discuss them in greater depth in the next chapter, where we will lay out what we believe to be the quintessential interests of the United States, Israel, Lebanon, a new Syria, a new Palestinian state, Jordan and Egypt. We will also discuss "the clear and present danger" to the U.S. and Israel posed by the ever increasing rise of Radical Islam, particularly in its most virulent form, The Islamic State.

On the flip side of that coin, is there any chance whatsoever that an American Statehood movement could even begin in Israel? In order for Israel to become an American state, this is a precondition, as this has always been the way any present state (after the first 13) has become a star in the spangled banner. But even if that were to happen, is there really any precedent for such a political move in American history? As we will show: yes.

Keep in mind that admitting Israel into the U.S.A as the 51ˢᵗ state would make the United States a permanent fixture in the Middle East without it being part of an empire there, the ephemeral roles that Turkey, Great Britain and France played in that neck of the woods for many centuries. Actually, it would simply extend the United States from Hawaii to Israel in latitude just as it extends from Alaska to Puerto Rico in longitude. In effect, *it would make the United States of America a unique and original kind of Global Nation, in large part due to its inventive federal system.*

Egypt was not an equal entity of the United Kingdom as Wales and Scotland have been for centuries. Iraq was not a sovereign part of Turkey during the Ottoman Empire., actually it was one of several provinces which were ruled unilaterally by the Sultans of their times. Neither Syria nor Lebanon were part of France. They were colonies of the French Empire, just as was French-Indo-China (Vietnam). America in the 17 and 18ᵗʰ centuries was not part of Great Britain, it was a rope of colonies. It had no members of Parliament.

Israel, as the 51ˢᵗ State, would be an equal part of the United States of America . . . .just as is Hawai'i, once an independent monarchy.

Theodore Herzl, the founder of Zionism, believed that the Jewish people could only be free of anti-Semitism if they would have their own state in which they would enjoy complete liberty to practice their own religion and nurture their own culture. A state (or as a province of the Ottoman Empire) governed by Jewish people would not persecute Jews; that was a key part of his thinking. Although he may well have envisioned it to be a nation-state at that time in the 19ᵗʰ century, we do not think Israel's being a state within the American constitutional framework would be antithetical to his dream and his political theory.

Thus, the Zionists would still have their "state", located in the heart of The Promised Land. It would be one heavily populated and run by people of the Jewish faith and culture, but it would transform from a nation state to one within the friendly confines and constitutional law of the United States federation. Actually Israel is about 75% Jewish. Likewise, in 2014 approximately 70% of Americans identified themselves as Christian. Both in Israel and the U.S., religious leaders do not control policy making at the national level, but in both places religion does play an important role in the affairs of government. Still, there are some governmental arrangements in Israel which would pose serious problems under the American constitutional doctrine of the separation of church and state. They will be discussed below.

So how does any political unit become a state within the United States of America? The U.S. Constitution provides a vague answer to that in its Article IV. Essentially, there are few basic requirements: (a) The United States Congress has the power to admit a new state. How is this done? The Constitution remains silent. History has shown that it takes a majority in both houses to agree. That's it.

Also, later in Article IV, it says that: (b) "The United States shall guarantee to every State in this Union, a Republican form of government." Is that the Platonic or Roman view of a "republic"? The Constitution remains mute. But by the standards of the various forms of government of the present day 50 states in the U.S.A., Israel's form of government could fit, although it would be the only "parliamentary" system and the Prime Minister would have to become a mere "Governor." Nebraska is the only state in the union with only a one-house (unicameral) legislature and no other state seems to care a lick. Plus nearly 50% of American states elect their judges, while a substantial minority do not whereas the federal government has all of its judiciary appointed. In other words, there is ample room for Israel's system to be incorporated into the U.S.A, although with some modifications.

Is there any legal precedent to allow an independent country into the union during American history? Well, as we say in law school, there may not be any single case of how a "territory" or "republic" or "break-away state" can be admitted into the American union that is "on all fours," i.e., which would be clearly binding "law" to make Israel the 51st state. However, there are several admissions of a polity into the union that provide some precedent to support America's doing this today with Israel, if the American and Israeli publics so desired.

There is actually an intriguing history of various political conflicts, dilemmas and varied solutions that were involved in the admission of the states of Vermont, Texas, Utah, Alaska and Hawai'i into the U.S.A. Each is a historical soap opera unto itself, extremely complicated, but each has one or more elements relevant to the Israeli-USA situation during our present era both in terms of advancing this move, but at the same time warning of the unexpected and/or difficult consequences that might ensue.

The History and Politics of Becoming a State in the U.S.A.: Five Short Case Studies.

Caveat to Professional Historians: What follows are just thumbnail sketches, not detailed histories, of events preceding their admission to the Union. They are only meant to show some resemblances to the problems and solutions to admitting Israel as a state that have occurred throughout American history.

Vermont: Exchanging Territory for Gold

Vermont's entry as the 14th state in the union was hardly a momentous decision . . . but there was a lot of stubborn independence among some leading Vermonters to becoming associated with their fellow British colonists in any "American" confederation or federation. Ethan Allen and The Green Mountain Boys were legendary for their role in helping the American revolutionaries defeat the British in the battle for Fort Ticonderoga. They were also legendary for fighting for Vermont's independence from New York and New Hampshire, due to various land grants bestowed upon those two larger colonies by the British Monarchy.

Partly due to a lot of animosity about which colony owned what land and because New York and New Hampshire had so much trouble with Vermonters, Vermont was barred from participation in The Continental Congress. It remained that way throughout the American Revolution (Vermonters fighting the tyranny of the King of England as well as that of the colonists of New York and New Hampshire).

The enmity between Vermont and its two bordering colonies was so great that a serious negotiation was held with the British in Quebec in the 1780s over whether Vermont might be best suited as part of Canada. Even the great Vermont revolutionary Ethan Allen was a delegate to those talks. Eventually, though, negotiations broke down—perhaps because they may have been a ploy to taunt and tempt the Congressional Congress. In fact, Vermont remained an independent political entity until after the new U.S. Constitution was formed in 1789. In its own mind, it was an independent republic with only its borders in dispute.

The long-simmering problem over land and boundary borders was not a small matter to the Vermonters or New Yorkers. The famous American poet John Greenleaf Whittier wrote a poem about the strong feelings of Vermonters about their liberty and freedom (maintaining their own postal service) during this period of time. Titled 'The Song of the Vermonters, 1779' the last verse went like this:

> *"Come York or come Hampshire, come traitors or knaves,*
> *If ye rule o'er our land ye shall rule o'er our graves;*
> *Our vow is recorded–our banner unfurled,*
> *In the name of Vermont we defy all the world!"*

However, by 1791 there was a strong support growing within the Vermont Republic to join the union, what we now call a "statehood movement". So they petitioned Congress for admission to the newly minted U.S.A. With the dispute over property still a sore point with New York, Vermont finally agreed to pay NY $30,000—in gold coins (a lot for that time) to settle the matter. The story of the transfer of that large amount of metal over trails and dirt roads is a saga unto itself. Once that deal was done, Congress agreed to admit Vermont into the Union with no grumbles from New York.

However, a few other lessons can be learned from the first new state to be added to the original Thirteen.

First, Vermont had been an independent "republic" for 14 years before its admission into the United States of America. It had its own unique history of being part of France and two other neighboring states. It had a unicameral legislature (just as Nebraska has today). It partially abolished slavery in its own constitution. And it had to settle some serious and long standing land issues with its neighboring states before it was allowed to become an equal part of the United States of America.

Admitting Vermont into the Union was, for its time, a multifaceted matter with a lot of emotional history and strong feelings one way or another. It took a lot of thinking, energy, and determination over an extended period of time to negotiate statehood. Such would also be the case as to Israel becoming a state, albeit even more complicated . . . and taking much longer as well. The case of Vermont becoming a new state set the first precedent that the statehood process could involve hot tempers on many sides and involve contested borders and monetary considerations before the deed was done.

Next Comes Annexing "The Republic of Texas": War and More War

To our mind, this case comes closer to the Israel situation, since it involved a long standing international dispute that the prospective new state had with very unfriendly neighbors who felt that their land had been stolen from them by force and violence and then occupied in a hostile manner. Of course, that was the Mexican view about Texas—the latter which declared itself to be an independent republic on land previously belonging to Mexico.. And, in fact, the formal admission of Texas into the American union actually was a major contributory factor to the vitriolic and very bloody Mexican-American War.

Also, admitting Texas was a very fiery and contentious issue among Americans at the time, with warnings of ominous, short-term and long-term consequences to come if Texas became part of America. For one thing, this became the single issue dividing America in a presidential race and decided the outcome of it as well. For another, it set the scene for two very bloody wars in America's future: the aforementioned Mexican war and the American Civil War.

Here is how this particular statehood procedure evolved.

As anyone familiar with American history should know, Texas was a large part of Mexico, and was heavily infiltrated by American settlers, mostly from the U.S. South, during the 1820s and 1830s. There was friction between at least some of the Spanish speaking Catholic Mexicans and the English speaking Protestant Americans from Day One. Eventually, this and a number of other factors led to a rebellion of the Americans against the Mexicans in 1836, followed by a series of blood-drenched battles that eventuated in an American military victory there and the establishment of the Republic of Texas in 1836.

The United States government quickly recognized this independent republic in 1837. The battle for statehood began for real at that time and took many years to reach a climax.

America was already deeply divided on the issues of slavery and its Westward expansionism. The South almost unanimously wanted Texas to be admitted as a "slave state". This would greatly expand the power of slave-holders in the union. Many in the North were just as vehemently opposed, both as a matter of anti-slavery in general, plus the idea of expanding it ever more westward, plus there was great nervousness that such an act would probably lead to an all-out war with Mexico.

As history would have it, given the way American and Washington, D.C politics seem to work, a presidential election provided the crucible for the inflammable chemicals to mix. The presidential election of 1844, which pitted James K. Polk vs. Henry Clay was fought almost entirely on the issues of annexing Texas to the U.S.A. and expanding slave-holding ever westward which was quite at odds with the religiously-based theory of "Manifest Destiny."

By electing Polk, the southern slavery expansionists won big, but on the other hand, the northern expansionists were on the verge of gaining Oregon, Washington, Idaho and parts of Wyoming as well. It was a political simile to a "Mexican Standoff." Nevertheless, in December of 1845, the U.S. Congress by joint vote annexed the Republic of Texas into the union. Only a year later in 1846, the next phase of the Mexican-American War broke out. It ended up with not only Texas as a state, but with Arizona, New Mexico, most of California, Colorado and Utah coming into the arms of America through various treaties, monetary purchases and cessations of title.

Of course, with this new power of Texas as a new member of the slavery states, this gave them more confidence in their desire to secede from the union and to bring about the horrendous War Between the States that began some 15 years later. Ulysses S. Grant, while dying and writing his memoirs, confessed his belief that the U.S. Civil War was God's punishment on the United States for the Mexican-American War. But whether by divine intervention or not, the addition of Texas to the United States was accompanied by lots of bloodshed, war, and a huge national wound and debt. Do the vast majority of Americans think that all that was worthwhile and good for the U.S.A. of today? Without a doubt.

So bringing a new state into the fold can lead to immense hard feelings among Americans and portend a great deal of fighting and dying over it. It was a risky move and led to many atrocities. Still, it is hard to deny that, in the long run, it did lead to the United States being a much greater nation. Texas, as an independent republic with many Americans living in it, had great potential as a new state in the Union, but lots of enemies across a disputed border and lots of controversy over such a statehood within the U.S.A.

The Israeli situation has an analogous set of plusses and minuses, not the least of which is that it is "a Jewish state." So is a different religion from the dominant American Christian religion a bar to statehood?

The Morman State Enters the Union: Descendants of the Ancient Israelites in "The New Zion"

So, would it be even remotely possible for a polity almost totally associated with one religion—a religion that differs dramatically from general American Christian beliefs (most assuredly those of the Pilgrims and Puritans)—and which was considered by many Americans to be a pure "theocracy"—to become a state within the United States federal system? Is it possible for a polity largely comprised of a religious group that has been despised and oppressed within the U.S.A. to ultimately become an American state itself? History says: yes. Utah is the epitome of an example.

Many Americans consider Utah to be "The Mormon" state even today. The Mormons are an unusual Christian sect which due to a horrendous persecution in parts of the United States in the early and mid-19th century, left for parts then unknown, in the heart of the Rocky Mountains (and which was at that time technically still a part of Mexico). They wished to practice their own religion away from the main body of American "civilization" and among the Native Americans (The Utes) who already lived there, likely for centuries before any White Man arrived.

Shortly after their arrival and settlement, the Mexican-American War ended and the Treaty of Guadalupe Hidalgo was signed, the Mormons held a constitutional convention in 1849 in which they formed the State of Deseret which included all of Utah and much of the present day states of Nevada, Colorado, Wyoming, Arizona, Southern California, Oregon and Idaho. They also named their top religious leader, Brigham Young, to be the Governor of Deseret and all of the state's officials were Mormons as well.

Partly due to this clear theocratic set-up, the "Representative" they sent to Washington to be their delegate to Congress was not permitted to be seated. We can all guess why. Congress relented some soon thereafter and did permit Utah and New Mexico to become official "Territories" of the United States in 1850.

Although the new Territory of Utah was almost homogenously Mormon, the then-sitting President Fillmore appointed both Mormon and non-Mormons as officials of the new territory, with Brigham Young still acting as the governor. The borders of this new Territory of Utah were far more limited than the more ambitious Mormon concept and boundaries of "Deseret." They were very close to what that state's lines are today.

In 1852, the Mormon Territorial government made it clear that it condoned certain fundamental Mormon religious beliefs and behavior, in particular polygamy, as it was being practiced in the Territory. This did not sit well at all in the Northeastern parts of America, where Congregationalists and Abolitionists were particularly devout and politically powerful.

Polygamy was not just something a few scattered Mormons did. This was a core belief in the Mormon religion at the time and was practiced earnestly by a substantial number of them. In fact, fundamentalist Mormons at that time, and especially prior to statehood, held that polygamy was a spiritually superior way of marriage to monogamy, which was by far the prevailing religious belief in the rest of the United States.

From the point of view of most Northerners, and particularly Abolitionists, this kind of "marriage" was tantamount to "barbarism" and to "slavery" of women. This deep detestation of fundamental Mormonism was an issue in the presidential election of 1856 and resulted in U.S. troops being sent to Utah in what has come to be known as "Buchanan's Blunder," since it really was a fool's errand, the military trying to stop polygamy. Nonetheless, widespread repugnance to this singular Mormon practice persisted long after the Civil War was concluded and especially so after the passage of the Civil War Amendments which constitutionally banned slavery.

However, this was not the only belief and practice system of the Mormons that made it difficult for many Americans to accept Utah as one of their own. Given the fact that America was in part based on "the separation of church and state" (via an article in the Bill of Rights, as well as being an article of faith as to what "Liberty" meant from the Puritan settlement of America), most Americans believed that there was an unforgivable mixing of religion and governance in the "Territory of Utah."

After all, hadn't the founder of the Mormon religion, Joseph Smith, proclaimed that the best form of government was "theodemocracy"? Did not the Mormon Church, in reality, actually rule Utah?

Despite Mormon denials of such being the truth, it was a widely held perception (and still is), one which is in direct conflict with a key part of America's constitutional political ideology. To the prevailing American way of thinking of the day, the Mormons practiced "theocracy," a form of government akin to: the British Crown and the Church of England; The Holy

Roman Empire; and many Islamic states. So there was stiff resistance to the prospect that any land or polity occupied by the Mormons would ever be allowed into the United States of America as a state, since it was not really what an American "republic" should be.

In fact, in 1862, smack in the middle of The Civil War, Senator Morrill of Vermont had a bill passed into law that made it unlawful for anyone to practice bigamy (much less polygamy) in any territory of the United States. Moreover, this Morrill Act of 1862 also forbid any church or non-profit organization from owning land that was valued in excess of $50,000. Of course, both of these provisions were a direct hit on the Mormon Church and its religious practices and the close-knit relationship in Mormonism between the church and the state in The Territory of Utah.

Obviously, the Mormons and their leadership were well aware of these seemingly impenetrable obstacles to statehood. So slowly, but surely, they altered their system of beliefs and laws to be more compliant to the requirements for American statehood. It took them nearly 4 decades to convince the American people and Congress to agree that they were finally in compliance with the separation of church and state, but it required Utah to make polygamy illegal. Once that was done, Utah gained statehood in 1890.

So, Utah is a state today and tomorrow. And it is an American state where many of its Mormon residents—who comprise a 60% majority of that state to this day—believe what its religion's founder, Joseph Smith said, that—yes, this is true—"The whole of America is Zion itself from north to south." Don't believe us? Read or Google it for yourself:

> "You know there has been great discussion in relation to Zion—where it is, and where the gathering of the dispensation is, and which I am now going to tell you. The prophets have spoken and written upon it; but I will make a proclamation that will cover a broader ground. The whole of America is Zion itself from north to south, and is described by the Prophets, who declare that it is the Zion where the mountain of the Lord should be, and that it should be in the center of the land. When Elders shall take up and examine the old prophecies in the Bible, they will see it." (Teachings of the Prophet Joseph Smith, Section Six 1843–44, p.362)

So does this mean that the Israel and the State of Utah have similar roots, Utah being the New Zion which has its ancestry with the ancient Israelites? Yes it does. Here is a quote from the actual teachings of Joseph Smith as archived at Brigham Young University in Utah by Dr. George Galbraith, a Ph.D. in experimental psychology from Northwestern University and presently a professor at BYU:

> . . . *we learn that our western tribes of Indians are descendants*
> *from that Joseph who was sold into Egypt, and that the land of*
> *America is a promised land unto them, and unto it all the tribes*
> *of Israel will come, with as many of the Gentiles as shall comply*
> *with the requisitions of the new covenant. But the tribe of Judah*
> *will return to old Jerusalem. The city of Zion spoken of by David,*
> *in the one hundred and second Psalm, will be built upon the land*
> *of America . . .*

So yes, indeed, the predominant religious beliefs of one of the present United States of America holds that Israel (Zion) are not only bound by history, but by God.

To us, this would indicate that many American citizens in the State of Utah would be avid supporters of our proposition to include Israel as the 51st state. After all, it is set forth explicitly in their scriptures, from the moment of their birth, that Israel and America are essentially the same. Having Israel apply for admission into the U.S.A. would be the sign that the Israelites have finally come to understand their Godly and political relationship to America in general, but Utah especially.

Old souls and new souls will marry as one.

Alaska and Hawai'i as Non-Contiguous States: Continental America Goes Arctic and Pacific.

In the 19th and 20th centuries, the United States of America set a couple of very crucial precedents that go a long way in supporting a union between the 50 present states with that of the nation-state of Israel so that the latter may enter this federal system and become an equal political partner in the federation.

The first was the acquisition of Alaska from Russia in the 1867 for a relatively paltry sum of money, i.e., a little more than $7 Million or about 2 cents an acre. At that time, Russia was well established in Alaska—being an actual part of Mother Russia—but it was so far from the central hub of that nation, i.e., Moscow, at a time when transportation and communication were nearly impossible . . . and the weather itself was a great impediment.

The Czar needed the money. A joint Russian-American fur company in Alaska had become unprofitable, and the Russians were apprehensive of an incipient conflict with Great Britain in that area (British Columbia). On the other hand, some people in Washington, D.C., being typical American traders and expansionists (particularly Secretary of State William Seward) couldn't turn away from what they saw as a "steal". (A good number of

Americans at the time saw it as a bad deal and mocked Seward.) They were wrong. He was right. Wily old Uncle Sam got a bargain.

The second precedent was the overthrow of the Hawaiian Monarchy by American planters, missionaries, commercial, and military interests who had settled and married into Hawai'i. Even though they had substantially "westernized" the Polynesian monarchy that ruled there—they still couldn't resist using the U.S. Navy to back a *coup d'etat* which took over the government in the name of the United States in 1893. They put the reigning queen into a life-long "house arrest" and established a "provisional republic."

What they coveted, and soon received, was some sort of "territorial status" by the United States, which occurred officially in the summer of 1898. This meant that the planters and other commercial interests could run the Hawaiian Islands pretty much as they wanted to their financial advantage and convert the non-American natives into second class citizens.

The overthrow, the annexation, and the original territorial status were done under Republican Party auspices and all those years saw the legislatures and governorships dominated by Republicans. That ended in the 1950s—post World War II. Then, the Democratic Party, strongly supported by those of Asian descent, particularly Japanese-Americans, became a major political player in the state and began agitating for statehood so that they could become first class American citizens.

Both of these states are poster children for a latter day worldwide "frontier" of American "Manifest Destiny," i.e., the continued advance of the United States outside its contiguous territorial boundaries. Moreover, Hawaii was even outside of North America and had been an internationally recognized nation state. So, once these two became states of the U.S.A., this was quite different from any "colonial system" and not even analogous to any "imperial system." That is part of the reason why they serve as a reasonable precedent for Israel becoming part of the United States of America.

Moreover, it should be noted that the "statehood movements" in both of these two outlying areas of the world really didn't begin to pick up steam until scores of years after the United States of America got seriously involved with them. That, too, is somewhat similar to the U.S.A.-Israeli relationship.

How Do These Lessons Apply to Start of an Israeli Statehood Movement and the Admission of Israel as a New State?

What we have noted above shows that the United States has suffered through some explosive quakes in admitting a variety of the 50 states within it today and has managed to survive some extremely painful after-shocks as well. In so doing, there are a number of important lessons or precedents for welcoming Israel into the United States of America as the 51st state, should Israel come to see that as being to its great advantage. Here they are:

1. A new state to the Union does not have to be contiguous to the original 48 (Hawaii, Alaska)

2. A new state may have a majority belonging to a single church and religious belief (Utah) who do not think, pray, or have a faith like the majority religion in the United States at the time.

3. The "statehood movement" process of a proposed new state to the Union may cause a great amount of dissension within the United States population, within the political system, and even impact presidential elections.

4. The proposed admission of a new state may cause great tension with some of its neighboring states (Vermont with New York) and the admission itself may inflame passions of a neighboring country (Mexico) which might even involve the start of a major war in that area (Texas and Mexico)

5. Several new states to the union had been independent republics before they sought admission. (Vermont, Texas, California, Hawai'i)

6. Monetary compensation to another state or country (Mexico, Russia, Great Britain) has been involved in admitting new states into the Union (Vermont, Oregon, Washington, Idaho, New Mexico, Arizona, Alaska, etc.)

7. Many decades may elapse between when the United States' first becomes involved with a non-American polity or place before a statehood movement begins, much less succeeds.

All of this being the case, we think that there is ample precedent, both legal, political and economic, which can serve as practical guidance to: (a) support the beginning of an American statehood movement in Israel and if that is successful to (b) either invite or accept an application from Israel to become a new American state. This is indispensible to understand before we delve deeper into the more complex issues of whether such would be in the special core national interests of (a) The U.S.A. and Israel; (b) The Palestinian State; (c) Other Middle Eastern nations that border Israel; (d) The general situation between Islam and the West; (e) The global geo-political situation of the past, present and future discussed throughout this book.

Yes, there is a cluster of sticky and thorny issues to resolve and a bunch of loose ends to tie up. Not the least of these are the Palestinian Muslims and what this would mean to and for them. This new option will have to take into account the deepest interests of the Palestinian diaspora as well as all the neighbors of this new state, one located in a very geographically, culturally and religiously distant part of the world from the mainland U.S.A.

A newly awakened United States would have to negotiate a brand new peaceful settlement with all its new Middle East neighbors as, in our view, THE major party. The reader should not be surprised that we believe that this process would be greatly helped by a staff of expert, experienced, and admired international mediators, a panel which all sides would greatly respect. Hopefully, the result would be a major realignment of the entire geo-political structure on the World Island to the advantage of everyone . . . Russia and China included.

How that can work out to be a win/win/win for the new neighborhood and the whole wide world is the task of this next chapter. So, read on.

CHAPTER 5

What's in this for the United States, Israel, Palestine, and All Its Neighbors by Redrawing an Obsolete and Lethal Map

NEWS FLASH!! WE ARE not the first people in the world who have seen the long, ambiguous relationship between the United States of America and Israel as perhaps evolving into Israel becoming a state within the American federal structure.

The Idea is Blowin' in the Wind

Obviously, the idea of having Israel become the 51st state is not a ping on America's radar in 2016.. One major reason for this is that the idea of American statehood has never appeared on Israel's political agenda in any way at this writing.

As we have alluded to above, some kind of "statehood movement" would have to start in Israel, in concert with some Jewish people on this side of the world, before the American political elite or American public opinion would even begin to take notice. This is because the United States government and the American people are glued to the idea that Israel must be a "nation-state" in the Middle East. Thinking of Israel as an American state is just a bit too unconventional in either nation's thinking, but not entirely.

According to *Google's* search engine, there have been several articles that have already advocated it for one reason or another. The first of these showed up in *The Seattle Times* in 1991. The article was written by the highly acclaimed journalist, Richard Reeves, the author of twenty-some books, the chief political correspondent for *The New York Times* for many years, and a man who was a senior lecturer at the Annenberg School of Communication at the University of Southern California. His column, the first serious piece floating this notion, needs be given full credit for the idea we are elaborating upon in this book. Its title says it all: "It's Time to Make Israel the 51ˢᵗ State." (Reeves 1991).

Reeves major argument was that the United States (at that time) had already spent a overly generous amount of money as a lifeline for Israel to remain an independent country. This came in the form of loan guarantees, outright grants, outright loans (many of which were and are "periodically forgiven") emergency grants and subsidies. What this amounted to, in his thinking, was that Israel was actually a "dependency."

He also observed, somewhat wryly, that despite being a "dependent", the Israeli government insisted on building settlements on Palestinian land contrary to international law, and that this was the kindling for future fires between the Palestinians and Israelis . . . which would cost the U.S. even more bundles of money in military support. All this has continued to be the case, if not more so.

Thus, he reasoned some 25 years ago, that all the financial aid given by America to Israel was counter to peace in that area and would be better spent as federal grants to a state which could be told or forced to stop causing trouble with foreign entities that might drag the United States into unwanted and unnecessary conflicts.

He also observed that many immigrants to Israel at the time, who were then steered into the new "settlements" were fleeing from other countries— at that time, notably Russia—but whose real destination was the United States. If Israel became the 51ˢᵗ state, Reeves reasoned, the Prime Minister of Israel could then tell these newcomers: "Welcome to the Promised Land: the U.S.A.". (Reeves 1991)

Even after all this time, he is still correct on all counts. The U.S. government continues to pour huge bundles of cash into Israel (mostly governmental, but with a lot of private funding as well) and the settlements continue to crawl further into illegal territory. They have become so widespread that they have all but quashed any dream of a "two state" solution. Moreover, the "dependency" of which he spoke has become a "co-dependency", since Israel is the only tried and true military and "democratic" ally the U.S. has in the Middle East and even that is being sorely strained by Israel's understandably fear-based foreign policy.

Much the same can be said of an article in the *Jewish Post and News* of Winnipeg, Canada written by Bernie Bellan. In classic Jewish style, the title of his article is a question: "Why Not Just Make Israel the 51ˢᵗ State?" His argument is basically that the United States and Israel are so closely tied in their national interests, republican values (that's a small "r"), and strategic interests, that they might as well conjoin formally.

However, his brief for Israeli statehood in America does center on Israel's key core interest which is survival . . . which we will explore more fully below. He is correct, though, in asking "whether Israel is a 'Jewish state' or a 'state for Jews?' If it's the latter, then is there much difference between Israel and states like New York or Florida?" (Bellan 2012, or 5775 on the Jewish calendar)

When he heard Republican candidate Mitt Romney say in a debate with President Obama in 2012 that there was "no daylight" between Israel and the United States, he made one of the connections we made above: "Why not just get it over with and make Israel a part of the U.S . . . .After all, if Hawaii was able to be brought into the fold, and it is separated from the mainland U.S. by a huge distance, why not another part of the world that is not part of the contiguous U.S. mainland?"

He also emphasizes, as do we above—and at much greater length below—that " . . . the problem of how to deal with the Palestinians might become somewhat easier to solve. Clearly both Israelis and Palestinians have been sloughing off onto Americans any real attempts to negotiate peace with one another. Why not simply dispense with the pretense that anyone other than the U.S. can bring about a lasting diplomatic solution to the problem?"

Another indicator that this concept is definitely in the ether was a recent article in one of the leading (liberal) Israeli newspapers *Haaretz*, not coincidentally published on July 4, 2013, again posing a similar question: "On this Fourth of July, it bears asking the question: Is Israel becoming more American? The answer is, unequivocally, yes." The author also notes that " . . . the writing is on the wall . . . and in English" (Prusher 2013). However, aside from showing that Israelis are becoming more and more like Americans in their way of life there, there is no discussion as to what core American interests—or core Israeli interests—would be served by Israeli statehood.

So, now that several different people in very separate parts of North America and Israel have broached the topic to think along these lines to solve a very perplexing international problem, this resolution, as Bob Dylan said early in his brilliant career, " . . . may be blowin' in the wind."

The remainder of this book is simply our attempt to kick-start the process of thinking it through on many levels and through many dimensions, including from a fuller historical perspective as to how this particular Middle East dilemma began, and by using mediation theory as a way to find common interests among ALL the directly and indirectly affected parties.

Previously, we laid out recent thinking that emanates from the rapidly evolving theory and practice of modern conflict resolution, and how that needs to be applied to the gnarly and global peace-threatening events in the Middle East of today. We applied them to show how they would fit into a new arrangement of the United States and Israel in the Middle East, with Israel's becoming a state within the United States federal structure. We showed how this could be done legally and gave some examples from past American history of statehood struggles and strategies.

However, even if this difficult process of gaining statehood for Israel in the U.S.A. should begin, evolve and eventually occur, this still would not answer questions that any true conflict resolution process would need to address. For example, what needs to be undone from the past, so that the parties can proceed into a "self-determined" future along some freshly imagined pathways?

In this case, the innermost, religious seeds of the pervasive conflict in this region were planted in antiquity and may endure into perpetuity. However, there are more recent and specific worldly causes to the ever more sore points and shifting battle lines of today—the first being the scurrilous intervention by two Western powers during and after the conclusion of World War I.

Let the Middle East Redraw All National Lines to Reflect the Best Interests of Those Who Live There in the 21ˢᵗ Century . . . by Whatever Means They Choose

As we stated earlier, one of the basic tenets of conflict resolution is to get the disputants to stop dwelling and reliving the past in concrete terms, as though what actually happened is "true" or thinking that laws and treaties made many years prior are immutable. Memories are faulty and times change. So many of the atrocities being committed today by people of one "nation", "state", "sect", "religion", "tribe", "transnational entity" or whatever are grounded on a century-old "treaty" or a resolution of a defunct international organization—each of which has as much relevance to reality today as Columbus' maps of The New World have to Google Maps. A little historical background about this will help.

World War I, sometimes billed as "The war to end all wars" and the "War to make the world safe for democracy." In retrospect, it had absolutely nothing whatsoever to do with protecting the American or any other democracy and instead of ending all wars it has dragged America into a parade of horrible and grizzly foreign battles.

If there was actually any "reasoning" behind that hideous episode in human history, it was about how Great Britain and France intended to (a) eliminate threats to their world-wide empires emanating from Central European, Balkan and Turkish ruling elites and (b) to divide up the spoils of that war, particularly that huge swath of the Middle East known as The Ottoman Empire. It's hard to see World War I in a more favorable light than that.

A Century Old British and French Imperial Plot Has Trapped the United States and Israel into Today's Islamic Quagmire

Well before the poorly branded "Great War" ended, the carving up of the Ottoman Empire in the Middle East in favor of British and French imperial interests had begun secretively in Paris in 1916. Led by French aristocrat Francois Georges-Picot and his equally aristocratic British counterpart Sir Mark Sykes, the scheming proceeded without the United States even present at that table.

Thus, it is of little surprise that the U.S.A. got very little if anything from the slicing, splicing and dicing of the Middle East at that time. Instead, several subsequent treaties and declarations consistent with the 1916 scheme were devised and enforced by the British and French after the First World War's conclusion. These made "nations" out of desert land populated by scattered bands, tribes, villages, towns and cities of Sunni and Shia Arabs, mainly, but with millions of Christians, Kurds, Turks, Assyrians, Jewish people, etc. lumped in.

Why did the British and French care so much about one of the most desolate areas in the entire world? Some Americans are aware of the exploits of "*Lawrence of Arabia*", a British officer who helped lead many Arabians in waging an insurgency against the Ottoman Empire so that they could gain "self-determination" for themselves after the Turks had been routed from their lands.

So is this what the British and French imperial elite wanted: free and self-determined Arab nations in the former Ottoman Republic? Hardly. Colonel Lawrence, who attended the official Paris Peace Conference in 1919, in flowing Arab robes, was not amused by what he saw and heard there. After his objections were ignored, he foresaw the coming train wreck in the Middle East as clearly as he saw the sleazy and corrupt motives behind the smiles of the diplomats who were completely blind to the long-term, contemptible consequences of their map-making game.

According to Dr. Bertram Wyatt-Brown, who was the Richard Milbauer Professor of History at the University of Florida, Sir Lawrence wisely warned that "*The people of England have been led in Mesopotamia into a trap from which it will be hard to escape with dignity and honour. They have been tricked into it by a steady withholding of information. Things have been far worse than we have been told, our administration more bloody and inefficient than the public knows."* (Wyatt-Brown 2008) So what did all these "states-men" from Great Britain and France really know? What information did they intentionally withhold from their own people?

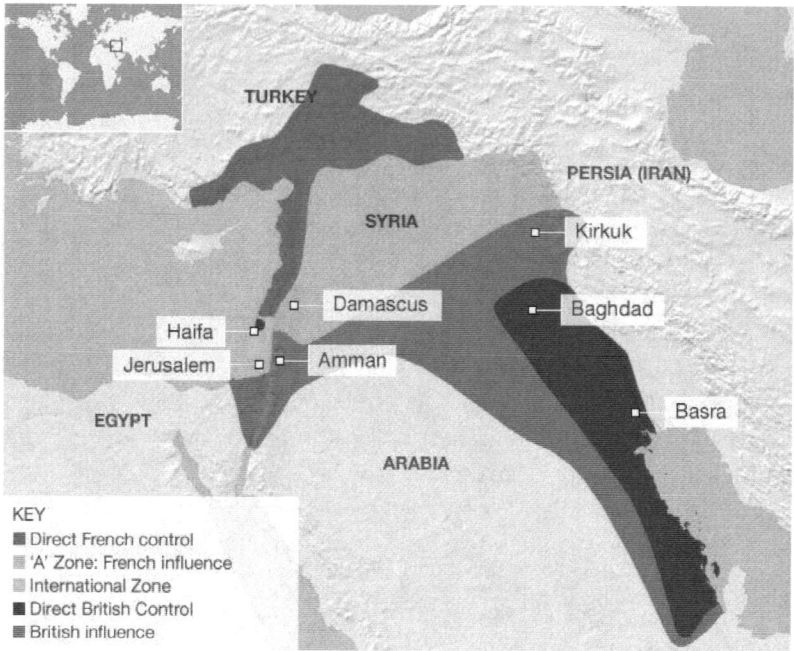

KEY
- Direct French control
- 'A' Zone: French influence
- International Zone
- Direct British Control
- British influence

What they concealed from their publics was their voracious lust for the spoils of "Mesopotamia" and "Arabia" and "The Levant," the exact same reasons that they "cared" about Africa, Afghanistan, India, and China. They wanted to "own" these distant lands, i.e., The Middle East—from "Mesopotamia" to Egypt to Saudi Arabia and Persia—for therein and thereunder lay the major energy materiel for certain future economic gains and uncertain future wars that would maintain and bloat their own imperial power. And what was that? Oil and natural gas. Thus, it came down to French and British politicians, generals, and scientists haggling over where a border should be or not be—and who was to get the lion's share of the wealth that lurked just below all that windswept sand.

This map can be found in an article by Tarek Osman, a highly regarded expert on "Islamism", which is the title of his latest book published by Yale University Press (2016). In that essay, which he wrote for BBC in 2013, he agrees with what we have said above about the perfidy and ignorance behind the maps that are at the bottom of the conflicts that abound there today. He includes this graphic of the lines that were "drawn with a ruler" and created "without any Arabic knowledge, (which) negated the main promise that Britain had made to the Arabs in the 1910s—that if they rebelled against the Ottomans, the fall of that empire would bring them independence." (Osman 2013)

Of course, there was the thorny question about what to do with millions upon millions of "backward" people who lived in that part of the world. The Franco-British objective was to create new "nations", each of which were patch-quilts of small ethnic groups who had little in common and, worse yet, even despised one another. Then they would put the head sheik or chieftain of some small minority in power and back them with their superior military force to harshly repress any dastardly uprisings against this new hierarchical order—usually a monarchy—from that much larger population, who were divided among themselves. That general theory which prevailed until the end of World War II was: conquer, divide, rule, and exploit to the max.

The geo-political mess they made then is plain to see in High Definition today on TV sets each and every day in 2016, *ad infinitum*. It is hard for either of us to agree with anything said by The Islamic State of Iraq and the Levant (ISIL). However, we both concur with what they proclaim as their chief goal in that region, to wit: to drive the final nail into the coffin of the insidious and infamous Sykes-Picot Agreement of 1916.

We hope this book is just another nail, albeit a paper and/or cyber one, in that very same coffin. After all, it was that insidious and perfidious agreement, plus *The Balfour Declaration*, plus the *Paris Peace Treaty of 1919* and the *League of Nations Mandates of 1920* which together created the spurious and dubious nations that remain at the eye of the current day political cyclone roaring through that region. These include: the mass murderous phenomenon known as ISIL; the perpetual distrust and enmity between Israel and the Palestinian Arabs; the proliferating wars between Shiites and Sunnis—from the Turkish border to Yemen and from Libya to Afghanistan—altogether a humongous storm system that shows no sign of relenting in its ferocity for the foreseeable future.

Further support for our thesis comes from David Andelman, who was a foreign correspondent for the *New York Times* and the Editor of *Forbes Magazine*. He wrote an in-depth book (including vivid descriptions of all the illicit sex and booze indulged in by the lead participants) at the Paris Peace Conference that produced the villainous Treaty of Versailles Treaty in 1919. He, too, emphasizes the huge impact it has had on the muddled, murky and murderous machinations in the Middle East at this moment. It is titled: *The Shattered Peace: The Price We Pay Today* (2007).

His book was meticulously reviewed by Dr. Claire Berllinski in *The New York Sun*. She has her Ph.D. from Oxford and is a journalist and academic and summarizes Mr. Andelman's major thesis as follows: "*The countries that emerged were not natural nation-states but contrivances to secure the Great Power's control over their colonial possessions and create buffer zones between themselves and their enemies. Their boundaries made no sense. They mashed together people who loathed each other and had always loathed each other. The world has been paying the price ever since.*" (Berlinski 2007).

So, what we see emerging today, according to a large group of Middle East experts, is an amorphous, multi-islandic "caliphate" which ISIL currently occupies that consists of very different boundaries than any concocted in 1916-19 with no Arab input. As it stands at this writing, the ISIL "califate" area includes: disparate parts of "Syria", southern Turkey, and northern and western "Iraq" . . . as well as parts of Mali, Somalia, and Libya. It also has devout adherents in non-Islamic countries around the world. It is a magnet for the most radical of Salafis.

If any Westerner—whether they be British, American, French, American, Russian or Israeli—is silly enough to get into this extremely deadly argument among Sunni and Shiite Arabs, Turks, Kurds, Alawites, Pashtuns, Druze, Uzbeks, Saudis, Houthis, Somalis, Wahhabis, Iranians, and on, about what their borders should be, then they deserve what will most assuredly come. This will include heaps of money thrown into military operations with no gains to be achieved; great confusion about who are allies and enemies; omnipresent hate and misunderstandings; plus a panorama of excruciating horrors that will descend upon the West for years to come.

In the year 2016, does anyone in their right mind really believe that the U.S., Russian, French, British, etc. daily bombings of Islamic fanatics in 5 or 6 countries at the same time will quell their revulsion against all things Western imposed upon their mislabeled and rudely and crudely constructed countries? Will showering high-tech munitions upon millions and millions of Islamic peoples, and creating millions upon millions of Muslim refugees, not lead to their savoring thoughts of revenge on "the infidel's" homelands so that they—or their children—can at least obtain vengeance and "martyrdom"?

The British and French, who cooked up this poisonous *potpourri*, and the Americans and Israelis, who have inherited it—and keep turning up the gas under the boiling pot—best keep as far away as they possibly can from the internal and perhaps eternal strife of Mesopotamia, The Levant, Arabia, Iran and North Africa. If the Russians want to get sucked in, let them. It will only come back to bite them in their posterior and interior. The Vietnam War was often called a "quagmire" into which the United States had stepped. Vietnam, as a quagmire, is but a mere puddle compared to the Middle East quagmire, the latter being the equivalent of The Great Lakes.

The rest of the world needs to let these people forge their own national, confederate, or tribal destinies and butt out. Does, China, Pakistan, India, Japan, Germany or Brazil have their troops on the ground there? No. True, the fighting between ancient antagonists, protagonists, and psychopaths won't be pretty other than to those who want to learn how to ritually sever a head on YouTube, but hopefully, sometime in the future, most of Islam in the Middle East and Africa will eventually sort and straighten themselves out. This is a conflict America needs to completely avoid.

Meanwhile, the maturing new Eurasian political entity discussed above will continue to expand to the North and East of this Zone of Hate and the oil will continue to flow to all and any who will pay spot prices to whoever is, at any given time, in charge of the spigots there and in other parts of the world. *Ergo*, the United States has only one genuine national core interest and meaningful foreign entanglement in that region, and that just happens to be Israel.

But won't that drag the United States into yet another Middle East heated and hateful border dispute? Under present day thinking that would seem likely, but there is an existent and widely accepted resolution to that issue, one we will discuss below.

What Core Interests of the U.S, Israel, the Palestinian Arabs and Their Neighbors Would Be Served by Israel Becoming an American State?

Americans have been told since the end of World War II that the United States has several important "strategic interests" in the Middle East and that these must be protected by military force, if necessary. The first of these is to protect American and allied oil interests there (local and foreign) and to keep the shipping lanes open for the oil to go freely to the U.S.A. and elsewhere.

The second is the dusty and rusty old saw that America needs to counter Russian and Iranian expansionism in that area. Both of these are strong tenets of belief among Washington Insiders, from the Pentagon to the White House to all those think tanks along the East Coast, which are little more than American military-industrial public relations hocus-pocus.

Americans are exposed to all this blather to the point of it being analogous to a litany. It emanates from the mouths and minds of politicians of all stripes from "liberal" to "conservative", "respectable" institutes and centers, prestigious academics, and "allies" from around the globe.

America's Core Interests in the Middle East Today Are neither Oil nor Geo-Political Positioning

On the other hand, there are many Americans and foreigners who are friendly to America's real interests—most of whom are not insiders—who disagree with this long outdated 'thinking', some of them being quite vocal and articulate in their reasoning that this is nothing more than elixirs promising eternal youth. We are but two of them. We do not think that insuring the oil supply from that region or any Russian or Iranian ambitions in their immediate vicinity in any way justify the huge expenditure of American wealth on military adventurism in that part of the world. None of this is in the American national interest in any way, shape or form . . . and is exactly the opposite from what many great Americans from the past have wisely what stated America's position on foreign affairs should be, that is, NO foreign alliances or other entanglements.

Many Americans still alive today became painfully aware of just how pitifully dependent the U.S. had come to be on Middle East oil in the 1970s when the Arab nations who were part of the international oil cartel called the *Organization of the Petroleum Exporting Countries (OPEC)* clamped an embargo on their oil to the United States. Why? They were very upset that the United States had sent arms to Israel to help the Israelis repel an Egyptian and Syrian attack on Israel to regain land lost in the 1967 war between Israel and them. This tactic caused an acute gasoline shortage in America. Prices at the pump skyrocketed in the U.S. and for many months, mile-long lines of cars had to wait to fill up their gas tanks.

Thus, it became clear then, as it is today, that the U.S. backing of the nation state of Israel is inextricably linked to the insecurity of America's oil interests in the Middle East. The American government's response to that, and another "oil shock" based on the explosive politics in that region (Russia's invasion of Afghanistan and the Iranian Revolution, both in 1979), has been to increase its military footprint in the Middle East. This has led to America's ever-increasing entrapment there and an ever growing national debt. How is this in America's core interest?

Another major "strategic interest" in the Middle East is the aforementioned "Grand Game." American military bases, air bases, naval bases, CIA bases, Special Operations outposts and surveillance stations are liberally peppered throughout the entire region as part of the "containment" strategy discussed at length above as well as part of the "Full Spectrum Dominance" tack still accepted as dogma by the Pentagon and its brigades of overpaid, "privatized" sub-contractors. This is merely a lavish, overpriced political position.

There are many reasons why this perpetually increasing military mission creep and "foreign entanglements" in the Middle East (and Africa) are definitely not in the national interest of America, but perhaps the biggest problem for the United States is that all this military presence and destructive activities are located among and waged upon Islamic people. Isn't it plain to see?

All the armed resistance to the United States in that region is coming from Muslims of all persuasions. If it weren't so tragic and destructive, American "policy" there is like a Keystone Cops silent movie comedy: How can America be siding with some Sunnis against the Shias in Syria (with Iran and Iraq as Shia allies) and siding with the Shiites (and their allies in Iran) against Sunnis in Iraq—when there is no effective border between Iraq and Syria anymore?

Unfortunately, one, if not THE key issue—and an attractive recruiting tool—for many of these religiously motivated Islamic fighters in IS, ISIL or the al-Nusra Front is: the ongoing policies of the nation state of Israel. Much of ISIS or ISIS's inflammatory but highly effective public relations campaign is based on TV clips for Islamic eyes about how the Israelis are: (1) abusing, imprisoning, terrorizing and killing the Palestinian Arabs; (2) steadily expanding new "settlements" into arable and already settled Arab land; and (3) making and threatening pre-emptive air attacks on perceived nuclear threats (past Iraq, past Syria, future Iran). The American Empire is effectively portrayed as Israel's enabler, supplier and close ally.

Thus, American support of Israel in its present status is contrary to America's so-called strategic interests in containing Russia and China by "controlling 'The Rimland'". China is not fighting against or enabling harm to Islamic people in the Middle East and is not widely despised there. In fact, they are helping many Arabs be relatively free of Western secular and industrial dependence. So without having lost a single soldier in Iraq, China is the leading importer of Iraqi oil in 2015, taking over 50% of its exports. (Arango and Krauss 2013)

Here's the way a former Defense Department official in the Bush Administration who worked on Iraq oil policy put it to *The New York Times*: "We lost out . . . The Chinese had nothing to do with the war, but from an economic standpoint they are benefiting from it, and our Fifth Fleet and air forces are helping to assure their supply." (Arango and Krauss 2013) So, all those gigantic military bases built in Iraq over a 10 year period have been abandoned; Iraq has become the close ally to Iran; and China gets the oil.

This is an "away" game for America. This is a "home game" for the foaming fanatics, who are legion. The United States cannot afford to keep at this for much longer. AK-47s and road bombs are much cheaper to buy, reload, and deploy than F-16s, B-1s, huge aircraft carrier groups, and predator reaper drones.

When the inevitable occurs and the U.S.A. is economically compelled to abandon its clearly self-destructive military strategy in the Middle East, where will that leave Israel? The United States and the UN Security Council made a deal in 2015 to lift all economic sanctions against Iran in return for "verifiable" U.N. *International Atomic Energy Agency (IAEA)* control over Iran's alleged nuclear weapons program for at least 10 years.

This pits Israel against a much stronger Iran who will have much more money to support present and future Israeli adversaries like Hezbollah and Hamas . . . all of whom want to "drive the Zionist entity into the sea" via whatever means they can use to do it (other than nukes). Does this leave Israel in a much more vulnerable position? Does this create a bigger headache for the United States in that region? Yes and yes.

Therefore, continued military and economic support for the nation state of Israel is actually weakening America's geo-strategic position in the Middle East against its purported "enemies" there and bestows a wide panoply of advantages for the rapid rise of The New Eurasia which wishes to exclude the United States entirely from that part of the world. If we are correct in this analysis, our proposed solution that Israel chuck its vainglorious notions of being a "nation state" in exchange for being a homeland in "The Holy Land" under the protection of being an American state, begins to make more sense, does it not?

So, what are the real core interests of the U.S. that would be served by such a deal?

America's Core Interests in Israel as a U.S. State Are Historical, Cultural, and Religious

History plays strange pranks on nations as well as in the personal lives of ordinary citizens and the deep interconnection of Israel and the United States has a long, tangled and somewhat ironic history. We have previously discussed the deep religious connections from 17th and 19th century American times with its Judeo-Christian past and we will dig into that a bit deeper later on in this chapter.

Historical: The more modern historical connection between America and Israel once again traces itself back to the World War I period both prior to and immediately after its conclusion. Manifestly, it really has little to do with oil and probably a lot more to do with, here's that word again, "destiny."

That brings us back to the preface to the Paris Treaty known as "The Balfour Declaration" of 1917. Lord Balfour was the British Foreign Minister and was well acquainted with the deals made by Picot and Sykes. For whatever reasons, he and the British Prime Minister were both positively inclined to help promote the Zionist agenda in The Holy Land after World War I was a memory shrouded in a nightmare. After much wrangling amongst various factions in the British foreign policy establishment at the time, Balfour went public and promised Zionists and their friends that there would be "in Palestine a national home for the Jewish people."

The Palestinian Arab and Christians who actually lived in Palestine at the time under Turkish rule were the vast majority of the inhabitants (about 90%) and, obviously, they were extremely agitated by this promise. This unease persisted even though the "Declaration" clearly omitted the word "state" for the Jewish people and promised with equal clarity that the political rights of those who lived there prior to this would in no way be diminished. No one living there at that time thought that this last part would ever be respected in a Jewish homeland and history has proved their fears justified so far.

Eventually, *The Balfour Declaration* was promulgated into international law by the League of Nations in 1920 when it assigned Palestine as a British "Mandate" with the League being: "in favour of the establishment in Palestine of a national home for the Jewish people, it being clearly understood that nothing should be done which might prejudice the civil and religious rights of non-Jewish communities in Palestine". The Brits were particularly keen on making sure that they did not guarantee a Jewish "state" in Palestine, much to the incredulity of Arabs living there. Perhaps the British word "home" was translated as "state" among the Arab population in residence at the time.

But, that was then, this is now. The principal cause of the present ongoing and growing disaster in the Middle East today are the silly lines and flawed if not false legalistic vows made by men who, when alive, greatly and gravely overestimated their power to shape the future . . . but their misdeeds and/or miscalculations live on long after their death. There is absolutely no reason today to adhere to anything they ever planned or did.

So where does American history fit into this muddle in Palestine? It is the necessary backdrop to the development of the cultural ties between America and Israel, which began to cohere even prior to America's entry into World War II discussed below. Moreover, if Israel were to become part of the United States, how could the United States stay out of re-making of borders in that part of the Middle East—something we previously said all Western nations should avoid like the plague? After all, so much of the fighting going on there today . . . and which will most likely intensify in the future . . . is precisely over what is the border of the nation state of Israel and a defined homeland for the Palestinian Arabs.

Any border between Israel, Palestine, Jordan, Lebanon and Egypt should not hark back to Balfour, Sykes or Picot or any League of Nations mandates or pronouncements. It should be the border that was the original one of the nation-state of Israel that was formally agreed upon as a result of the agonizing Israeli-Arab War of 1947-48, a boundary which remained finite until the 1967 war. This is the border that the United States considered to contain Israel when the American government recognized Israel as a nation state in 1948 and was conceded as such by involved Arab nations in 1949 in an armistice agreement. Here is a map of it found on a website called *Middle East Facts* (which can be accessed online by the URL found in References) which claims that is there by courtesy of the Israel Ministry of Foreign Affairs. Of course, that map puts Gaza under Egyptian rule, which is not the case today, as it is under Palestinian rule, as are the West Bank areas of what are loosely referred to as Samaria and Judea.

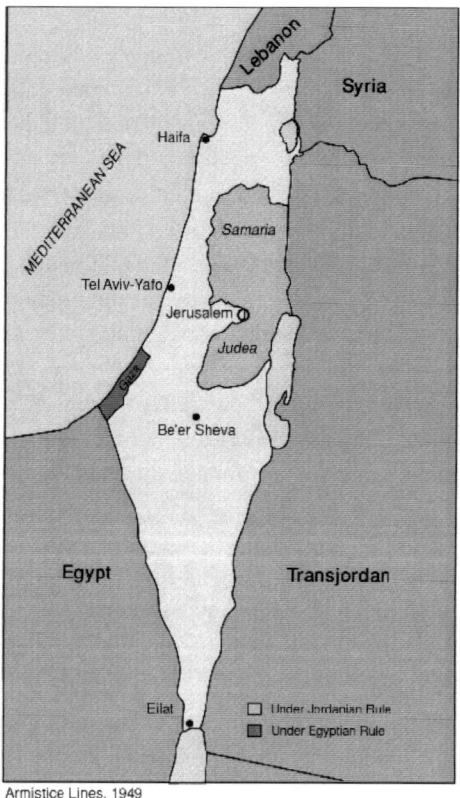

Armistice Lines, 1949

This is also the border that was legitimized by the UN General Assembly Resolution in that time period. This set of boundaries—which divided Jewish Israel or Jewish Palestine from Arab Palestine— were also the lines that were reaffirmed as Israel's legal borders by the International Court of Justice in 2004 and agreed to by the President of the Palestinian Authority, Mahmoud Abbas, in 2011. Likewise, it is the border agreed upon by the Saudi King Abdullah Plan.

Thus, thanks to all this history, including the official U.S. recognition of the nation of Israel being delineated by such borders, there would not be a serious "border" issue involving THAT Israel becoming an American state in the Middle East with any of Israel's neighbors (The Likud Party, Prime Minister Netanyahu and the opinion of many Israelis notwithstanding). The United States has been dealing with that particular outline of Israel for nearly 70 years now as the Jewish homeland and has built deep economic and cultural ties with it as well.

Are the pre-1967 lines—the legal and original borders of the nation-state of Israel—too small to be an American state? No. Dr. Becker's home state of New Jersey (the 5th smallest of the 50 states) has 7,850 square miles, while the original nation of Israel has slightly more than 8,000 square miles. Is the original configuration of Israel too small to accommodate its 8.2 million people? Not if New Jersey compares, which manages over 9 million inhabitants. The narrow "neck" that can be seen in the map on this page posed a major "security" problem for Israel as a nation state but would not as "The 51st state," as we hope to demonstrate by what we say below.

However, the main reasons why President Truman decided to recognize Israel as a nation back then was not a position taken based on any sense of biblical or modern history or as a step taken in The Grand Game. Instead, it came from a deep sense of cultural identity between this new "nation" of Jewish people that had really begun after World War II. Thus the American historical tie to Israel is connected to the Second World War.

Cultural: We believe that the close cultural ties between America and Israel today would best be described to be of the emotional and spiritual variety. Becker recalls vividly, since he was a teen-ager at the time, the almost universal American loathing and disgust of the Nazis when the newsreel footage of the liberation of the Dachau and Auschwitz concentration camps began to filter into the American consciousness in the immediate post-World War II times.

We are also of the opinion that those shocking scenes of barely living Jewish skeletons seared a permanent scar into the collective American psyche. Those motion pictures, taken by American soldiers who liberated these poor souls from the Nazi concentration camps, enhanced a sense of national guilt about how some 2,000 Jewish refugees escaping Hitler's Germany were turned away from American shores in 1939. They were passengers on board a ship named *The St. Louis* and many of them ended up in gas chambers and became part of landfills of human remains.

After World War II, with the advent of television as a powerful means of stirring emotions, the saga of the emaciated victims of the Nazi "final solution to the Jewish problem" returning to their "homeland" in Palestine also tugged at the heartstrings of Americans, and has ever since. Just as Becker was deeply moved by their struggle to "return" to Judaic biblical roots, and the way they were thwarted by the British and the Palestinians there, so were most Americans. Just as Hollywood and politics collaborated to engrave negative stereotypes of the Germans and Japanese in World War II, so they mixed various stories like the Warsaw Ghetto and "The Diary of Anne Frank" to conduct an American symphony of empathy for the Zionist cause.

Core interests, as Ury and Fisher make abundantly clear, involve guttural emotions. In the case of the U.S.A's feelings towards Israel, it was not fear, anxiety and national identity, it was national compassion and empathy . . . which are subconscious and powerful feelings, not to be dismissed because they are sentimental and/or altruistic. They started manifesting themselves right at the beginning of the new Israeli nation when President Truman, ignoring the heated advice of his most trusted military and State Department advisors, officially recognized Israel anyway. Why?

President Truman was an astute politician who found a way to resonate well with the American people. He must have sensed that many of his fellow citizens were going to be on his side.

A distinguished professor of American foreign policy at Bard College and Yale University, Walter Russell Mead, put it like this: "Truman's support for the Jewish state was 'wildly popular' throughout the United States. A Gallup poll in June 1948 showed that almost three times as many Americans "sympathized with the Jews" as "sympathized with the Arabs." *That support was no flash in the pan. Widespread gentile support for Israel is one of the most potent political forces in U.S. foreign policy . . .* " (Mead 2008, emphasis ours).

So why did the brilliant American general and statesman, George C. Marshall, actually threaten Truman that he would not support him for his 1948 presidential race if he recognized Israel? Well, Marshall was a supreme macro-strategist and knew the United States was in for a ton of trouble with the Soviet Union in the near future and knew that this move would infuriate many Arabs in the Middle East. He foresaw the American recognition of Israel as giving the U.S.S.R. an opening to make political gains in the Middle

East and that it would be a root cause for a bevy of wars involving Israel in the future if Truman did this. And he was right on all counts!!

But even so, was Truman wrong?

Not according to an article in *Foreign Affairs,* the flagship journal of the *uber*-elitist *Council on Foreign Relations,* in an article published in 2012. "Truman was a brave man, and in my view a correct one—but (recognizing Israel) did lead to the wars that the others feared recognition would ignite. Today political Islam is on the rise . . . and . . . creation of a state of Palestine remains a consequential, bleeding global ulcer." (Clemmons, 2012)

So how could Marshall who opposed the recognition of Israel and Truman who supported it, both be right? In our view, that is because in the American heart and soul, the geopolitical costs to America in the Middle East over the past 65+ years have been worth the spiritual umbilical cord to the state of Israel in the Middle East. There is a core national interest that the overwhelming majority of Americans feel in the continuation of Israel as a state in the Middle East because: (1) they are the only "democracy" there"; (2) "they are our most reliable ally in that part of the world"; (3) "they are the most Western culture in the Middle East" and therefore most like "us."

There are other, more recent, major cultural factors in the long standing intimacy between the United States and Israel. One is the rather small, but well integrated and relatively influential American Jewish community that is now deeply ingrained in modern American history. Jewish Americans only make up about 2% of the U.S. population, and in actual size, that comes to roughly 6-7million. The exact number is not important, but it is about the same size as the Jewish population of Israel, which comprises 75% of that country's populace. Together, though, they comprise over 80% of the world's population of Jewish people. Thus, it is hardly surprising that there is a close affinity between Israel and the American Jewish community.

The latter, for its relatively puny size, has influence in professions far beyond its proportion in the American population. These include such as the practice of law, medicine, Academia, finance and banking, the fashion industry, and the mass media, which would include the motion picture industry, TV entertainment and news, and theatre. It is clear that having disproportionate power in these areas of American life would lend immense support to a Pro-Israel narrative in the United States since the former became a nation state in 1948. This influence on "the collective subconscious" of the United States continues, if not grows, to the present day.

Obviously, this robust Jewish presence in these areas of American life is going to be felt in the American political system, not the least of which would be its foreign postures and activities in The Middle East. Although American policy towards Israel is rarely an issue that is fought in Congressional or presidential elections, the strength of the pro-Zionist position of some in the American Jewish community impacts the electoral and political process through substantial and strategically placed hefty campaign donations and well-funded and intense lobbying.

Whether or not this heavy-handed pro-Israeli position has been and is in the national interest of the United States has been seriously questioned, in minute detail, by two eminent professors at the University of Chicago and the John F. Kennedy School at Harvard in their book *The Israeli Lobby and U.S. Foreign Policy* (Mearsheimer and Walt, 2008). But this serious issue about how American foreign policy is really made rarely rises above Ivory Tower haggling. It surely has not risen to the level of a candid and debatable issue in American public discourse—so intertwined are the cultures and actual core interests of Israel these days with those of America.

We should also note that there is an active "liberal" Jewish-American minority which is extremely upset about Israel and its perceived punitive, tough and rough treatment of both the Palestinian citizens of Israel and the Palestinians in Gaza and the West Bank . . . their critique being acerbic and acidic, to say the least. There are also many liberal gentile Americans who chastise Israel for having established an "Apartheid" system reminiscent to that of the white rule in South Africa.

Former president Jimmy Carter, a frequent visitor to Israel and Palestine, devoted a whole book to make this very same case. It's title says it all: *Palestine: Peace Not Apartheid*. (Carter 2006). Similar charges are hurled from some notable Jewish-American academics like former MIT Professor Noam Chomsky (2013), All of the above, who might be called "The Moral Minority," do not think it is in America's core interests to keep supporting Israel's continued expansion into the "occupied territories". But, the general and generous love affair of the U.S.A. with Israel carries on despite these scathing criticisms.

Thus, in many ways then, the Jewish and American cultures have bonded together a great deal from the mid-20th century to today and there is a growing sense of mutual identity in both Israel and American cultures, possibly enough to support a vigorous statehood movement from Israel.

Religious: As we described in Chapter 3, there has been a very close religious connection between the early Puritan settlers in The New World and Jesus of Nazareth and his teachings. Of course, Jesus was Jewish and was considered by some in his time, as The King of the Jews and/or as the Jewish Messiah. His teachings during his last year on Earth, in pretty much what is now Israel and Palestine, were central in John Winthrop's speech on the Arabella, and thus influenced traditional Christian teachings in America to this very day.

Up to this day, in the United States, there is a deep belief among many Americans, that America itself was founded upon what they believe to be "Judeo-Christian" beliefs. The Old Testament, which is in large part derived from the ancient Jewish Scriptures is considered by many American Christians to contain pretty much the history of humankind from Genesis and a noteworthy, relatively accurate story of humanity on this planet up to the birth of Christ.

Indeed, the more fundamentalist the sects of American Christianity, the more they cite and believe that the historical narrative of the Old Testament has more truth to it about human evolution on this planet than Darwin's "Theory of Evolution." These "fundamentalist Christians" and/or Evangelicals who hold sacred these views are known both to themselves as well as their detractors as "Creationists"—the more extreme of whom believe that planet Earth, all humanity's common habitat, was literally created in 7 days.

They are so devoted to this Old Testament, Jewish biblical version of Genesis that they openly discount all the work of the countless modern Earth scientists who through various scientific methodologies, techniques and high tech instrumentation can prove beyond any reasonable doubt that the geological Earth is millions and millions years old. The most extreme of these American creationists equally dispute Darwin's theory of Evolution and insist that God created humankind in one day via Adam and Eve.

In fact, there is a large, loosely organized group of what is claimed to be millions of Americans who actually call themselves "*Christian Zionists*" and their organizational name is *Christians United for Israel* or *CUFI*. (Norton 2015) These people are really not too far from an equivalent belief system that was at the core of a lot of anti-Semitic thinking in America up to mid-late 20th century (i.e., that the Jewish disbelief in Christ's word led to his crucifixion).

Today's Christian Zionists are devout believers that the Jewish Semitic tribe are God's "Chosen People" and that God, indeed, promised them "The Holy Land." There are many bountiful monetary donations to Israeli Zionist causes from these Americans. They also organize numerous tours of The Holy Land and Jerusalem in order to be in that most sacred of places to them.

At their conventions, including the most recent in July 2015, thousands of American and Israeli flags can be seen waving from the crowd. Despite the many contradictions that seem to abound even in their name, much less their belief system and practices, Christian Zionism is an extant phenomenon of how many devout American Christians see an ancient and unbreakable bond between the United States and Israel. It is likely that many of them would welcome Israeli statehood.

Israel's Core Interests in Abandoning its National Identity and Becoming an American State.

There is substantial body of thought that the right wing Prime Minister of Israel, Benjamin Netanyahu, took a rash gamble by coming to the United States in March of 2015 to address a Republican dominated U.S. Congress while making it perfectly clear that he was publicly snubbing the Democrat president of the United States, Barack Obama. The two men can barely conceal the fact that they harbor an intense dislike of one another.

But this was more than personal, it was about a political issue that is deemed to be by many Israeli's, as well as many Americans, as the core interest at stake in Iran's nuclear program, i.e., the future existence of Israel. Nothing could be more central to Israel's psychological, if not material, security. So, since President Obama and the entire Security Council of the UN were in ongoing and promising negotiations with Iran's new President, Hassan Rouhani, Netanyahu was determined to undermine any American position that relented on the total denial of any nuclear capability for Iran whatsoever.

Netanyahu used this speech, given before a doting and approving Republican-led U.S. Congress, to shore up Israeli support for his political future as Israel's Prime Minister. He guessed right and was re-elected once again. Plus, should Iran actually obtain "the bomb" in the future, Netanyahu assured that the onus and blame would fall on President Obama's head.

Obviously, an existential threat to the existence of any nation state is the primary core interest of that country. Many of Israel's neighbors, in addition to Iran, have made statements saying that they want to drive "The Zionist Entity", a/k/a "Israel", into the sea. In other words, it is their hope and/or plan to destroy Israel as a Zionist nation-state in the former Palestine in the future.

Israelis live with this mortal threat every day. It cannot be pleasant to contemplate. Thus, the Likud Party of Israel and other very right wing and religious parties remind the populace of these statements regularly and run and gain and keep office by threatening to bomb Iran's nuclear facilities and extinguish that possibility. Public opinion poll upon public opinion poll in Israel prove that Jewish Israelis overwhelmingly feel exactly this way at the present point in time.

An article in *Haaretz*, analyzed several surveys on what Israelis thought about the Iran nuclear deal between the U.S., U.K. France, Russia, China and Germany in the summer of 2015 and concluded that approximately 70-80% were opposed to it with similar numbers believing it would not keep Iran from constructing such a weapon. These findings are also supported by Peace Index Surveys conducted by the *Evens Program for International Conflict Resolution at Tel Aviv University* which also pointed out that these numbers were across the political spectrum, that is, regardless of party affiliation. On the other hand, only about 40% in various polls wanted Israel to attack Iran's nuclear facilities with or without U.S. promises of support. (Maltz 2015).

Since the 1967 War, Israel has proved to all its Arab neighbors and even those far from Israel, like Iran and the ever mutating Islamic State, that it has an overwhelming military capacity to inflict devastating damage upon them first. One of the major restraints on war-minded Israelis which keep Israel from attacking Iran is not knowing what would be the U.S.A's response. If Iran retaliated by air and sea, would the United States military come to their aid? Have American presidents told Israeli PMs that they would not unless the U.S. gave a clear and official OK first? No one is saying yes or no. However, no one in American power circles has ever said that Israel's existence as a nation is in America's core interests either.

So, Israel's very existence is THE "core" interest for Israel, though only a "strategic" interest for the United States. Netanyahu's speech to Congress was meant to gather enough American public support to cut off any further negotiations with Iran and promise Israel that it would attack Iran alongside Israel, thus making an Iranian threat to Israel's existence an American core interest. He failed.

There are a few other countries who feel the same as Israel does about Iran, with Saudi Arabia being the foremost leader of them. But the Saudis would dare not attack Iran directly. Instead, they will simply wage proxy wars against them, as in Yemen and Syria.

No Western, Latin American, African, Eurasian or Asian nation wants to see such an attack on Iran for fear this could usher in the start of World War III. As we noted above, Iran has some very powerful close allies like China and Russia, and are close to belonging to *the SCO*.

Therefore, Israel must remain on edge about its continued existence as Iran continues to gain strength on the global scene, which it most likely will. The stronger Iran becomes, the more nervous Israel gets, with no guarantee of American support for an Israeli first strike and subsequent mutual defense of an inevitable retaliation from Iran.

So, here's the big question: If Israel became part of the United States, as its 51st state, would anyone in the Middle East or anywhere, even in their wildest dreams, think of launching a military attack on Israel ever again? Would Israeli statehood in America guarantee the continued existence of the "promised" homeland-state of the Jewish people for as long as the U.S.A. and NATO (an attack on any NATO country is an attack on NATO) existed?

The answer to that is: Yes! As The 51st state, Israel's existence becomes an American core interest. Does Israel have that kind of blue ribbon warranty right now or is it likely in its present or other form in the future? The answer to that is: perhaps, but that is far from a guarantee.

Israel's independent foreign policies in recent years—particularly concerning its invasion of Lebanon in 2006, its extremely destructive response to a hail of frightening rocket fire and a series of secret tunnels from Gaza into Israel in 2014—have had enormously negative consequences worldwide. They have handed Israel a very black eye in the sight of just about all of the United Nations. Fair or not, Israel, as presently constituted along with its present policy positions in the Middle East, is in great danger of becoming an international pariah.

Almost the entire United Nations has backed the plight of the Palestinian people over the past few years by recognizing them *de facto* by admitting them to "Non-member observer state" status by a 138-9 vote. In fact, Palestinian President Abbas called this resolution "The Palestinian State's birth certificate." This is hardly a resounding vote of confidence by the "international community" for the nation state of Israel and its foreign policy towards the Palestinian State.

Prime Minister Netanyahu himself proved Israel's growing global isolation and shunning when he verbally lambasted the entire U.N. General Assembly in October 2015 for its "deafening silence" to explicit threats to destroy Israel within 25 years by the Supreme Leader of Iran a few days before his speech. What he received in response from all those present, to prove our point, not his, was the now famous "44 seconds of deafening silence" from that very same General Assembly. (Netanyahu Speech to UN General Assembly, 2015).

The reader can watch that telling moment on a link we have in References. One could hear a pin drop; not a sound was audible. That is proof of where Israel stands in the mind and actions of the world at that point in time. That is not good for Israel's deepest core interests. No one seems to care at all about Israel's existence as a nation, other than the United States, Canada, Micronesia and Palau.

Another actual menace to the very existence of the state of Israel in its present form, is the admission of the Palestinian State into *The International*

Criminal Court (The ICC is a UN entity). Although this was not to take effect until April 1, 2015, the admission had a retroactive date of its jurisdiction extending back to June 13, 2014, when Israel had retaliated against Hamas's rocket barrage and tunnel construction in Gaza—killing somewhere in the vicinity of 2,000 people and bombing out a UN school with many civilian deaths as a result.

True, neither the U.S. nor Israel are members of the *ICC*, but Israel's leaders can be prosecuted for war crimes committed outside the ICC's membership. Although no one really expects (at this writing) that Israeli government leaders will end up in the dock at The Hague, there is some strong sentiment around the world that they should be.

One of the most recent examples of this sentiment is the *UN's Human Rights Council* Resolution which states that Israel should be held "accountable" in all appropriate forums for its violations of international law and human rights for its actions in Gaza in 2014. (*Times of Israel Staff*, 2015. For the entire resolution see References.) The vote was 41 in favor (including: Germany, France, China, Brazil, Indonesia, Mexico, Saudi Arabia, Estonia, and Japan) with 5 abstentions and only 1 "No" vote—the U.S.A. Is a nearly unanimous global animosity a good sign for the future existence of the nation-state of Israel? The world is turning a thumbs down on Israel as a decent nation. And Israel, as a nation, is sticking it tongue out at the world.

In other words, these scornful reactions to Israel's muscular military might and aggressive foreign policy—whether truly in their self-defense or not—ironically undermine the core interests of Israel's existence as a nation state as presently configured. We are not making any moral judgments here, we are simply describing the empirical dynamics, which could be described as a classic case of "the law of unintended consequences" operating against Israel's positions and core interests.

In addition, this inflated global enmity towards Israel is having a negative effect upon a large swathe of the Jewish diaspora. Exhibit A in 2015 is the fact that the French government is presently being charged with the heavy duty of protecting all Jewish schools, synagogues, cultural centers, and even kosher butcheries throughout France from attack by vengeance-minded Islamists goaded on by the increasingly hostile Israeli-Palestinian relations.

Jewish people around this Earth are not to blame for Israel's foreign and military policies and actions. But there are Islamic fanatics around this Earth who cannot vent their rage directly against "The Jewish State" itself, but they can against Jewish buildings, businesses and innocent Jewish people in every niche and crevice on the planet, otherwise known as "soft targets." Thus Israeli actions in Palestine especially have led to, and more than likely will continue to precipitate, violent responses against Jewish men, women and children everywhere.

In our view, if Israel became the 51st state, it would automatically become the most secure state the Jewish people could have in all the world, while they would still be within their state boundaries in The Holy Land, their Promised Land. Their foreign policy would vanish into the foreign policies of the United States of America and give them no further problems like the ones which they are now confronted every day and are compounding into the indefinite future.

This is not to say that the foreign policies of the U.S.A. are brilliant and positive and well received in that part of the world, but that whatever they may come to be, they will not be those of a Zionist Nation State that is viewed by its neighbors as wanting more and more of their territory in the heart of the Middle East. Israel needs to decide if it wants to be viewed and treated as an expansionist, occupation-oriented militaristic nation or a small, democratic American state in harmony with its neighbors.

Furthermore, the tremendous amount of money Israel spends on its military capabilities, which is a heavy burden on its financial, social and mental health as a nation, would be drastically reduced. There would no longer be the massive Israel Defense Force (IDF). That would just become another American state's 'national guard.' If it follows the other states' model, Israel would not be any more of a front line of American defense than Texas.

This long range deterrent, would also result in no more Israeli need for the world to believe that it has sequestered a few hundred (more or less) nuclear weapons into well-fortified bunkers. Any nuclear capability and liability that Israel may possess would have to be merged into the American arsenal (and formally and transparently removed from Israeli territory). The charge that "if Israel has the bomb, then why not Iran", would no longer have any merit. A lot of genuine "core interests" concerning Israel's peaceful existence, health, wealth and public welfare would be addressed in many ways if it were to become an American state, as we hope to demonstrate below.

In point of fact, the Israeli government of today and tomorrow is under great domestic pressures to make a major pivot in its governmental policies, both social and economic. This became crystal clear in the autumn of 2011—at exactly the same time "Occupy Movements" were burgeoning elsewhere—when hundreds of thousands of Israelis (largely young people) took to the streets in that nation's largest political protests ever.

According to an article in *Reuters* the following day, this monster nationwide demonstration had nothing to do with the IDF or the Palestinian problem, it was about the rapid deterioration of living conditions in Israel, especially Tel Aviv, for the middle class. According to the *Reuters* report: " . . . a grassroots movement . . . has swollen (in about 6 months) from a cluster of tent-squatters into a countrywide mobilization of Israel's middle class." (Rabinovitch 2011).

The major issues then, as well as now, for a large percentage of the Israeli population are the same: affordable housing, affordable higher and professional education and a domestic economy that provides hope of a brighter future for Israel's youth. These will not vanish with more money being spent on further settlements in the occupied Palestinian lands or with fresh assaults on or responses to whatever new methods Hamas, Hezbollah, or Iran conceive to harass, fatigue and plague the Israelis.

American statehood for Israel would create a far better political, economic, and social environment than the most grandiose prayer that Theodore Herzl could have made on bended knee to Almighty God when he wrote Der Judenstatt (1896). It is a far better option than his desperate and failed attempt to get Kaiser Wilhelm to convince the Sultan of the Ottoman Empire to grant a "Protectorate" to the Jewish people in Palestine. A state of Israel within the loving embrace of the United States? We think that would have been Herzl's dream of dreams on steroids. Those who interpret the name of his book to be "A State of the Jews" rather than "The Jewish State" have more wiggle room to agree.

Just substitute the idea of being a state in the U.S.A. for Herzl's conclusion to *Der Judenstaat* as the culmination of his dream of dreams for the Jewish people and the whole world: "*Let me repeat once more my opening words: The Jews who wish for a State will have it. We shall live at last as free men on our own soil, and die peacefully in our own homes. The world will be freed by our liberty, enriched by our wealth, magnified by our greatness. And whatever we attempt there to accomplish for our own welfare, will react powerfully and beneficially for the good of humanity.*" (Herzl 1896 as translated into English online in the Virtual Jewish Library, emphasis ours).

By the way, we hope the reader can see how close Herzl's vision of this new Jewish polity equates to John Winthrop's speech on the Arabella before the founding of his colony in Massachusetts. From where we sit as mediators, they have exactly the same interests in the founding of their new nations.

In any event, his vision of the good for all humanity that would derive from having a Jewish State has not and is not likely to happen as long as Israel insists on remaining in the 19th and 20th century political modality of being a "nation state" in the hub of the Middle East. It could much more easily become the great reality he envisioned by seeking and being granted statehood in the United States of America.

What a blessing that would be for "the good of humanity" as well as all Jews living in Israel and for Jewish people living worldwide. Plus this move could well inject new vigor into both the Israeli and American economies. Israel would now be part of free "interstate commerce" with the other 50 American states . . . no free trade agreements with exceptions and no passports needed.

So, what's the downside of American statehood from the point of view of many Israelis and is it or are they a deal-breaker?

The Interaction of the Government and the Dominant Religion

The key here is what Jefferson advocated and argued for vigorously, "the absolute separation of church and state." This separation between the state and any official religion is guaranteed all Americans against the national government of the United States in the First Amendment to the U.S. Constitution. The same freedom of religion is guaranteed by the Fourteenth Amendment to all American citizens against any such discrimination by any state in the Union as well.

So, does this violate the core interests of the Nation of Israel? No, it does not if we are to believe that such tenets set forth in Israel's Declaration of Independence mean what they say. Here is what is stated to be the absolute, basic mission of the State of Israel concerning the liberties and freedoms of all Israeli citizens:

> "THE STATE OF ISRAEL will be open for Jewish immigration and for the Ingathering of the Exiles; it will foster the development of the country for the benefit of all its inhabitants; it will be based on freedom, justice and peace as envisaged by the prophets of Israel; it will ensure complete equality of social and political rights to all its inhabitants irrespective of religion, race or sex; it will guarantee freedom of religion, conscience, language, education and culture; it will safeguard the Holy Places of all religions; and it will be faithful to the principles of the Charter of the United Nations."

Naturally, as in all grandiose political tracts, the words are vague enough to allow for an array of interpretations. This is no less true in Israel today than it is with the U.S. Constitution from its ratification to today in the United States.

For example, can American states give educational vouchers paid for out of state taxes to parents so as to give them the ability to pay tuition at a Baptist or Catholic school? Does not a Christian chaplain open every session of Congress with a prayer? How can the U.S. Senate and the U.S. House of Representatives have "chaplains" as officers of the Congress and what about the fact that, somehow, every single one of them have been Christian? There is a cornucopia full of other examples to prove conclusively that the "absolute" Jeffersonian wall between church and state has some canyon wide cracks in it.

Another good example of a U.S. state breaching the wall of separation between church and state would be Utah. As we wrote above, it was founded to protect and nourish a particular religion, particularly one that had a history of persecution in America. Since its induction into statehood, though, it has managed to deal with the complexities inherent in the separation of church and state in a nation that has multiple religions and many very religious people.

For instance, though "polygamy" is officially prohibited in Utah, it is still practiced by many thousands of Mormon families—in Utah and elsewhere— in one way or another. However, as recently as 2014, the ban on polygamy by Mormons was struck down by a United States federal judge as being against religious liberty and an infringement on privacy. (Holpuch 2014) We need not go into details here, but there are many ways to chip away at constitutional proscriptions and prescriptions. Here's another example.

The State of Utah, which is still heavily influenced by The Mormon Church, also has a ban on how alcohol must be served, even in restaurants throughout the state. To most modern Utahns, this is an absurdity. Thus, a political movement is forming to *"Tear Down the Zionist Curtain,"* (believe it or not) because booze cannot be mixed or prepared at the table, but can only be prepared in the kitchen or a closed bar area. This religious relic will probably not last too much longer, despite the fact that the church's website has a major leader calling for upholding the ban since such a practice is "closely tied to the moral culture of the state." (Glionna 2014)

The Mormon Church also had a long standing policy of banning almost all commerce on the Sabbath, for them Sundays. This had a few exceptions to it and became the main reason that the U.S. Supreme Court struck it down as being "arbitrary" and no doubt in violation of the "equal protection of the laws" of the United States Constitution.

So, what's the lesson here for Israel as being a "Jewish state" or "state for Jews" and entering into a federal system that has many laws separating the church from the state and protecting individual liberties against governmental establishment of religion and intrusion into private life?

Aside from the soaring prose in its founding documents, the Jewish state is a state that is intrinsically Jewish in that the purpose it serves is to direct the powers of the state to "dealing with the problems of the Jewish people." In past and present practice, this principle meant the promulgation of a substantial number of particularistic "Jewish" laws and policies. These include:

- the Law of Return granting the right of free Jewish immigration into Israel;
- the State Education Law mandating the inculcation of "the values of Jewish culture" and "loyalty to the Jewish people";
- the involvement of the Israeli armed forces and security services in rescue operations of non-Israeli Jews in foreign countries;
- the use of Israeli courts to try and punish Nazi war criminals for "crimes against the Jewish people";
- mandating the state's adoption of Jewish symbols, as well as the Jewish holidays and Sabbath; and many others.

Of course, one could argue about the specifics of any of these particular "Jewish" policies. But virtually all Jews embraced the idea that Israel had been established as a "Jewish state," not only in terms of its demographics, but also in its purpose, values, policies and institutions. But so it was with Utah, "The New Zion."

So would Israel have to abandon some—or even the great majority— of the intermixing of church and state that actually exists there? Here is the way a Shimon Shishtreet, Professor of Law at the Hebrew University in Jerusalem, sees this "*hybrid*" secular/religious state. First and foremost he states clearly that "Judaism has not been proclaimed the official religion of Israel." Thus, it is not a "theocracy" along the lines of Iran, where the top religious leader is also the head of state. (See Shishtreet's website VirtualJewishHistory.org, link is in References.)

Professor Shishtreet goes on to emphasize what has been said above, that there is a guarantee of freedom of religion in Israel, according to what Herzl would have wanted and according to its founding beliefs, vows and fundamental charter. However, he goes on to explain that Israel is in reality "*a hybrid between non-intervention in religious affairs, on the one hand, and the inter-involvement of religion and government on the other.*"

Let us be perfectly clear: That "inter-involvement" in its many forms in present day Israel would never pass muster under Supreme Court interpretations of the First Amendment and they would have to be jettisoned, just as the Mormons had to dispose of some fundamentally cherished religious tenets of their own to become an American state. So what might some of these be? Well, pretty much all of what we mentioned above would have to be scrapped.

Some other traditional Jewish Israeli practices would have to be abolished as well. If Israel becomes a part of the United States, any American citizen who moves there becomes a citizen of that state after they establish a permanent residence there and they need not have a Jewish mother or grandmother to do so. There is a long lineup of other legalities of the Israeli government that would also have to walk the plank. Here are just a few others that would need to go which were part of an understanding between the first Israeli president, David Ben-Gurion, and Jewish religious leaders at their founding in 1948:

- No public transportation on the Sabbath. Unconstitutional.

- Ban on the importation of non-Kosher foods. Unconstitutional.

- No civil marriages; only religious ones. Unconstitutional.

- State funding of religious schools. Unconstitutional.

There are lots more such laws which would take a lot of time to negotiate before statehood and even some litigation afterwards to settle. On the other hand, whether to strictly or liberally interpret many of these laws would depend largely on the composition of the U.S. Supreme Court at the time. If the majority of the Court is comprised of those with a more liberal bent, some of these religiously discriminatory practices might pass muster, as has been the case on occasion in Hawai'i where the state makes exceptions for both Native Hawaiians or for permanent residents vs. mainland Americans. Even after 55 years of statehood, there is still a great deal of friction between Hawaiians, locals, and mainlanders. (Kasindorf 2007) This leads to lawsuits and this would probably hold true in Israel for many decades after statehood. Such a prospect, however, need not be an obstacles towards or a bar to statehood. It would, however, be a boon to Israeli attorneys.

The fact that most residents of Israel today consider themselves to be religious in the Jewish persuasion does not mean that any of the above, or even all of the above, if thought to be important to these people, would be considered by them as core interests of the Israeli state. They are traditional Jewish "interconnections" to be sure, but they are not vital to the existence of the state or to freedom of religion in Israel.

Israel was founded primarily to be a state where Jewish people would not be persecuted, imprisoned, exiled or murdered for practicing their religion, openly be discriminated against, or be second class citizens simply because they were Jewish. Those are the innermost core interests of a

Jewish state right alongside the existential one of security from outside attack or invasion.

Thus, if any Jewish person in Israel, after statehood, wanted a Rabbi to marry them and it would be enough to be a legal marriage, then this is not necessarily a violation of the U.S. Constitution. If any Jewish person refused to travel or carry money on a Saturday, this would be none of the government's business. If there are multitudes of Jewish schools—as well as Muslim and Christian schools—this is none of the government's business under the U.S. Constitution. If there are many kosher butcher shops and restaurants and they have a good enough clientele to be profitable, this is none of the state's concern either.

This is the only kind of freedom of religion that Theodore Herzl and persecuted Jews throughout the ages in the diaspora deeply craved and deserved. Yes, the state of Israel would almost certainly have to surrender some of the state's financial and moral support to the Jewish synagogues, institutes and schools (and other religions as well), but that was not fundamental to the original need for Zionism. Freedom and religious liberty, a public pride in Jewishness, was what was to be cherished. And that key core interest of Israel, would be served well—if not even better—if Israel became the 51st state.

Very orthodox religious Jews in Israel might have a very hard time in coming to terms with this ceding and diminution of their power in and through the state. However, there are equally religious Jewish people in the United States, like the many branches, communities and sub-groups of the Hasidic Jews, and they practice their religion perfectly well without the assistance of their state governments and have no trouble with state authorities oppressing them.

Rampant, state-supported Anti-Semitism is what Herzl saw in France during the Dreyfus Affair. This is what he saw throughout Western and Eastern Europe. This is what millions of Jews in Eastern Europe flocked to him to plead for: freedom to be Jews. That's the quintessential core interest. That would in no way be threatened by Israeli statehood as the 51st state.

Therefore, it should be manifestly clear that all of the above religious positions, practices and orthodoxies together are not inimical for American statehood and for a Jewish state. Altogether, from our viewpoint as mediators, these are "religious positions" well worth yielding for the core interests of (a) permanent existence and security; (b) freedom of religion from state discrimination and/or persecution; plus (c) the economic advantages of being the only American state in The Middle East. Israelis and Jewish Americans should know a good bargain when they see it. As for Israel's neighbors, we will discuss what's in it for them below.

However, there are also about a quarter of Israelis who are not Jewish. We believe that most of them would come to look upon American statehood favorably, since they would more likely than not benefit from the legal disassociation of the state from Jewish religious institutions which exist in the Israel of today.

Such a cultural and religious merger could also be interpreted as a shiny new element in the American theory of "Manifest Destiny," since looking at it from the American historical, expansionist perspective, Israel would be its most western state after Hawaii. As we have pointed out before, many American religious visionaries have seen America as a "New Zion" and a legacy of the biblical Israelites. To have the "Old Zion" become part of the United States would be the closure of the American dream of the "city on the hill" showering its light across the globe.

Israel becoming part of the United States could turn out to be a match made in Heaven.

The Two-State Solution Is Dead.
Long Live the New State Solution

As we noted above, whether Israel becomes a 51st state of the U.S.A. is entirely an internal matter between Israel and the United States, however to ignore the core interests of Israel's immediate and even somewhat distant neighbors in thinking about such a radical political move would be politically and morally foolish. Surely, it would neither be in America's nor Israel's core interests if such a political maneuver inflamed the passions and sense of national security of each of Israel's present or potential future next door or next block neighbors.

So, we'll commence with the most intimate neighbor of Israel's, the amorphous "quasi-state" of the Palestinian "Authority" (Fatah and Hamas). It is this neighbor whose fierce rebellion against the nation state of Israel, as we have mentioned frequently above, feeds widespread Islamic distemper and contempt for both Israel and the U.S.A. as close allies.

The infectious relationship between the Jewish people of Israel and the Palestinian people who have been forced from their land, driven into exile, or live in Gaza or the "West Bank"—in various situations from misery to third class citizenship—most assuredly will continue to fester unless adequately treated with the healthy new tonic of Israel being part of the United States. The idea of there being a "Palestine" for the Arabs who used to live in that vicinity, their children and grandchildren, who yearn to come back to it, and who still reside in various parts of it, needs to be handled empathetically and delicately by the United States consistent with its own core interests in the Middle East, particularly as a potentially new and permanent resident there.

All the former elements of what was mistakenly conceived as the only possible remedy, i.e., "The Two-State Solution," have been grounded in misguided, imperialistic and surreal borders based on interests that no longer exist. Many new "special interests" have vested since then within and between these borders and pseudo-countries, but they need to be erased and redrawn from a politically astute point of view. These need to be based on the increasingly obvious realities on the ground there, within that region, and throughout the entire world as expeditiously and sensitively as possible. (We offer some potential "options" below, so read on).

As matters now stand with that perennial global septicity on Eastern Mediterranean shores, the present Israeli government has made it crystal clear to one and all that it now considers "The Two State Solution" to be DOA (or, dead on arrival—a hospital emergency room acronym). Prime Minister Netanyahu was re-elected in 2015 with that as an explicit and major plank in his platform and we can be certain that he will maintain that position for as long as he is in office, and probably for as long as Israel remains a nation state.

For empirical proof of this death notice, a British journalist quoted all of Netanyahu's cabinet for their views on this subject in the Arab news giant, *Al Jazeera*, and here are a few morsels to dispel any remnants of nostalgia for that "solution" to the contrary:

a. The deputy foreign minister: "opposed to a Palestinian State";

b. The defense minister: "chemotherapy" is needed against the "cancer like" Palestinian state;

c. The justice minister: (to *The New Yorker* Magazine) "I will do everything in my power to make sure they never get a state."

d. The Rural Development minister: " . . . there won't be a Palestinian state west of the Jordan River."

e. In an interview on *Israeli National Radio*, the Science and Technology Minister said that "The Oslo Process is finished . . . .Enough with the two-state solution. Land for peace is over. We don't want a Palestinian State . . . we need to apply Israeli sovereignty over (the West Bank)." (Hasan 2015).

So where does that leave the Palestinian Arabs in 2016 and in years to come? They are already feeling the steady march of Israeli "settlements" as a "death by a thousand cuts." In return, Israel is feeling the increasing bitterness from various and sundry nations, Islamic sects, and official and non-governmental wrath from various world governments, not the least of which is the Obama Administration.

The world seems to be saying in unison: "Stop the Settlements." The Israeli government and most of its voters seem to be saying: "All the old Palestine is ours for the taking." So what's the next round in the bout: Israel vs. The World?

According to some reasonably objective and pragmatic sources in that area: more and more Palestinians are beginning to feel that the only solution is some kind of "one-state" solution, i.e., that the Palestinians must become equal citizens of Israel—perhaps in some federated or confederated union. In this scenario, Israel then would be comprised the old Palestine of British Mandate days, including The West Bank of the Jordan and the Gaza Strip, and once again the population of the unified nation would be split between Jews and Arabs.

Two young Middle Eastern researchers based in Washington, D.C., Grant Rumley and Amir Tibon, analyzed this situation during the summer of 2015 in the CFR's *Foreign Affairs*. They see this idea ballooning in popularity among the younger generation of Palestinians, particularly those living on the West Bank. A burgeoning cohort of young Palestinians see the "two-state solution" as belonging to the older "Tunis Crowd" of exiled PLO and Fatah people and know that it has failed miserably. Younger Palestinians want to enjoy the civil benefits of being Israeli NOW. So what would that entail?

"*This veiled reference to voting rights would give Palestinians access to the Israeli Knessset, where decisions regarding their lives are really made . . . (This) alternative strategy would put Israel on a dangerous path: the country would have to deal with approximately 4.5 million Palestinians in the West Bank and Gaza asking not for land of their own, but for a voice and role inside (a bi-national) Israel itself.*" (Rumley and Tibon 2015)

This sentiment among Palestinian Millennials will become tougher and tougher for Jewish Israelis to swallow since, as Rumley and Tibon note: "(Israeli) officials would not be able to argue against it by appealing to security." Thus, " . . . *it would be far harder for (Netanyahu) or any future Israeli prime minister to say no to a new generation of Palestinians who called for Israeli citizenship and voting rights but no change to the existing security structure.*"

And how do they think Israelis would respond to such a growing movement? Not well. "*Granting Israeli voting rights to the Palestinians living under Israeli control in the West Bank and Jerusalem would mean the end of the Jewish state and there is no chance Israelis would agree to it."* (Rumley and Tibon 2015, emphasis ours)

So what options will that leave the Israelis in the future? There are two: (a) slaughter and/or expel all the Palestinians living on the West Bank and in Gaza (a/k/a genocide); or (b) devise a wholly novel kind of two-state solution acceptable to the Jewish and Palestinian Arab communities.

The first is unthinkable and would trigger an even bigger war in the Middle East. No better two-state solution than previously proposed and completely rejected has been seriously offered because Israel will not consider it as an option to be negotiated. Question: what does that leave?

The only answer to this utter impasse is what we have proposed, i.e., The New State Solution with Israel as the 51st state, within its 1967 borders, and a brand new version of a Palestinian state reconstructed, expanded, modernized and supported by its great and beneficent new neighbor, the United States of America.

In conflict resolution terms of win-win, that would mean "expanding the pie," or to put it into geo-political terms, already artificial borders would have to be re-conceived and newly vested interests would have to get something of great value to them in return for surrendering past "rights" and privileges. The United States of America has more than enough resources to accomplish this elusive feat given that it would be re-prioritizing its budget from militarily destructive uses to people-friendly constructive ones. What? That's insane! Never!

Yes, yes, we know that does not seem like it will ever be in the cards, otherwise: bring on the fire and brimstone!!

The Jordan-Egyptian "New Palestine"

The history between Israel, the Palestinians, Egypt and Jordan since the 1940s has ranged from extremely violent to an uneasy, sometimes peaceful co-existence. Multiple "facts," "events," and agreements are as malleable as putty at best and we do not profess to be able to distinguish which particular "truths" are so or not. So what follows is simply a sketchy view of what most agree as to being so and using that as a basis for future negotiations to decide where human-friendly and realistic borders might go and what kind of governmental structure might be best for everyone involved.

What appears to be the case in 2016 is: (a) the U.S. brokered Camp David peace agreement between Israel and Egypt seems to be holding, with radical Islamist activity in the Sinai peninsula being a worry about escalating violence on the Sinai-Israel-Egypt borders; (b) a peace agreement between Israel and the Jordanian government (the Hashemite monarchy) also appears to be relatively stable for the time being bolstered by looming threats to both from the Islamic State; (c) the Palestinian population of Jordan is overwhelmingly considered to be a majority with estimates ranging up to 2/3s, although the Jordanian government's last official count in 2004 low-balled it at 43%. The most accurate guess is a bit over 50%; (d) the United States contributes large amounts of "foreign aid" (many billions annually) to both Egypt and Jordan that helps maintain relative "stability" (tight hierarchical control) in both regimes up to 2016 . . . albeit cracking down hard on occasional uprisings.

This confluence of factors makes it a reasonable step into a future to establish a new state of Palestine that includes the present "Authority" of Palestine's West Bank territory plus some of that included in present day Jordan. This is not a new idea and history does not have to be an irresistible obstacle. The River Jordan is a natural boundary, but need not be a political one.

There are contiguous parts of West Jordan that are overwhelmingly populated by Palestinian exiles...many living in refugee camps for generations. There is no reason other than relatively recent political ones for them not to be united with their countrymen living on the West Bank. Jordan and Trans-Jordan were mere figments of British imperial megalomania. Modern day Jordan needs the population, vim, and vigor of their Jordan-Palestinian citizens, but they would surely continue in their role as economic generators as a neighboring partner nation. Plus, both what remains as Jordan, and the New Palestine (West Bank + some parts of current Jordan), will be financially and technologically helped by Israel, the 51st United State of America, the Old and New Zion fused at last.

This is a somewhat more nuanced version of what some have already proposed, i.e., that Jordan disappear in favor of becoming a majoritarian Palestinian state. There is no need for such a radical step and it is highly unlikely that King Abdullah II is going to play Mr. Good Guy and humbly abdicate. It is equally unlikely that he will hold a referendum on whether to be Jordan or Palestine.

After all, the minority Jordanian Bedouins exclusively staff Jordan's military, police, government, and intelligence agencies. A Palestinian takeover of all of Jordan will not happen no matter how intently and intensely one peers into a crystal ball. An expanded Palestinian state into PARTS of Jordan heavily laden with Palestinians and descendants of Palestinians makes sense given their sheer presence there. In addition, both the Jordanians and Palestinians who live in that country now have many essential economic ties to both Israel and the United States already.

According to a recent article in *Middle East Quarterly*: *"There is, in fact, almost nothing un-Palestinian about Jordan except for the royal family. Despite decades of official imposition of a Bedouin image on the country, and even Bedouin accents on state television, the Palestinian identity is still the most dominant—to the point where the Jordanian capital—Amman—is the largest and most populated Palestinian city anywhere. Palestinians view it as a symbol of their economic success and ability to excel."* (Zahran 2012).

The writer of the above thus advocates the shooing of the Hashemite monarchy into the dank dungeons of history and making all of Jordan into Palestine. As we observed above, that would likely feed even more conflict. Figuring out how to enhance the Palestinian state out of part of Jordan, but maintaining, if not strengthening, Jordanian independence and relevance—with the assistance and support of Israel and the U.S.A. to supplement long existent 21st century manufacturing deals—opens the possibility of a "Confederation." This is not just a wild idea out of nowhere.

According to Uri Savir (who was a lead negotiator in the Oslo process, a member of the Knesset, and is a director of the *Peres Center for Peace* in Jaffa, Israel): " . . . *Palestinians are looking for creative ideas to revive international interest in the resolution of the conflict while actively engaging Arab countries. One senior Palestinian official told Al-Monitor of a deus ex machina concept he had in mind that could salvage the Palestinian predicament. The official, who entertains good contacts within the Jordanian court, would like to rekindle the idea of a Jordanian-Palestinian confederation, an issue he has apparently raised lately with Palestinian President Mahmoud Abbas and with the entourage of the Jordanian king."*

He continues:

> *"The characteristics of the confederation, according to the senior source, would be outlined in an agreement between two independent states — each headed by an independent executive, two capitals (one in Amman and one in East Jerusalem), two parliaments, a joint parliamentary institution dealing with confederative issues, a joint economic area of free trade, joint economic ventures (including enterprises in the Dead Sea region) and joint water and energy mechanisms. There would also be joint security and anti-terror measures and arrangements, mainly along the Jordan River."*
>
> *"The confederation, according to this source, would come about only after the establishment of the Palestinian state. Yet, an understanding in principle could be achieved prior to that, so as to give Jordan a central role in the negotiations on statehood.*

Jordanian involvement in the negotiation is considered by many of its officials as essential in several aspects." (Savir 2015)

Now we are not endorsing this recipe as containing the perfect and exact ingredients of The New Palestine. However, it certainly seems to have more than enough merit to deliberate, tweak and negotiate and its finished details should take care of that longest border of Israel—as the 51st state—without embroiling the United States in what might portend to be a certain and incalculably difficult dispute in that part of the world. It also throws a bright spotlight on how to revitalize that entire area economically, culturally and politically and would present to the entire Middle East an attractive alternative to Radical Islam's vision of "End Times" in Jerusalem (to be discussed below).

But what about Gaza—an integral part of the New Palestine, yet separated from its larger part by a great distance. Well, what about Alaska and Hawaii? They are part of the United States and separated by tremendous distances . . . not just a few kilometers. So, geographical distance alone is really not problematic in this day and age.

The biggest question is: how can this new, expanded America help transform Gaza, as part of The New Palestine, into a glittering showplace instead of the world's largest bereft and bedraggled refugee camp? That is where Egypt would come into the picture, keeping in mind that Egypt, Israel and the United States already have a long and mostly friendly relationship . . . particularly since the U.S.-brokered Israel/Egypt Camp David Treaty.

Just brainstorming this, one possibility that comes to mind has a historical backdrop, and that would be to split the Palestinians in Gaza from The New Palestine and make it an autonomous state or province within Egypt. As such, it could be a self-governing polity domestically, with all tax monies going for domestic health, educational, and welfare programs as well as infrastructure. Gaza would pay a fee or tax to Egypt to handle its "foreign affairs" and thus rely on the Egyptian military, heavily subsidized by the Pentagon, for border and domestic security.

There would be free "interstate commerce" between them. This would be a boon to Egypt, since Gaza—whether under this arrangement or as a confederate part of The New Palestine—could easily be invested in as a major Eastern Mediterranean tourist competitor to Dubai and/or Doha. Both of the latter two are far much longer jet trips for Europeans—western and eastern. After all, Gaza's entire western border is open sea and tropical beaches . . . with an excellent year round climate.

The biggest problem in this scenario is that Gaza is, at least under present political pressures, ruled by Hamas, an offshoot of The Muslim

Brotherhood, which is illegal—and persecuted— under the current Egyptian military regime. This violent and injudicious suppression of the Muslim Brotherhood in Egypt has caused a sizable, steady (if not growing) insurrection in Egypt against the militarized government . . . as well as fueling Radical Islamic resistance in the Sinai and on the Libyan border regions.

Thus, the removal of a guarded border between Gaza (and its Muslim Brotherhood sympathies) and Egypt at this point in time, or for the foreseeable future, would not be seen by the Egyptian government as a workable idea since it would add avowed enemies into the Egyptian polity. On the other hand, things change as rapidly in that part of the world as the swirling sands, and the Muslim Brotherhood could be back in power, or become part of a new governmental power structure (as might the Taliban in Afghanistan) in the future. In that possible event, Egypt could welcome Gaza as at least a step-brother.

Either situation we have broached above would drastically improve the living conditions of the million plus Palestinians in Gaza and make the relationship with the United States and its 51st state far more positive and of mutual economic benefit, if not socially and culturally as well. Are not these few potentially viable solutions—and they are merely a hint of the wide array available through the "Principled Negotiation" techniques and attitudes discussed in Chapter 3—not infinitely preferable ways to live in the future than the way things are playing out under present American and Israeli imperial thought? Gaza squalor seems equated with Israeli valor, but such conditions are counter-productive to a peaceful and prosperous Middle East with the U.S.A. as a "good neighbor" (an American policy that worked elsewhere before under similar conditions which will be discussed below).

So, these or better reconciliations would make the Eastern and Southern borders of the 51st state far more secure and happy places than they are at present and are likely to be under "Full Spectrum Dominance" and persistent Israeli expansion into Arab lands. Forever anxiety and retaliations is not the way to go on those two Israeli borders. But that still leaves us with the problem on Israel's Northern borders: Hezbollah and Syria.

The Northern Border: "South Lebanon"

Simplistically, under the fictitious and fractious Picot-Sykes and League of Nations proclamations, the northern border of Israel is bounded by Lebanon and Syria. In actuality today, it is more like a Rubik's Cube. Think of it in three dimensions with lots of different colors and moving parts.

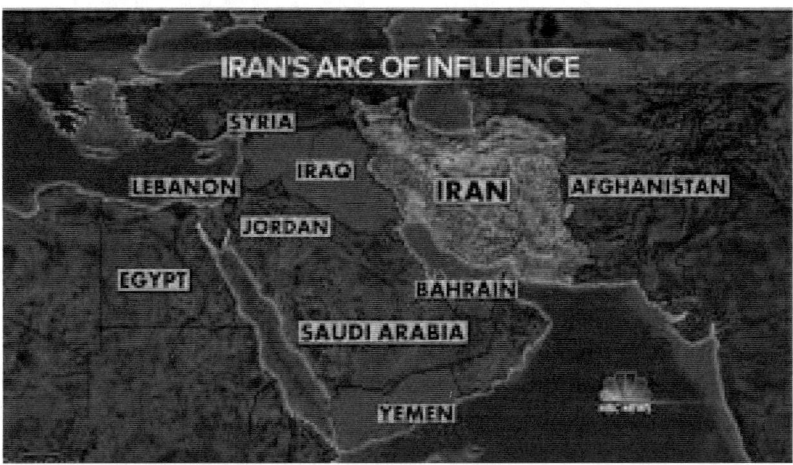

The trick would be how to make this into a functional border between America's 51st state and the Shia Muslim's fondest dream: "The Shia Arc" of alliances from Iran to the coast of the Mediterranean Sea. This Shia Arc became close to an ephemeral reality with the Assad dictatorship of Syria and Anbar Province of Iraq under legal dominion of a Shiite dominated government in Baghdad. The map on the left is on the website of *The Consortium of Defense Analysts* and is the best and most recent image of "The Shia Crescent" or "The Shia Arc" that we could find posted on the Internet at present (*Consortium of Defense Analysts*, 2015).

This *Consortium* sees such a Shia "alliance" as being a haven for a great "terror" threat to the United States, Latin America and the Middle East. We do not. What is true is that the "control" of Syria in 2016 and beyond by a Shia or Shia-friendly regime is far from certain in 2016 and will probably stay that way for some time to come. Whether that Shia linkage could or would be re-established or redrawn more realistically in the future remains to be seen as a potentially feasible solution between the expanded United States, Iran and whoever else is in between.

Under present U.S. and Israeli thinking and alliances, i.e., The New World Order, NATO and the Pentagon's wildly fantastic "Full Spectrum Dominance," having a Shiite political entity at the Northern border of Israel is The Impossible Dream. America's and Israel's only somewhat reliable "allies" in the Middle East are Sunni national governments. The present Iraq political system (constructed by the U.S. to be American-friendly), is run by the majority Shiites, and is really a kissing cousin of Iran who, under present day circumstances, merely tolerates what it deems as a temporary American intervention in the region.

It is undoubtedly true that the cardinal planner and enabler of "The Shia Arc" idea and ideal is Iran. And Iran is the nation that is now most closely allied with the biggest bugaboo on the northern Israeli borders of today: Hezbollah in Southern Lebanon—as well as what is left of the besieged remnants of the Syrian regime in Damascus and any link it may still have to The Golan Heights in what used to be called Syria. Israel has been in intermittent deadly contact with both Hezbollah and The Assad Regime of Syria for many decades along its northern borders and the hatred between them seems to be of the "fight to the death" brand.

It is our view, though, that the huge problems and tectonic shifts in store for humanity in the very near future which we have discussed in depth above will make the U.S.-Sunni governmental alliances much less fruitful. Conversely, a *rapprochement* with the Shiites in Iran, Iraq, Syria and Lebanon will become a far more palatable and digestible menu item for the United States of America in the new, future Middle East.

After all, despite Iran's Supreme Leader's grand strategic plan of his own laid out in his recent *magnum opus* called *Palestine* (to be discussed below), Iran did negotiate with the West a deal to jettison a large portion of its present day nuclear capacity in return for near future material and political gains. Great visions of imperial sway or foreign ambition don't always work out well. As a relatively recent historical example, consider Japan's illusion of a "Greater East Asia's Co-Prosperity Sphere", *circa* 20th century. Sometimes the stomach betrays the appetite.

As matters presently stand in 2016, Syria as a "nation" configured after The First World War is like all sand castles built at water's edge at low tide, dissolving as the high tide rolls in. Wracked with both a civil war, proxy wars, and various forms of invasion and assault from the air, the former Pan-Arab Socialist regime in Damascus will not maintain authority throughout the entirety of "Syria" as planned in Paris in 1916 . . . especially in the south, towards the border of Israel. This could develop a perfect political void for what we have to offer as a potential solution for a neighborly, peaceful, if not collaborative border between Israel, the 51st state, and a new nation to be constructed there that we will tentatively dub: "South Lebanon."

It is well known that Hezbollah was formed in Lebanon in 1982—although it took some time to reach the boiling point—in part as an angry and extremely aggressive response to the Israeli invasion and occupation there along with what was widely perceived in Arab lands as Israel's ill treatment of the Palestinian refugees in Lebanon. Hezbollah has been funded, armed and trained by the Iranian Revolutionary Guard from its inception.

Although Hezbollah has been and is considered and labeled to this day as a "terrorist" organization by some nations (the U.S. and Israel included), it has become over the years the most potent and powerful political, economic and religious force south of Beirut. Approximately 2/3s of the population from South Beirut to the Israeli border are Shiites, with most of the rest being Christian.

However, Hezbollah has achieved great political power inside the country of Lebanon today since it was—and continues to be—a much more powerful military force than is Lebanon's national army. According to political terminology, it is officially a national political party and it is guaranteed, after a highly successful mediation between Hezbollah and the Lebanese government by the Qataris in Doha in 2008 (Kamrava 2011), one third of cabinet seats at the national level and the power to veto any law passed by the majority.

This odd arrangement kept the peace relatively well within Lebanon between Hezbollah and its national government since the settlement was reached. It is evidentiary that Hezbollah (that dogmatic, implacable "terrorist" organization) can actually negotiate a fair agreement (like Iran over its nuclear program) with a range of sectarian and political foes (in Hezbollah's case, at least if there is a trusted and skilled mediator at the table).

Up to the summer and autumn of 2015, Hezbollah was perhaps the main fighting force that kept the Assad regime in formal power in Syria, that is, at least until President Putin intervened with a large Russian military presence in North Syria in mid-late 2015. Its fighters—along with Iranian equipment and more than token assistance from The Revolutionary Guards—have been and are taking heavy losses in their attempts to help shore up Assad's Syrian government, particularly against the fanatic Sunni brigades of the al-Nusra Front and the Islamic State.

This significant depletion of fighting-age men, however, is weakening Hezbollah domestically and surely has greatly fatigued their future fighting capabilities against the Israeli Defense Force. However, they remain a strong quasi-governmental entity and a legitimate Lebanese political force since they provide many health, educational, and spiritual services to the mainly Shiite community they serve and rule in Southern Lebanon.

During the 2006 war with Israel in the southern part of Lebanon, Hezbollah displayed much greater military prowess than the Israelis expected. This included the launching of thousands of large missiles on Israel and inflicting unusually heavy casualties on the invading Israeli army and more than token harm on Israel proper. Everyone knows that Iran has reinforced Hezbollah's depleted missile arsenal—which was far more deadly and accurate than those in use by Hamas in 2015. Indeed, it is widely assumed that Iran has improved Hezbollah's stockpile with much more long range and more precise missiles for 2016 and beyond.

To be sure, Israel today remains somewhat wary of any repeat armed advance into South Lebanon and rightfully fears some maniacal jihad from the Lebanese skies. After all, there is no peace treaty between Hezbollah and Israel and the entire region is embattled. Peace on Israel's northern border, if present day conditions project into the future, is a fairy tale at best.

So what, if anything, could be done to reconstitute that border so as to be satisfactory to both Hezbollah and the new U.S. state we propose to be on its southern border? For one thing, a peace treaty between the U.S. and Lebanon itself would be in order. Given Hezbollah's power, though, perhaps a better way would be by all interested parties there agreeing to a new, independent Shiite political entity called "South Lebanon", which would secede from what is now delineated as Lebanon and become a new Shiite Republic between the U.S.A. and whatever thereafter constitutes Lebanon itself.

With Israel no longer being the hated "Zionist Entity" on its border, but just a part of the U.S.A. with whom it has a peace treaty, Hezbollah would no longer need to be a warrior surrogate for Iran, Syria, or any other country. It could devote itself to its many economic, cultural, and welfare projects in its own country. It would have its own international identity and dignity.

So what would a revised Lebanon get in return? For one thing, they would have their own coalition of ethnic groups without a strong Shiite opposition. As for the lost land, this could perhaps be replaced from ethnically friendly parts of what is left of Syria after its ruination and reconstitution. That could the substance of negotiations between various factions in Lebanon and the remnants of Syria (all of whom would have to deal with a strong, permanent Russian military presence in their vicinity.) Thus, this is more a Russian and Eurasian problem than one for the U.S.A. as Israel.

Indeed, from the Lebanese perspective, the political detachment of the Shiite part of Lebanon from the Lebanese political spectrum could easily be viewed as an "addition by subtraction" and a remedial revocation of the by-now infamous Sykes-Picot plan. The biggest issue between the new Lebanon (whatever its contours may end up being) and South Lebanon would be the border between the two, since Hezbollah and the Shiites are strong in Beirut and Beirut—or a good part of it—would still be the capital of Lebanon.

With Shias dispersed as they are in Lebanon, and Beirut the capital, another possibility could be for South Lebanon either to be part of a confederate system or it could become an "autonomous region" and designate its own capital from which it can decide its own foreign policies. There are numerous paths available. We are just testing some.

It has already been demonstrated that the United States and Iran can negotiate some pretty serious matters and come to an agreement, and it is pretty clear that Syria will not be any kind of military threat to Israel in whatever form it becomes in the future. Thus South Lebanon could cease to be a proxy warrior against Israel as The 51st state and still be part of a peaceful and stable "Shiite Arc" in the Middle East—even though it may lack a land bridge with Shiite parts of Iraq, Iran and northwestern Syria. Hassan Nasrallah, as the "supreme leader" of this Shiite polity, has shown his willingness to negotiate with political enemies in Qatar and with international economic powers, including the *International Monetary Fund*, as he did in 2009.

We think this kind of re-alignment of national borders much more closely reflects the ethno-religious map that is a reality on the ground there today than the 1919-20 colonial-political map that has fueled such hostility and passion in that area. South Lebanon and the U.S.A. can be peaceful neighbors, and America can induce a collaborative, pro-active partnership with it would work best if it includes our proposal for a new *"Good Neighbor Policy"* and *"New Marshall Plan."* This truce will allow Iran to turn most of its energies into its Eurasian partnership with Russia and China and simply be a cultural, economic and religious ally of South Lebanon.

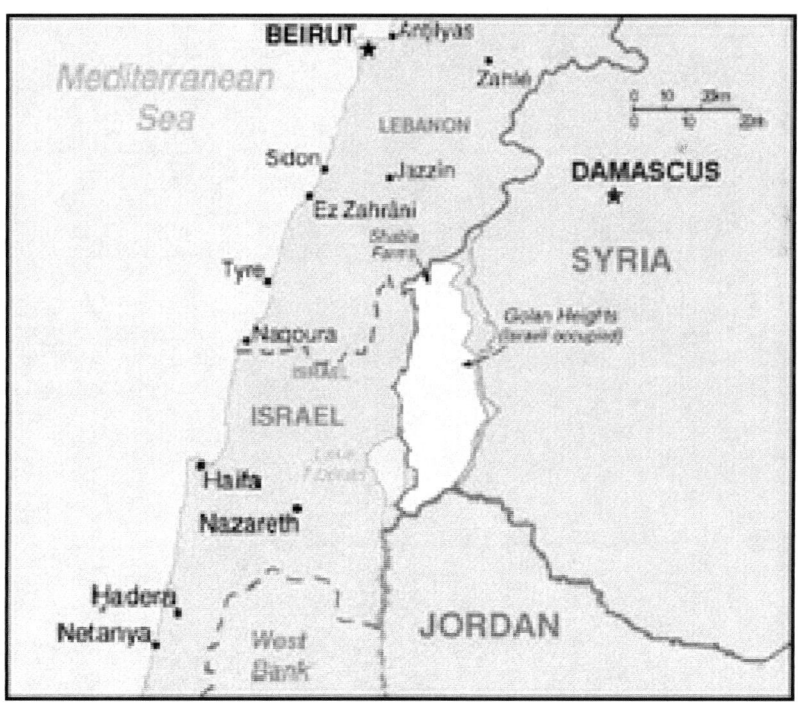

In the future, the more complex ethno-religious problem that exists in what used to be called "Syria" are the Shab'a Farms and Golan Heights. Such a negotiation over their contours would have to include, as requisite future stakeholders: an emergent South Lebanon, Jordan, the New Palestine, whatever is left of Syria, and the U.S.A. before any final Northern border of the 51st state can be formally etched on maps.

In 2016, this hotly contested region depicted on the Wikipedia map of The Golan Heights is a hodge-podge of Islamic religious sects, thousands of Jewish settlers and Druze. Israel has imposed its view of legal and administrative rule over this patch of land, but the U.N. Security Council in Resolution 497 declared Israeli occupation there to be "null and void." Therefore, under generally prevailing interpretations of international law, it remains an illegal occupation.

Obviously, this is much too fluid a situation to work out in any detail at this point in time. However, with all of the other borders becoming relatively secure, and with the U.S.A. showing its "exceptional" values and "exceptional" nature to the other parties in the region—consistent with our recommendations below—we feel as though ethno-religious details can be drawn fairly from the point of view of those who reside there, particularly if a mediation team is agreed upon and works its usual magic.

CHAPTER 6

The United States as the First Global Nation in the New Multi-Polar World: From the Apocalypse to Manifest Destiny 2.0

B EFORE WE GET INTO the meat of this chapter, which will conclude the book, it is imperative to make some other notes about the severity of the situation into which we are advocating a permanent and official American presence. The mad-scientist flights into some dream-world about world domination, which have characterized Western European and American geo-strategies for centuries, are hardly unique in their trance-like qualities. We have already explained how they have violently impacted the billion or more people who live in that part of the world and have contributed mightily to the ongoing virtual invasion of Europe by impoverished and traumatized peoples from there as refugees or people seeking political asylum. Among them will surely be a multitude of potential recruits into Radical Islam.

However, there are some much more recent "ideologies" of national expansion and religious salvation in that region that add a whole new dimension of danger to such an American-Israeli merger smack dab in the middle of those troubled lands. One is a home-grown Israeli one, which though confined to its own specific region, needs to be chucked overboard along with its first cousin, the American global model of Full Spectrum Dominance.

Another is Iranian and needs to be taken seriously posthaste if this new alignment in this part of the World Island is to become pacific and bear the fruits of the tree of peace. The third is a transnational political/religious ideology that needs to be minimized and /or contained, which is, in the words of *Getting to Yes* (1980), a BATNA (Best Alternative to a Negotiated Agreement). The fourth is a strictly American affair that has nothing to do with the American military-industrial complex but its goal is a grand opera of demolition and horrors.

After we expose all of these as unrealistic, nihilistic and implausible flights of fancy, which is not an easy task, we will proceed to show realistic options of how the new, expanded and improved United States of America, the world's First Global Nation, can be a truly "exceptional" addition to that region. We see it as being a positive force to synthesize a harmony with some major variants of Islam as well as with the emergent Eurasian Economic Union, multiple Chinese Silk and Belt Roads and the rest of the nascent Multi-Polar World.

The Four Horsemen of the Apocalypse Meet in the Holy Land: Ground Zero or Eulogy for Old Myths?

Although we will treat each of the following Middle Eastern "visions" separately, their greatest threat to all of humanity lies in their convergence in time and place, plus the fact that they are undergirded by the incubating geo-political confrontation between the early 21st century global powers: The USA/NATO/Gulf States vs. Russia-China-Iran/SCO. The following listing and discussion is in random order, since we consider them all equally incendiary and menacing to the peaceful co-existence that is essential to that part of the world, if not global survival.

The Oded Yinon Plan for a Greater Israel and Its Neo-Con Supplement

We have used some of Theodore Herzl's thinking before to guide us towards some kind of non-belligerent solution to the increasingly perfidious war games presently being waged in the Middle East. Unfortunately, Herzl, like many visionaries and theorists, was quite a prolix author and said many things—some contradictory or subject to competing interpretations—over his lifetime. Thus, he can be used by people with very different goals, just as Jesus, Buddha, Martin Luther King, and Nostradamus are mutually quoted by antagonists.

The Israel of Theodore Herzl (1904)
and of Rabbi Fischmann (1947)

One thing Herzl did say, and which is quoted *ad infinitum* by those Zionists (Jewish and Gentile) who maintain an extremely broad view of what would constitute "The Promised Land" given—so the story goes—to the Jewish people by God Almighty is this:

"*The area of The Jewish State stretches from the brook of Egypt (Author's Note: probably the Nile) to the Euphrates.*" Taking this literally, arch Zionists in Israel and elsewhere use this as a rough road map of what they think of as "Greater Israel." The map of that is pretty much the one we display here and can be found all over the Internet. This one is from Sizer, circa 2006 (See References)—and is from a Christian Zionist blog. (We'll get to them later in this chapter).

In the Winter of 1982, an article appeared in *Kivunim* (Directions), a journal of the Department of Information of the *World Zionist Organization*. It was written by a journalist with close ties to Israel's Foreign Ministry.

His name, Oded Yinon, has become legendary, largely because of that essay titled: "A Strategy for Israel in the Nineteen Eighties." (Shahak 1982).

Yinon's piece was translated into English by Israel Shahak, an Israeli Professor of Chemistry at the Hebrew University of Jerusalem and is widely available online (For a link, see Yinon in References). Some question important nuances in Shahak's English version, due to his very liberal and anti-Israeli policies at the time (he was, by the way, a Holocaust survivor as well). However, given what has transpired since its publication in that region of the world, we feel Shahak's translation is exact enough to accept as at least a generic "strategic plan" for what its author (Yinon) felt was for the greater good for the future of Israel, as well as to fulfill God's promise to the ancient Israelites.

This strategy was improved and elaborated upon in 1996 by an Israel-based Washington, D.C. "think tank" called *The Institute for Advanced Strategic and Political Studies*" (*IASPS*) in a paper produced by it titled: "A Clean Break: A New Strategy for Securing the Realm." (*The Institute for Advanced Strategic and Political Studies,* 1996) The study group that synthesized this report was led by Richard Perle, one of the prime architects of the George W. Bush Iraq War strategy. The strategic goal in this document was the necessity to expand Israeli power in order for Israel to become the leading military and political power throughout the entire Middle East.

Surely, avowed enemies of Israel—a nation-state which has moved into the West Bank, the Golan Heights, encircles Gaza, has invaded Lebanon, bombed Iraq, is bombing Syria, and threatens to obliterate Iran's nuclear industry—fervently believe that these two documents contain the key elements to the Israeli "Grand Game." In their mind, it is not coincidental that they just happen to square neatly with U.S. Neo-Conservative and Christian Zionist values, opinions and strategies. That so many denizens of the Middle East believe that this plot is now in full swing and explains to them vividly what Israel has done, is doing, and threatens to do, is way more than enough for Americans and people around the world to take "The Yinon Plan" and its successor's objectives seriously.

In essence, what they can easily be interpreted as saying is that there must be a Greater Israel which is destined to be a, or the, major nation-state in that corner of the planet. What stood in the way, back when this was presented in 1982 and updated in 1996, were nation states like Iraq and Syria and, of course, Egypt. So, one of the major tenets of the strategy is that the phony borders of the Sykes-Picot arrangement must be erased and the pseudo nation-states of Iraq, Syria, Lebanon and Jordan must be divided into much smaller, quarrelling, and thus weaker, polities that could easily be dominated by the nation-state of Israel.

Thus, according to Yinon's thinking, Iraq—which actually does have at least three decidedly different parts: The Sunni West, the Kurdish north, and the Shiite South—should be decomposed into its constituent areas. Syria should probably be broken into even smaller bits . . . .as should Lebanon as well.

Obviously, then, there are many professional analysts in Israel, the U.S., Russia, China and Islam who see the American and NATO attacks on Iraq and Syria as being in league with this "new divide-and-conquer" mentality. As we write this, mass mayhem and erupting chaos are engulfing Syria and Iraq.

"The Yinon Plan"—and its American cousin "A Clean Break"—has apparently been implemented by the Likud Party over the years (although it denies it) and supported by its allies in America (knowingly or coincidentally). In any event, these strategies are slowly coming to be the stark and hard reality. Unfortunately for the people who live today and tomorrow in that "promised land" on the map above, to attain what God-has ordained, a torrential downpour of flames must ensue. The firestorms continue to this day with more to come.

So does this mean that we agree with this idea, given that we also have written at length herein about the folly and sinister motivations in creating the old borders of Iraq and Syria? Obviously not. We are in the conflict resolution business, not the war-making and global-conquest business, no matter what euphemisms the war-hawks try to capture in order to sate their territorial and power yearnings.

We do not want to see Iraq and Syria split into splinter mini-nations so as to make them weaker vs. Israeli hallucinations of grandeur and Western *uber-menschen* schemes to exploit their natural resources forevermore. We want to see realistic, independent polities as set forth above which may well entail some deconstruction and reconstruction of their borders, but which can be sustainable and prosper on their own. That is because they will have compatible cultural and economic interests, be mutually respectful of religious differences, and be free to work with other nations in their region for the betterment of all. This solution is in the core interests of all who live in that area.

The other way, the Yinon Plan + "The Clean Break", are constructs for never ending wars. Israel is not going to be The Super Power of The Levant without severe unintended consequences for the whole world, and most assuredly for Israel and the U.S.A. What we have tried to offer is a peace plan for that area of the world which is absolutely necessary for all humanity to find a common-sense and practical way to confront the ecological disasters that threaten humanity on this planet in the all too near future. Modern warfare is probably the greatest environmental polluter of all time.

Isn't is crystal clear that our proposal is infinitely superior as a preferred future—one that keeps America and Israel as major actors in the Middle East, but as peaceful and helpful neighbors? But read on. There is yet another new, grand strategic plan recently revealed that—as being directly opposed to The Yinon Plan—would greatly aggravate matters in the Middle East should it be put into motion, as well it might, and soon . . . .and lead humanity ever more quickly to ruination.

The Supreme Leader's Plan to Destroy Israel and America

Not soon after Iran negotiated a deal with the UN Security Council + Germany (disguised for some strange reason as the P5+1), which was ratified by the for-real United Nations Security Council in the Summer of 2015, out of the blue comes a 400+ page book penned by none other than Ali Khamenei himself. He is, no questions asked, the Supreme Leader (Numero Uno) in Iran, the top religious and political leader who has the final word on all foreign, and many domestic, matters. The book, ominously, is titled: *Palestine* (Khamenei 2015).

Only a fool would believe that the Grand Ayatollah of Iran is unaware of the Yinon Plan + "The Clean Break" strategy and how they appear to be in the heart and mind of the current Israeli Prime Minister, Benjamin Netanyahu. One only need to look at that map of "The Promised Land." See? One contour of that "Promised Land" nestles right up to the Persian Gulf and comes to rest at the tip of Iran. Does the reader think that the Grand Ayatollah and all his generals, admirals, Revolutionary Guards, the Council of Experts, and the Guardian Council have not seen that map . . . and that it did not burn an indelible hole in all their souls and kick their brains into high gear?

The Grand Ayatollah and his minions are no doubt keenly aware of deep ache in the minds of some Israeli supra-nationalists to destroy Iran's nuclear ambitions, and forever diminish the Persian homeland to little league status in the Middle East. They need only know what is well known in Israel and in other higher circles, to wit: that Netanyahu has been overruled by his own cabinet, the Israeli military and the great Mossad director, Meir Dagan, several times from ordering a "pre-emptive attack" on Iran in the past 2-3 years . . . with or without American consent or direct collaboration.

Indeed, Dagan himself was described in an interview with the *Associated Press* as a "fierce critic of Netanyahu's approach to Iran . . . a key opponent of a potential Israeli attack," a tactic which at another time he proclaimed as being "idiotic." Dagan was also quoted in the *New York Times* as saying that 'the person who has caused the greatest strategic danger to Israel is the prime minister." (Associated Press 2015) And for good measure, he added that such a plan " . . . is the stupidest thing I've ever heard." (Weitz 2015) Nonetheless, since Netanyahu was re-elected in mid-2015, the race to disaster in the region has legs well into 2016 if not beyond that.

So, is Iran being "clinically paranoid" about being attacked by Israel? No, they are perfectly normal human beings to want to protect themselves against any foreign country which regularly threatens to bomb them mercilessly from the air (with or without the U.S. in the lead); which has waged an effective cyber-war against their nuclear centrifuges and scientists for years (Stuxnet and friends); and which almost everyone believes possesses a nuclear capability to inflict woeful carnage on their beloved land.

To add to their "paranoia", the hard line of American Neo-Conservatives—which is chomping at the bit to co-launch such an assault—keeps getting more and more informal support from various major U.S. media outposts, including the *New York Times* and *Washington Post*—two very influential newspapers in American internal and external affairs. Thus, within a two month period of time in mid-2015, two articles by prominent Neo-Con stalwarts—one by John Bolton, a former UN Ambassador under George W. Bush and the other, Joshua Muravchik, a fellow at the *Foreign Policy Institute* at Johns Hopkins University— brazenly called for immediate bombing and war with Iran. (Bolton 2015; Muravchik 2015).

It should be noted that these two are among the very same insider D.C. clique which claimed absolutely no doubt that the first days of the Iraq war would create global "shock and awe" at America's invincible military might. One or another of their colleagues also publicly announced that the 2003 war against Iraq would be a "cakewalk"; that Saddam had weapons of mass destruction (WMDs); that Iraqi oil would completely pay for the war; that Iraq would become a model Middle Eastern democracy and America's close ally; and the next logical steps were to instigate regime change in Syria and Iran.

To emphasize the last point, David Remnick, a senior editor of *The New Yorker* magazine, wrote this shortly after the "successful" invasion of Iraq: "One senior British official dryly told *Newsweek* before the invasion, "Everyone wants to go to Baghdad. Real men want to go to Tehran . . . Richard Perle, one of the most influential advisers to the Pentagon in the George W. Bush administration (and the lead author of "The Clean Break"), told an audience not long ago that, with a successful invasion of Iraq, 'we could deliver a short message, a two-word message (to Iran): You're next.' " (Remnick 2003, emphasis ours)

At this writing, U.S. planes are bombing Syria every day . . . and have been joined by the Russian, British, French, and Jordanian Air Forces (a volatile mix). Whatever reason the Americans give for it and its allies' aerial assault, Iran is not amused and, actually if they are the least bit logical, need to take this never ending barrage of threats and acts of war—aimed at their core interests— very seriously.

Thus, Ayatollah Khamenei's thick, new book is not just a knee-jerk reaction to The Yinon Plan, or platoons of "intellectuals" and "Pentagon-friendly analysts" for American Imperialism, or other grand visions about supremacy in the Middle East coming from their mostly deadly enemies, the Saudis. The Grand Ayatollah is not considered to be among the elite theologians in the scholarly world of the Shia. This *magnum opus* of his is more of a long-term strategy based on many speeches he has given at his weekly Friday evening sermons and religiously grounded columns and blogs posted on his website (www.khamenei.ir)

That said, what he writes—which is being translated in the West as rabid Anti-Semitism (and sensible people could easily read it that way if they are so inclined)—must be causing some level of consternation in Tel Aviv, London, and Washington, D.C. Why? Because it is an explicit design to erase the nation-state of Israel from the political map. Here are some of its elements.

Authors Note: The translator of the book from which we are quoting, Mr. David Reaboi, is a young research associate previously affiliated with a very pro-Israeli NGO and presently associated with a very conservative political policy think tank in Texas. Despite his bias, we chose to use his version because it is a far more detailed translation than what ALL Western news outlets and politicians reported and analyzed as the content of the book upon its publication. See Reaboi (2015) in References for a direct link to this article online.

First and foremost, according to Khamenei: Any land that has been the province of Islam, i.e., once occupied by Islam, and thereafter was occupied by infidels (Christians, Jews or whomever) must be "emancipated" and restored to Islamic dominance. This is known in conflict resolution terms as "a bottom line position."

Second, this means that Iran is 100% opposed to any two-state solution and that any Palestinian Arabs who agree with the proposed two-state solution in Palestine are apostates, and are subject to the murder of themselves and their families by Allah-commanded Jihadists.

Third, the United States, due to its collaboration and support of the Jewish State in former Islamic land, is complicit and all Americans are therefore subject to similar retaliatory treatment. In the Introduction to the book (according to a website called "*Iran Truth*" which claims to have posted "The First Translation" of Palestine), one of the Supreme Leader's closest and most influential advisors, Dr. Ali Akbar Velayati states clearly that: "*Cutting the hand of the United States from Islamic countries, establishing Islamic government and restoring Islamic values, and emancipating the whole of Palestine are our objectives.*" (Reaboi 2015). By the way, Dr. Velayati is a physician who held a fellowship in pediatrics at Johns Hopkins University Medical School, one of the top in the U.S.A.)

Fourth, The Supreme Leader is cognizant of the strategic importance of Palestine/Israel in The Grand Game: "*Another reason is that the establishment of this Jewish government, in other words, Zionist government, in this region was to fulfill the first stage of a bigger plan. Palestine links three continents of Asia, Africa, and Europe.*" He also observes that America "inherited" the old British plan. (p. 51)

Fifth, "*Our position against Israel is, as always: Israel is a malignant cancer gland (sic) that needs to be uprooted. In contrast to what shallow people believe, it is not impossible to defeat Israel and the United States. Superpowers have come and gone throughout history.*" (p. 68 emphasis ours). Yes, please note that all of the above diatribe . . . .setting forth this Master Plan . . . is in the translator's own English word: a "position"—and despite its deep religious and historical significance to Islamic people, not a core "interest."

The Supreme Leader continues by proposing a protocol for Iran to follow to exorcise this cancer. Is it chemo, radiation, surgery or all three? For the actual answer we do not have to turn to the Western media who employ quicker and more adroit translators than can we. But, believe it or not, Khamenei has a *Nine-Step Plan* on how to perform this feat and the reader does not have to read a biased Western account or be fluent in Farsi or fractured English to read all about it. Indeed, it is in chart form—in passable English—on his very own website albeit a bit repetitive with the book translation above.

However, to spare the reader the difficulty of accessing it, we present it below for the reader's perusal. We advise the reader to go into it thoroughly and think it through. A lot of people discounted what Hitler said clearly in *Mein Kampf,* much to their regret.

Here it is: (See page below)

No.	Questions	Ayatollah Khamenei's response
	9 key questions about elimination of Israel	
1	Why should the Zionist regime be eliminated?	During its 66 years of life so far, the fake Zionist regime has tried to realize its goals by means of infanticide, homicide, violence & iron fist while boasts about it blatantly.
2	What does elimination of Israel mean in the viewpoint of Imam Khomeini?	The only means of bringing Israeli crimes to an end is the elimination of this regime. And of course the elimination of Israel does not mean the massacre of the Jewish people in this region. The Islamic Republic has proposed a practical & logical mechanism for this to international communities.
3	What is the proper way of eliminating Israel?	All the original people of Palestine including Muslims, Christians and Jews wherever they are, whether inside Palestine, in refugee camps in other countries or just anywhere else, take part in a public and organized referendum. Naturally the Jewish immigrants who have been persuaded into emigration to Palestine do not have the right to take part in this referendum.
4	What happened to the non-Palestinian emigrants?	The ensuing government, which comes into power after a referendum among the original Palestinians, once settled will decide whether the non-Palestinian emigrants who have immigrated to this country over the past years can continue living in Palestine or should return to their home countries.
5	How will the proposed referendum succeed?	This is a fair and logical plan that can be properly understood by global public opinion and can enjoy the supports of the independent nations and governments. Certainly we do not expect the usurper Zionists to easily surrender to this proposal and this is where the role of governments, nations and organization of resistance is shaped and defined.
6	Until a referendum is held, how should Israel be confronted?	Up until the day when this homicidal and infanticidal regime is eliminated through a referendum, powerful confrontation and resolute and armed resistance is the cure of this ruinous regime. The only means of confronting a regime which commits crimes beyond one's thought and imagination is a resolute and armed confrontation.
7	What is the most urgent action to take for militarily confront Israel?	The West Bank should be armed like Gaza and those who are interested in Palestine's destiny should take action to arm the people of the West Bank so that the sorrows and grieves of the Palestinian people will reduce in the light of their powerful hands and the weakness of the Zionist enemy.
8	What solutions are not acceptable?	We recommend neither a classical war by the army of Muslim countries nor to throw migrated Jews at sea and certainly not an arbitration by UN or other international organizations.
9	Why do we oppose compromise proposals?	That the rockets of Gaza have led to the crimes of Israel is a wrong conclusion. In the west Bank, people's only weapon is stones and there are not many types of weaponry. But this regime massacres and humiliates people there and destroys their houses and farms. The fact that Yasser Arafat was poisoned and killed by Israel while he had the most cooperation with the Zionists proves that in the viewpoint of Israel, "peace" is simply a trick for more crimes and occupation.

KHAMENEI.IR

As the reader can plainly see: There are no warnings, threats or intimation of nuclear annihilation or mass extermination of all Jewish people. In fact, his first weapon of choice is a referendum, albeit one limited to all who lived in Palestine up to the end of World War II, a completely unacceptable precondition to any authentic negotiation on the wording of a referendum concerning the future of "Palestine". But the really scary part comes later, which is his stated intention to give military muscle to Fatah—or Palestin-ian Jihadists—on the West Bank.

This latter plan, let's call it Plan B, is to be implemented only after Israel and the U.S. refuse his offer of the limited referendum (a sure thing) because that would obviously transform Israel into Palestine under Islamic rule (The Bad State Solution). Unfortunately, it has that tinder-like element: arming an insurgency on the West Bank as Iran has already done—and keeps on doing—with Hamas and Hezbollah.

Such an overt (or even covert) move would be all Prime Minister Ne-tanyahu would need as a "rationale" to order a major (tactical nuclear?) air strike against Iran and, perhaps light up World War III. But, then, he might not last much longer as Prime Minister either. In a parliamentary system, his tenure is uncertain and who might follow, and with what popular Israeli mandate, no one knows, surely not Khamenei.

According to several other "interpretations" of this book—which are consistent in their views and are definitely consistent with the above rendi-tion of the Grand Ayatollah's website—his strategic plan is to wage a "low intensity" war over an extensive period of time, which would be calculated to tire the Israelis out and induce many of them with dual citizenship to move to the safer American mainland. Likewise, this grinding struggle would ultimately become too pricey for the U.S.A. and lead to "Israel fatigue" thereby compelling America to diminish—if not terminate—its financial and other support of Israel.

This analysis is consistent with two reviews of the book which ema-nate from a pro-Israeli site (Noble 2015) and the rabidly anti-Iran news-paper, the *New York Post* (Taheri 2015). They agree with us that Khamenei has presented a plausible strategy and set of Iranian tactics in opposition to the Israel and U.S. partnership in the Middle East. How many years of protracted "low intensity" warfare along these lines is America and Israel prepared for: 5? 10? 20? 50? Iran has been around for a long, long time. Like China, they know how to take the long view and are not worried about annual profit reports.

Fortunately, though, the Supreme Leader is not Adolf Hitler. He can-not do any of this on his own, given the fragmented power structure that is The Islamic Republic of Iran. It is not a strict theocracy. It is not a one-man dictatorship. The vast majority of Iranians do not want to be wiped off the face of the Earth . . . and probably do not want to engage in a costly, endless "low intensity warfare" with Israel and the U.S. either.

Many leading top Shia clergy and "reformist" political leaders in Iran are undoubtedly strongly opposed to The Supreme Leader's plan of pro-longed low-intensity warfare . . . but for understandable reasons do not write about it or take to the streets in protest these days. The 2015 nuclear deal with the Security Council has the wherewithal to harvest great wealth for Iran in the next decade. The Supreme Leader can say what he wants in his book and website, but he is not going to commit national suicide—or to resource-draining wars just when things are looking up.

After all, Iran is on the verge of being admitted into the *Shanghai Cooperative Organization* as a full member (probably soon after the U.N. lifts economic sanctions on Iran) and thus will become a major part of the fast developing Eurasia, probably the key member in Iran's part of "The World Island". This development, which at this point seems quite likely, will itself stall or roll back any Greater Israel-U.S. plan and, in fact, will keep them "contained" in pretty much the old Palestine Mandate area. If this is the long-term prospect, it cannot pose much of an economic, cultural or military impediment to the New Eurasia, in which Iran will play a leading role.

We see Iran's Islamic Republic's "core interests" as being (1) survival as a Shia nation; (2) maintaining the Islamic Republic with the Supreme Leader and Revolutionary Guards in control; (3) increasing Shia security and collaboration in the Middle East mainly to protect themselves against the Sunni radical Islamic fanatics (Al Qaeda, Islamic State, Saudi Wahhabis) who want to torture and decapitate all Shia as apostates; and (4) maintaining a close and harmonious relationship with the Shia majority in whatever remains of Iraq. None of this threatens Israel or American core interests in Israel and all of the Ayatollah's and Revolutionary Guard's illusions of restoring Persian glory are negotiable positions.

Actually, this seems to be President Obama's view as well. Here is the way President Obama responded to Khamenei's Islamic views of Jews, Christians, Buddhists, Hindus, etc., i.e., they are inferior peoples who need to be under Islamic rule by force if necessary . . . particularly if the land in question had once been under Islamic control. The question was put to him in an interview in May of 2015 during the ultimately successful negotiations with Iran and Khamenei himself. It also demonstrates that the president is pretty familiar and sympathetic with at least some of the basic tenets of conflict resolution. Here is a short excerpt from that interview to illustrate this point:

> *"Well the fact that you are anti-Semitic, or racist, doesn't preclude you from being interested in survival. It doesn't preclude you from being rational about the need to keep your economy afloat; it doesn't preclude you from making strategic decisions about how you stay in power; and so the fact that the supreme leader is anti-Semitic doesn't mean that this overrides all of his*

other considerations. You know, if you look at the history of anti-Semitism, Jeff, there were a whole lot of European leaders—and there were deep strains of anti-Semitism in this country—"

"I interjected by suggesting that anti-Semitic European leaders made irrational decisions, to which Obama responded, 'They may make irrational decisions with respect to discrimination, with respect to trying to use anti-Semitic rhetoric as an organizing tool. At the margins, where the costs are low, they may pursue policies based on hatred as opposed to self-interest. But the costs here are not low, and what we've been very clear [about] to the Iranian regime over the past six years is that we will continue to ratchet up the costs, not simply for their anti-Semitism, but also for whatever expansionist ambitions they may have.'

"That's what the sanctions represent. That's what the military option I've made clear I preserve represents. And so I think it is not at all contradictory to say that there are deep strains of anti-Semitism in the core regime, but that they also are interested in maintaining power, having some semblance of legitimacy inside their own country, which requires that they get themselves out of what is a deep economic rut that we've put them in, and on that basis they are then willing and prepared potentially to strike an agreement on their nuclear program." (Goldberg 2015)

Along these lines, from the Iranian point of view, there are those there who realize that there are equally stubborn and extreme people in the United States (mostly in The Republican Party and/or *AIPAC*), who think of Iran as a "terrorist" state which harbors lunatic intentions to become the Hegemon of the Middle East. Such people there are also aware that different American administrations can have different ideas and can change American long-established foreign policy even towards Iran. If there are many prominent people in Iran who comprehend this, and we think there are, then Iran might be quite willing to negotiate with the United States about Israel as the 51ˢᵗ state.

After all, the U.S., Israel, Iraq and the Kurds could all be seen as their "allies' against the Islamic State, Al Qaeda and other Sunni fanatics, particularly including Saudi Wahhabism. It would just take a different perspective and stance on the part of the America foreign policy establishment about Iran and the Wahabi movement, something that the Iranian leadership does not expect to happen any time soon, but perhaps some time in the future. So, for now, the Grand Ayatollah in Iran will stick to his position.

Thus, in July of 2015, shortly after his Foreign Minister successfully negotiated the nuclear deal with the Security Council of the UN, and particularly with the U.S.A., the Supreme Leader made it manifest to one and all that he did not have any intention of re-establishing any friendly or commercial relations with America because of, according to CNN, the U.S.A.'s "arrogance." (Spark and Youssuf 2015). Then, a month or so later, when the British were allowed to re-establish its Embassy in Tehran, that very same Foreign Minister who negotiated the deal that broke the ice between UK and Iran (and the rest of Western Europe) was quite clear about what Iran wanted from the U.S.A.

He said that there was no thought of re-opening any new American Embassy in Tehran until the United States began to make some substantial changes in its "attitudes and behavior" which he also noted were "illogical." (*Times of Israel Staff and AFP* 2015 emphasis ours). After all, it is Saudi Wahabbism that is the basis of the ideologies of both Al Qaeda and Islamic State which are mortal enemies of all Western values, i.e., core interests.

Thus, as two people well versed in mediating hate-filled conflicts, this is almost a normal set of 180 degree divergence of opinions about "the other side's" beliefs, actions, reasonableness and/or mental health that mediators deal with on a regular basis. The Supreme Leader's book is a very intense and minutely detailed position about Iran's future foreign policy towards Israel and Palestine. That's all.

He may be the Supreme Leader of Iran right now, but several things we know for sure are that: (a) he is not immortal; (b) he will have a successor (whom he appoints) but who might not think and feel precisely the same about Iran's strategic goals—for better or worse; (c) there are other Iranian strongholds of political power which are not at all in agreement with him; (d) times change; and most importantly, (e) the fundamental "core interests" of Iran will not be threatened by Israel becoming the 51st state but will forever remain threatened by Sunni fanatics of all stripes in Iran's immediate neighborhood who are there to stay. A friendly U.S. in Israel could be perceived to be a powerful friend in the long run.

Thus, there is plenty of room for the American government to negotiate with Iran in the future before, during and/or after Israel becomes a new state in the United States of America. There is a much more difficult dilemma to handle in that neck of the woods, though. We are referring to none other than the newest nasty on the block: The Islamic State, which has been heavily backed by Iran's other arch-enemy, Saudi Arabia (as well as Qatar). In fact, our guess is that Iran would much rather have the U.S.A. in its vicinity as a friend than the Islamic State and Saudi Arabia, which are its eternal and infernal, religiously avowed enemy of enemies.

The Islamic State (ISIS) and Their Apocalypse

By now, everyone on the planet must know about the Islamic State (IS) and its rapid rise to "power" in Iraq and Syria, as well as its well-publicized pride in its barbarity and cruelty to all who do not strictly obey its—to the Western mind—diabolical, didactic dictates of Sharia Law. What most people do not know about the Islamic State (IS)—or as it is sometimes called The Islamic State of Iraq and Syria (ISIS)—is that it also has a grand theory for that region and a large part of the world as well, i.e., the establishment of a Grand Caliphate. Below is a map of its global "vision".

A quick glance at this map of the, shall we say ambitious, Islamic State Caliphate should make the reader scratch his or her head with amazement. How can a small group of "fighters" in Iraq and Syria who seem to be well equipped with the world's most fearsome weaponry—Toyota pickup trucks toting large machine guns—conquer Spain, Morocco, Algeria, the Balkans, Turkey, Egypt, Arabia, Iran, Pakistan, India and the Caucuses—AND then dominate it ruthlessly under draconian Sharia Law? Answer: This is as likely to happen as Peru declaring war on Switzerland.

The above map was taken from a June 2014 issue of *The Daily Mail* in the UK, but it is all over the Internet in many languages and colors. There is no doubt but that it is an "official" graphic concoction of IS or ISIL who do not shy away from *braggadocio*. As the news article reporting the IS statement accompanying this map states: "The group insist the carving up of the Ottoman Empire by Allied forces after the conflict - commonly known as the Sykes-Picot Agreement - was a deliberate attempt to divide Muslims and restrict the likelihood of another caliphate being established. Muslim extremists have long yearned to recreate the Islamic state, or caliphate, that ruled over the Middle East, North Africa and beyond in various forms over the course of Islam's 1,400-year history." (Hall 2014).

So, should IS be taken seriously at all—aside from their contemporary control of some strips and clusters of Eastern and Northern Syria and Western Iraq and their appeal to violent Jihadists from all parts of the globe? Are they a realistic material threat to the United States of America's presence in that part of the world with the addition of the new state of Israel? Of course, nothing can be predicted about this with certitude, but we think that they will be able to pull off "terrorist" bombings and shootings occasionally, but not pose an "existential threat" to the more positive American presence in the Middle East.

Of course, there little doubt but that the fundamentalist ideology of Islamic State is spreading beyond The Levant. One can find seedlings of it sprouting all over that map of their aspirations: The Sinai, Somalia, Mali, Libya, Jordan, Afghanistan, China, the Balkans. As a strong theological force that re-enacts the roots of Islam back to the time, words and actions of Muhammad, they are not easily extinguished . . . and have lands well fertilized with human blood to flourish.

So, what we say below is not to discount their ideals, their objectives, their tactics—after all, if God really wants the world to experience an Apocalypse, who are we to scoff? And if God is truly on one side and not another, what mere human being can really know which? Plus, as the reader will see, there are others with the same end game in mind and even, in another way, advocating similar tactics to The Ultimate Show-Down between God and the Devil, Christ and the Anti-Christ.

What we are saying is that barring some cosmic or other-worldly Fate of the Destruction of the Earth that must precede The Second Coming of Christ, the probable development of supra-regional secular entities like China's Silk and Belt Roads, Russia's Eurasian Economic Union, UNASUR and the Latin American community, the Shia Arc, and the like are far more likely "enemies" of The Islamic State than the U.S.A confined to its small region (in its new state, Israel).

But, given what we've said above, and will say below: Israel knows how to defend itself quite well in that area; there must be a "*cordon sanitaire*" of friendly collaborative nations around Israel; and the more IS pops up to confront other major regional entities, the more friends the new United States will have around the world . . . and particularly in The Middle East.

In other words, the New Multi-Polar World will be far more amenable to the new United States as a Global Nation and less than hospitable to the overzealous ambitions and map of The Islamic State's Caliphate. But the overarching reason we do not see IS as an existential or permanent threat to Israel as the 51st state has nothing to do with whether or not such a move will lead to "End Times" of the Islamic or Revelations varieties . . . and does not need global alliances. The Islamic State, as a modern manifestation of the time and practices of Muhammad Himself, may manage to create a number of quasi-imitations of itself here and there, but the world of the original Islamic Caliphate will not be recreated in the 21st century world-as-we-know-it, and here's a specific reason as to why.

In order for "The Caliphate" of the Islamic State to exist as a legitimate caliphate—and maintain the fidelity of its followers—it must conquer territory upon which can impose its dogmatic, orthodox, mega-draconian Islamic rule. As only a cursory glance at the map above reveals, the goal of Islamic State is hallucinatory. This is explained well by Graeme Wood, a lecturer at Yale University and editor of *The Atlantic*:

> "*One way to un-cast the Islamic State's spell over its adherents would be to overpower it militarily and occupy the parts of Syria and Iraq now under caliphate rule. Al Qaeda is ineradicable because it can survive, cockroach-like, by going underground. The Islamic State cannot. If it loses its grip on its territory in Syria and Iraq, it will cease to be a caliphate. Caliphates cannot exist as underground movements, because territorial authority is a requirement: take away its command of territory, and all those oaths of allegiance are no longer binding.*" (Wood 2015, emphasis ours)

These lads, as fierce and barbaric as they may be, do not appear capable of defeating the Shia of Iraq and Lebanon or the Kurds of Kurdistan—particularly their well-armed and equally devoted-to-Muhammad militias. They really do not seem to be a much of a match against the Iranian Revolutionary Guards, Hezbollah, the Peshmerga, the Badr Brigades, and on. So how can they re-establish a 7th century theocracy by force of arms throughout this modern world of Weapons of Mass Destruction, so widely dispersed and available to wipe them off the face of the earth within seconds at the flip of a switch from afar—from space or way below the sea?

They will not win their wars by scary blustering, occasional terrorist attacks near-by or far-away, nauseating beheadings on YouTube, or blowing a civilian Russian airliner out of the sky (for which they will pay dearly). We also have zero doubt, nor should any reader, that any of their tactics could bring about their most avidly held desire that their last fighters, cornered in Jerusalem, will be saved by—the reader will never guess this one—Jesus! Yes, it the very same Jesus Christ who, in IS theology, will slay the anti-Christ and bring about their final ecstatic victory. Yes, the Jewish Jesus is a revered prophet in Islam too . . . even The Islamic State. Who knew?

So, although these worshippers of the caliphate and activists for The Apocalypse, who would never negotiate anything with the Americans or Israelis or Shias or any apostates, need real estate, and a lot of it, to legitimize their whole theology and maintain their "army". As Graeme Wood observes correctly in his article, "Properly contained, the Islamic State is likely to be its undoing." (Wood 2015) And if the Shia and the Kurds can't finish them off with the help of the U.S. and several other modern air forces, they can get the Taliban (Sunni apostates) and the Egyptian army (more Sunni apostates) to lend a hand grenade or two.

This is not meant to deprecate their resolve, resilience or reserves. For as Dr. Anne Speckhard, who teaches psychiatry at Georgetown University School of Medicine—and is the author of a book that did in-depth interviews with hundreds of terrorists—states with conviction: "one must also be aware of the power of apocalyptic dreams in spurring on the violence of men who are completely convinced they are bringing in the final apocalyptic vision of the "end times". (Speckhard 2012, 2014)

Islamic State may be the bearer of End Times, except it will be their own . . . .as a caliphate. There is little doubt that defeated in achieving their greatest objective in the immediate and/or intermediate future, they may well transition back into their previous translucent and decentralized form as Al Qaeda and wage guerilla warfare and commit many acts of martyrdom for an even longer time to come. But that will be a global problem for the long haul regardless of whether Israel is or is not an American state.

The Christian Zionists' Rapture

It is unlikely, though, that Dr. Speckhard ever did any interviews with another major group who get giddy over the specter of The Four Horsemen riding roughshod over the burning corpses of millions of human beings as the appetizer for the main course: The Second Coming of Christ and Heavenly Redemption.

We've mentioned The Christian Zionists—*Christians United for Israel, or CUFI*—before and pointed out that they have gained greatly in American popularity in recent years (Norton 2015). Indeed they claim to have a membership in the millions, and filled a huge convention center in Washington, D.C. in 2015 to listen to stem-winding speeches from Prime Minister

Netanyahu (live via Satellite from Israel) and several prominent American Republican politicos, including several running in the presidential primaries in 2016. Israeli and U.S. flags waved from every seat.

These particular American Christians, who love Israel so much, are staunch allies of the nation state of Israel and heap praise and lucre upon it as the land promised by God to the Chosen People. Yet, they are also great believers in the biblical books of Revelations and Ezekiel, each of which are pretty much End Times predictions of complete and total annihilation of all creatures in human bodies—except those who are saved in the ruins of Jerusalem by the Second Coming of Christ.

So, yes, both they and ISIS (arch foes) have a common dream of apocalyptic obliteration followed by the coming of the holiest of the holies: first (from the IS point of view), The Mahdi returns and completes his mission, then comes Jesus . . . to cleanse the sins of all the wretched of the Earth. The Christian Zionists) don't have anything to do with the Mahdi. It's only Jesus and The Rapture.

Are we saying, then, that the Christian Zionists, such good pals with their Jewish "friends" in Israel, might be setting them up because they sincerely believe that most of them are surely doomed to meet horrific ends except for a virtuous few who will see "the light" and convert to Christ and rise to Heaven? If that isn't exactly correct, it is pretty close. One is tempted to say that these "Christians" are willing to help bring about this apocalyptical genocide by supporting the present-day Jewish nation in all its military escapades thereby incurring the implacable overflow of wrath from all of Islam. This will most likely precipitate The Final Reckoning and Judgment Day. And that person's temptation would be pretty close to the truth.

There is some reasonably credible evidence coming from France, that President George W. Bush, in trying to convince the French to join in the invasion of Iraq, told the then-president of France that all Christians (and President Jacques Chirac of France, being a Catholic, fit that bill) needed to do whatever they could to prod the world along to End Times as quickly as possible. The invasion of Iraq would be the righteous catalyst. The primary source of this is Thomas Romer, a Professor of the Old Testament at Lausanne University, who was asked by higher ups in the French government after that meeting about who "Gog and Magog" were, the forces Bush kept referring to in his *tête-à-tête* with the French President.

Chirac is quoted as conveying the same message about President Bush to a highly regarded French journalist who interviewed him for a book (in French) titled, in a loose English translation as: *If You Repeat It, I Will Deny It* (Maurice 2009). All of this is covered extensively throughout the Internet, but an article in *The Guardian* reports that Chirac could hardly believe he was hearing such ancient biblical predictions from the president of the United States who truly believed this to be Reason Number One enough to invade an Islamic country. "Chirac wondered how someone (with such power) could be so superficial and fanatical in his beliefs" (Brown 2009).

The point of all this is to emphasize that there is a strong contingent of American Christians—some in very high positions of power—who are spurring Israel on in its wars with Islam because they see it as their calling to bring their version of The Apocalypse to fruition. Thus, they can help facilitate Christ's encore and they or their offspring can transcend to Heaven with Him. Does this make them anti-Semitic, which many see as being true? No, they just want to play their divine role as set forth in the book of Revelation.

They revere the Jews as the Chosen People but know full well that the vast majority of Jewish people (with the exception of a sect who call themselves "Jews for Jesus") reject Jesus as the Messiah. The Christian Zionists see this as a fatal error, one which most Jewish people will pay dearly for during apocalyptic times. However, those Jewish folk who finally accept Jesus as the Messiah will join them in their joyous rapture into the better world as brothers and sisters in God's love. Finally, Jerusalem will be the new capital of Jesus' Kingdom on Earth. There will be billions of tons of suffering for a long time, but it will all be worth it in the longest run.

However, a big question remains. Would these Americans, who are so sure of this final scenario for all humanity, want Israel as an American state—if it will bring such misery upon America and everywhere else? Can the future capital of The Kingdom of God be an American state? We think the answer is inherent in the questions. Why not, given that America was fervently believed to be the New Zion in the first place. Both the American evangelists, Christian Zionists, and Mormons, it seems to us, would have zero problem with Israel as the 51st state . . . .even if it takes an era of tarnation and damnation to get to where the world needs to go. We're talking about "faith" here, not scientific logic or empirical evidence.

Besides, with Israel as an American state, current Israeli laws prohibiting proselyting in Israel will become null and void and open all Israelis to the word of these Christian Americans loud and clear, beckoning errant Chosen People to Christ. Israel's statehood would be as a golden gate thrown wide open for evangelicals, Christian Zionists and Mormons alike. It would be hard to resist and would, instead, be a gift from On High to them—to spread the word before The Second Coming so as to convert as many as possible before they die agonizing deaths in the fire-from-the-sky sure to come.

As for the Israeli Jews, they've heard it for a long, long time before there ever was an America. They didn't believe it then, and by and large and for the most-part, they won't believe it now or ever. But by becoming an

American state, they will just have to let those "meshuga" (crazy) Christians rave on. If these Bible-thumping Americans pine to see the return of a 2,000 year old delusional Jewish boy, who cares?

The "Exceptional" United States in the New Eurasia and the Multi-Polar World: The Fulfillment of Its "Manifest Destiny" Materially and Spiritually

So, what would be the place of this New United States of America, now a fixture in the Middle East in the form of the American state of Israel? Where does it fit in, particularly with the growing specters of a bulked up New Eurasian Union (with one participant, Iran, being a pushy neighbor); the ongoing and infinite internecine wars among the Shias and Sunnis throughout the Middle East; and the onrushing, unpredictable and increasingly chaotic catastrophes of Climate Change? Aside from just being there, what would this new configuration of the U.S.A. offer that part of the world?

Let us count the ways.

The Lesser of Many Evils and a Force for Good

The United States of America, in so many ways, has been a "force for good" in this world, despite its many hypocrisies, deceits, conceits, shortcomings, conquests, subversions, regime changes, occupations, espionage, mass deportations, slavery, genocide, torture, and its normal gross inequality of wealth. Hold on, one should say, that's an incredibly heavy debit side of the ledger, deeply in the red. What could possibly balance it back towards at least an equilibrium, much less make America come out on the profit side, as a "force for good"?

We think World War II and the Cold War victory over Soviet Communism are hefty and positive counter-weights on the "good" side of America's existence in this world over time. Would the world be better off today had Nazi Germany and Imperial Japan won the Second World War? If it wasn't for the heroic stand of the Russians at Stalingrad; the gritty determination of the Chinese people for a decade or so; some celestial good fortune for the U.S. at Midway and Normandy, it could easily have gone that way.

Who knows how long the horror of a world dominated by the Axis Powers (Germany, Italy, Japan) would have lasted and might even be dominant today had the United States not sacrificed the lives of over 500,000 Americans to help defeat them. After all, the Roman Empire lasted for centuries and they didn't have nearly the weapons of mass extermination and subjugation as did the Germans and the Japanese.

And what about the Soviet Union? Consider the nature of human life on this planet at this moment should Josef Stalin's perversion of Karl Marx's notion of "Communism" prevailed as the predominant philosophy and practice of political economy throughout the world. Imagine the entire world with governments like that of North Korea (which proudly practices the Soviet model) starving and oppressing their citizenry for the benefits of their small Communist Party elites.

Without the United States—and its NATO allies—that might have been how the "workers of the world" got united, in submission to "Great Leaders" of every nation kowtowing to the loathsome Soviet Communist Party which was bent on crushing individual freedom and religious belief worldwide. That cost the United States a great deal in blood money over 40 years. In that sense, America was the only nation who could play the role of "the leader of the Free World." Instead: Can the reader imagine the Ruler of the World being Kim Jong-un? God Bless America!

Going further back, keep in mind that the indigenous people living in the New World before the British settled in Virginia and Massachusetts had encountered the Spanish Empire, as bloodcurdling and rapacious a crew as ever conquered any people. Though sanctioned and accompanied by The Catholic Church of the Inquisition, the Spanish Conquistadores of the early 16th century were mesmerized by conquest, lust, enslavement, mass murder and gleaming gold.

Here is one small nugget from the *U.S. Public Broadcasting Company* documentary film on the Spanish conquest, about the Spanish Way of imperialism in The New World: "On Easter Day 1519 near today's city of Veracruz, Cortés was greeted by envoys from the Emperor Montezuma who offered him gifts of gold: *Cortés could not, of course, let such a momentous meeting end without asking if they had more gold. 'It is good for a bad heart,' said the supreme ironist. 'You see, my men suffer from a disease of the heart, which can only be assuaged by gold.'* "(Riding 2001).

Keep in mind, this was more than 100 years prior to the Puritans arrival in Massachusetts. In that interim, the Spanish had pretty well annihilated the native populations of the islands of the Caribbean as well as the highly advanced Incan and Aztec civilizations.

How does that compare to John Winthrop's speech on The Arabella? How does this kind of "empire" compare even with the worst way that the English settlers in Massachusetts dealt with the aborigines with whom they mingled—who were not nearly as friendly and yielding as the ones Christopher Columbus betrayed and obliterated in the Caribbean. Did the Spanish warriors beholden to their Church have the same Christian faith and behavior of the Puritans—who wanted to build, stick by stick and stone by stone, that shining "City on the Hill"? No, they were much too busy looking for shiny stones under the hills and hacking to death those who didn't dig for them or hampered their search.

There is no religious justification or redemption for The American Empire of today, running helter-skelter on this globe under the euphemism of "Full Spectrum Dominance" and a militaristic masquerade of "exceptionality." There is also no denying the tremendous cauldrons of misery and destruction being spilled worldwide by these still relatively adolescent American imperial urges. But as we noted above, all empires are evil at heart, some being much worse than others.

Yes, the Puritans took possession of land from the Native Americans whose land they coveted, and engaged in "imperial wars" with them, but for far different reasons and with a much different mind and spirit. And it is this difference that Americans somehow, even today, believe makes the United States, albeit a *nouveaux*-imperial force in the world, an "exceptional" nation . . . or "exceptional" empire. So is it?

We believe that in some ways it is and in others it is not. We also have made it clear enough in earlier chapters that there was a great departure in American history from its earliest days as colonies of the British Empire and its century long period of Manifest Destiny, to the incipience and growth of its present Empire starting with the Spanish American War of 1898. The early American quest for land (and other riches) was tied to a strong motive for religious and political freedom, a spiritual prodding that the new American Empire utterly lacks.

This relatively new America, to most of the world, is super-materialistic and excessively haughty in its ways, not the least bit humble, devout or self-sacrificing in its surge outward from yesteryear. Thus, if a deal was worked out with Israel to come under the American federal structure, it would be either welcomed by the new Multi-Polar World or rejected by it.

We believe that the difference would largely depend on which U.S.A. wanted to settle in the Middle East and what would be its true—not self-delusional—intentions. If it was related or closer to the earlier more religious and deity-inspired America, it would be more likely accepted. If it was to continue to make—and even strengthen—Israel into a regional military power as part of America's quasi-empire and in synch with the Yinon Plan, it would be detested, encapsulated and eventually expelled.

So are there any examples in recent times, post Manifest Destiny, that might be used as examples of a modern America that is devoted to a more peaceable and spiritual path and be willing to share its riches with less fortunate peoples to shore them up and make them stronger, more independent, and more prosperous? Yes there are. We will present two short illustrations of how America, as a far superior military power, could place at least partial humanitarian needs above purely material or imperious ones to benefit less fortunate countries and help them attain some level of independence, economic strength, and national dignity.

Both are far from perfect examples of how such a transformed United States of America, modelling itself as a truly Global Nation, can not only improve its relations with its new neighbors in the Middle East . . . including what we have (for the sake of discussion) dubbed as the "New Palestine" and "South Lebanon" . . . .but become a resourceful colleague as well. This turnabout in America's strategy and reversion to genuine, deeply rooted American values can make that relatively small region of the New Eurasia a template for other nations in that and other regions.

In so doing, the future United States as a Global Nation can become—what else?—a shining example that others might admire and even emulate, the 21st century realization of "The City on the Hill." With at least a section of Jerusalem, the holiest city of three of the world's most ancient and major religious, being the capital of the new state, Israel could be seen in a far more moral (rather than militaristic) light as well. This won't matter to IS or the Grand Ayatollah of Iran, but it would lessen any threats to Israel's core interests.

In other words, to trump the billionaire hotel and casino developer Donald Trump, a leading contender for the Republican nomination for President of the United States in the earliest stages of the presidential contest of 2016, it isn't about "Make America Great Again," it's about making America live up to its original meaning of being an "exceptional" nation. Like living up to Jesus' Sermon on the Mount, that is easier said than done.

It is also about being true to the collaborative and cooperative spirit of some of the first American settlements in the New World who lived among, worked with and even helped some Native Americans who had lived there for many centuries. Roger Williams in Rhode Island and William Penn and the Quakers in Pennsylvania are brilliant and admirable examples of this spiritually positive American story. (University of Virginia Crossroads Project, current)

The New "Good Neighbor Policy": Middle East Edition

Obviously, somewhere down the line would be the necessity for a Middle East reconciliation process which is mediated by a panel that all immediate and concerned stakeholders agree are trustworthy neutrals. People like Pope Francis, The Dalai Lama, and former president Oscar Arias, of Costa Rica, come to mind. The subject of the remediation—with the issues of Israel's pre-1967 border and Jerusalem's openness to all religions previously agreed upon by the U.S. and Israel—would be what the Global United States can do to help develop a viable and sustainable political and economic community of nations in that region.

The United States of America did that, unilaterally, twice in the 20th century. The First time was under President Franklin Delano Roosevelt in the 1930s, and it was called "The Good Neighbor Policy." It worked then, and it can work again, perhaps even better and last much longer.

Actually we believe that this 1934 turn in American foreign policy is eerily similar and pertinent to the situation in the Middle East in 2016 and beyond. Back in the 1930s, the United States was heavily engaged in Central America and the Caribbean in what was known at the times as "Gunboat Diplomacy." This is generally understood as the use of military threats by a super power against much inferior martial powers in order to gain control over the weaker countries' resources and to gain a compelling influence over the smaller power's leadership.

The U.S.A. has been practicing this—with air, sea and land power in the Middle East for decades now—with no end in sight. Whether the rampaging chaos, failed states, and widespread emigration of Arab populations away from their homelands is the intended result of the Yinon-Clean Break plans described before, or a superb example of The Law of Unintended Consequences, is beside the point. The point is that the "American Empire" is almost universally recognized as a principal engineer of this darkness with no light at the end of any tunnel.

A similar strategy and set of tactics was practiced extensively by the United States in Central America and the Caribbean from the first years of the 20th century to 1933. In today's geopolitical lexicology, according to the The Encyclopedia of U.S. Military Intervention in Latin America—(believe it or not) edited by the ConocoPhillips Chair of Latin American Studies at the University of Oklahoma—the term "Gunboat Diplomacy has been currently superseded by the more euphemistic phrase: 'power projection.' (McPherson, 2013, p. 262). In actual practice, there is little difference other than in the greater deadliness and sophistication of the weapons of destruction and the much greater numbers of non-Americans whose lives have been ended, crushed or paralyzed.

A brief history of Gunboat Diplomacy is in order. It was only by the backing of the U.S. armed force that insurgents in Panama had enough power to secede from Colombia in 1903 and thus make a deal with America to cede land for the Panama Canal. The United States also used its navy and land forces, in true Mahan-Teddy Roosevelt vogue in Nicaragua 1912-33; Haiti 1915-33; Cuba on and off up until 1933. The goal, everywhere, was to attain and maintain hegemony over its southern neighbors so as to be able to extract and export many natural resources cheaply at the expense of the indigenous people. There were invasions, repressions of insurgencies, and occupations. Let us remind the reader of how U.S. Marine Major General Smedley Butler, who fought in many of these battles and won two Congressional Medals of Honor, bluntly stated what was really going on: It was all a "racket" run by U.S. big business.

This original Latin American form of Yankee Imperialism, or Gunboat Diplomacy, was abruptly ended in 1934 by none other than Teddy Roosevelt's cousin, Franklin, shortly upon his assuming the presidency of the United States. Why did President Franklin Roosevelt, an ardent admirer of his cousin Teddy and the great geo-political theorist Mahan, decide to openly reverse decades of American military colonialism in that region?

Probably the most compelling reason at the moment was internal economic necessity. The United States was in the midst of the Great Depression and the money used for such nefarious purposes abroad could be put to better use to help FDR yank his country out of the depths of economic dysfunction that threatened the entire capitalist structure of the United States at that time.

Well, the reader might say, that's not a very altruistic, idealistic, spiritual or religious reason at all, it's pragmatic. We think it was all-of-the-above for the second coming of the Roosevelts.

Although one of the explicitly moral reasons given for pulling all American troops out of Nicaragua and Haiti in 1933 and 1934 was that America should no longer intervene and interfere in the domestic matters of any countries in Latin America, surely a noble purpose, there was a mutually beneficial materialistic motivation as well. Roosevelt knew America needed to rejuvenate the U.S. domestic economy and the whole New Deal was about that. The Good Neighbor Policy became an important adjunct to it.

In good capitalist terms, he wanted to develop friendly foreign markets and cultural and trade exchanges that would add to and supercharge the U.S. economy. That's what we have in mind for America and the Middle East—that entire region is ripe to become advanced and thereby contribute to bilateral trade, commerce and cultural exchanges with the U.S. and everywhere.

In some ways, it is similar in concept to Henry Ford's innovation of doubling the wages of his workers. Why did he do that? For one thing, it gave his small army of employees enough money to buy his Model T

Ford automobiles and created a significant market for this new assembly line mass produced machine. For another, it won him a dedicated, hard-working labor force.

A prime example of "The Good Neighbor Policy" in action was when the Mexican government seized American oil companies in Mexico in 1938 and converted them into the property of the Mexican government. One can imagine the fury of the American oil barons who had weathered a storm of Mexican oil worker unionization and protests for years before this dastardly act of Mexican "socialism" occurred.

If anything called for an ornate display of "Gunboat Diplomacy," this was it. However, under "The Good Neighbor Policy", FDR refrained from blockading Mexican ports or levying economic sanctions and instead negotiated an acceptable compensation for the takeover of American assets from the Mexican government. The oilmen got at least a half a pound of flesh and the U.S. didn't waste a lot of taxpayer money invading a foreign country, or leading a coup to overthrow it, so as to retrieve a huge monetary windfall for big private interests. The Good Neighbor Policy allowed Mexico to construct its own capital economy through oil revenues and become a more prosperous trading partner with America.

The Good Neighbor Policy intended and did make numerous other efforts to stimulate industry and commerce in the poorer nations so as to bolster the economy of the entire southern region of the Western Hemisphere. And it worked. Here is the way the *International Relations Center* in Washington, D.C. puts it:

> "*Being a good neighbor for Roosevelt and for Secretary of State Cordell Hull, had economic implications as well as security ones. Hull believed that a good neighbor policy meant offering U.S. markets for the region's exports. If political relations were to improve, the United States had to open its doors to the Latin American and Caribbean economy, according to Hull.*
>
> "*For their part, Latin American and Caribbean nations were eager to access U.S. markets for their agro-exports—such as sugar and cotton—and applauded Roosevelt's initiatives to lower tariffs and remove quotas. Working collaboratively, the U.S. State and Commerce departments launched a campaign to sign reciprocal trade agreements with all the countries of the hemisphere, and during the 1930s intra-regional trade boomed.*
>
> "*The trade agreements which we are now making are not only finding outlets for the products of American fields and factories,*" Roosevelt declared, "*but are also pointing the way to the elimination of embargoes, quotas, and other devices which place such*

pressure on nations not possessing great natural resources that to
them the price of peace seems less terrible than the price of war."

The *IRC* also notes that in the 1934-41 period, the trade between the U.S. and Latin America tripled. *(IRC*, current, see online link in References, emphasis ours). So how does that stand today, in 2015? According to the *Congressional Research Service:*

> *"The economic and trade relationship with Mexico is of interest*
> *to U.S. policy makers because of Mexico's proximity to the United*
> *States, the high level of bilateral trade, and the strong cultural and*
> *economic ties that connect the two countries. Also, it is of national*
> *interest for the United States to have a prosperous and democratic*
> *Mexico as a neighboring country. Mexico is the United States'*
> *third-largest trading partner, while the United States is, by far,*
> *Mexico's largest trading partner. Mexico ranks third as a source of*
> *U.S. imports, after China and Canada, and second, after Canada,*
> *as an export market for U.S. goods and services. The United States*
> *is the largest source of foreign direct investment (FDI) in Mexico.*
> (Congressional Research Service 2015)

All of this indicates that there can be a strong interaction between the withdrawal of American armed forces from an area of the world, correlated with an enlightened and mutually advantageous set of economic policies between America and its neighboring nations, which results in relative harmony and peace amongst them for a long time to come. So, what kind of military maneuver do we suggest might be an important first step in the Middle East that is similar to what FDR did back in the 1930s?

Putting this in the context of negotiations and economic interactions with Israel's neighbors in the future, the initial military facet of this second coming of "The Good Neighbor Policy" could be that America extracts all nuclear weapons from Israel as soon as it becomes the 51st state. This would be the death knell of "Nuclear Diplomacy" ("all options are on the table") and end the threat of nuclear war emanating from that region. Such a good faith gesture to change a long-standing, American-Israel bottom line position should satisfy the abutting neighborhood, as well as all New Eurasia, about the truly peaceful intentions of the United States as a friendly country in that part of the world.

Yes, yes, everyone knows about America's Trident submarines and the global span of its ever more stealthy stealth bombers, so negating nukes from Israel would have no effect on America's or Israel's core interest of existential survival. The nuclear pull-out from Middle East soil would be meant as a "goodwill" signal on the part of the United States. Let's call it a "symbolic retreat," much like the Good Neighbor Policy's transfer of American troops back to their bases in the U.S.A. in the 1930s.

The Supreme Leader of Iran, as well as many other important figures in the Middle East (especially Saudi Arabia) and world-wide, have long pleaded for The Middle East to be a "nuclear free zone," and this would be an American show of deference in that direction. Israel would not be in any worse situation by this action since as an American state, any attack upon it would require instantaneous retaliation by NATO. Thus Israel's security from military attack is assured without there being any nuclear weapons on or under its turf. Plus the U.S. would not have lost a millimeter of its strategic nuclear range.

Last, but definitely not least, there was a definite, strong, and traditional American spiritual motive behind The Good Neighbor Policy. The author and prime instigator of it was not FDR himself or any of his Ivy League "brain-trust". It was, instead, none other than FDR's wife, Eleanor Roosevelt. Mrs. Roosevelt was a devotee of what was called for some time in America, the "Social Gospel movement." As the religious underpinning of The Progressive Movement of the early 20th century, it had significantly altered the American "free enterprise" landscape to consider Jesus' principles in how labor and people in general should be treated humanely in society.

Dr. Sheila D. Collins, who was a political science professor and Director of the Graduate Program in Public Policy and International Affairs at William Paterson University (New Jersey) wrote that the American Social Gospel movement had embraced the teachings of Jesus Christ in order to transform the great injustices of the early stages of the industrial revolution in the United States. It held that society should be "organized on principles of justice where workers would be treated as valuable ends and not a means to a commercial end, and parasitic wealth and predatory commerce would be abolished." (Collins 2014, p. 4)

This spiritually based movement—in large part carried forth by American women—had profound effects on the social consciousness of government in the early part of the 20th century and supported such new policies as prohibiting child labor, establishing safe workplaces, the 40-hour work week, and government regulation of the food and drug industries. Later on, it had a profound impact on President Franklin D. Roosevelt and his concept and innumerable policies of the *New Deal* including such major social programs like social security and the legitimation of American labor unions to collectively bargain with capital.

So it was in this Christian social spirit that Eleanor Roosevelt helped birth and mother "The Good Neighbor Policy." Here's how *The Eleanor Roosevelt Encyclopedia* (2001) puts it:

> *"From the 1920s, until her death in 1962, Eleanor Roosevelt's in-teractions with Latin America were conducted in the context of furthering U.S. policy goals in the region. She served as a highly successful goodwill ambassador, and interpreter of Pan-Ameri-canism to the U.S. public, and was a critic of Republican interven-tionist policies in the Caribbean and Central America.*
>
> *"Eleanor Roosevelt's January 1927 editorial in the Women's Democratic News, "Our Foreign Policy: What Is It?" charged that there was no 'constructive effort' to build up 'good feelings with our hemispheric neighbors . . . and towards rethinking of U.S. relations with Latin America."* (Beasley, et al. 2001, p. 310, emphasis ours).

To remedy that deficit in traditional American Christian values, she worked intimately, diligently, and persistently with various and sundry Hollywood and New York media and entertainment moguls to get them to transform their negative stereotyping of Latin Americans into much more realistic and American friendly images. Conversely, this persistence paid off handsomely as the United States became to be viewed in a far more favorable light throughout Latin America and the Caribbean, particularly during World War II, when they greatly assisted in the American war ef-fort against Germany.

But it was not all Eleanor applying the pure teachings of Jesus that prompted FDR into executing his "Good Neighbor Policy". Indeed, Freder-ick B. Pike, a noted Professor of History at the University of Notre Dame, in his definitive study *FDR's Good Neighbor Policy* (1993) states:

> *"While some biographers maintain that FDR's concern with re-ligion was dictated primarily by expediency, others insist that he was profoundly influenced by the New Testament's emphasis on social responsibility . . . whether sincere or not, FDR did frequently draw on what appeared to be a biblical spirit as he stressed that social obligations must supersede mere private interest."* (Pike 1993, p.51).

We believe that it was in him to be sincere about this, given his entire body of political rhetoric and works. Jesus berated the rich all the time and made it a Christian mantra that it was the poor who, although they would always be with us, were his principal concern. So if one is a Christian, and studies American politics, then *The New Deal* is the closest American gov-ernment has ever come to heeding the words of The Savior.

Also, if one visits one of FDR's favorite spots on Earth, "The Little White House" in Warm Springs, Georgia, and goes to his favorite lookout nearby, one would understand the spirit of humbleness that had to be in large part a deeper motivation for both *The New Deal* and the *Good Neighbor Policy*. *The Good Neighbor Policy* was smart politically and economically—under the situation at the time—but also consistent spiritually in American terms with Franklin and Eleanor Roosevelt's personal American Christian traditional American religious beliefs.

The political-economic situation in the Middle East today is reasonably close to what it was like in the 1930s in Latin America. It is a crucible of desperation, depression and despair. Lebanon, Syria, Palestine, Jordan and Egypt are in extremely dreadful condition with unemployment among the youth in those countries reaching astronomical proportions. None of these nations are oil rich, but all are sun drenched.

Therein lies the exceptional promise for a better future for all humankind and where the United States (including its new state Israel) can excel at helping its new neighborhood prosper through a combination of renouncing military means and occupations, developing economic assets and markets, and inspiring spiritual brotherhood. Furthermore, this new Middle East America can assist monumentally the rapidly growing world population obtain solar energy at very low costs thereby transforming the global energy grid from being cursed with an overabundance of oil and coal but blessed by an even greater bounty of sunlight.

This is the nexus between the *Good Neighbor Policy* and *The Marshall Plan*. This is where America once again can become perceived by foreigners as "the exceptional nation"—as a Global Nation—as it was prophesized to be by its spiritual founders—and no longer be miscast as "exceptional" because of its Star-Wars-like military might.

As one of the, if not THE, leading nation that has helped catalyze disastrous climate change for over a century, America can help bring a new "light" to the world through its spiritual, industrial and entrepreneurial involvement in the Middle East in partnership with its only state there: Israel. After all, the leading Jewish prophets are also revered in Islam (Abraham, Moses and Jesus) and the Jewish people are world renowned for their intellectual, technological and commercial prowess.

The New "Marshall Plan": Middle East Edition

Mainly because of the overlapping set of competing megalomaniacal ideologies and strategic lunacies described at some length before in this book, a large part of the Middle East has been bombed into debris today . . . with heaps more ash and millions of cadavers in the offing. The tidal wave of refugees heading towards Europe surged in 2015, but there is little reason to think that it will get anything but worse in 2016 and beyond. This rising flood of Islamic migrants will most assuredly cause greater inner turmoil and escalating tumultuousness throughout Europe and probably well beyond.

As we pointed out in an earlier chapter, there is plenty of blame to spread around. Just like World War II, the carnage in the Middle East and Central Asia has been sponsored by current major powers like Russia and the United States, but Radical Islam and Radical Right Israel are more than willing and able partners in the massive massacres and wild fantasies of caliphates and promised lands.

Is it as bad in the Middle East today as it was in the aftermath of World War II throughout Europe? Well, if you look at the photos of all the demolished buildings and people living in the crumbled bricks of what used to be their homes, it looks pretty similar. True, the sheer number of people living in the rubble of Berlin, Warsaw, Leningrad, Dresden, Normandy, and throughout all of Europe was much greater than those scratching out existence in Aleppo, Fallujah, Mogadishu and Gaza right now.

But the contemporary immigration level from the Middle East and Central Asia is constantly being referred to as "the worst refugee crisis since World War II." So it's bad enough to be comparable. And it will only double or quintuple if the same kind of thinking persists among those presently calling the shots.

So how did the United States come to the rescue of an obliterated and prostrate Western Europe nearly a decade after World War II had concluded? Here is the short story:

With European capitalism in great disrepute among the European stragglers, strugglers and survivors, Western Europe had become a fertile ground for Soviet-style Communism to become the dominant political ideology and gain political-economic control of all of Europe. The Red Army was huge, flushed with victory, and a real and imminent threat to American forces still in Europe.

Something had to be done, and fast, to counter this philosophical and military threat to the now feeble European capitalist system. America was a close partner to Western European capitalism prior to and during that war and it needed Western Europe as a lucrative future market and major manufacturing supplier, as it had been throughout the early to mid-20th century.

President Harry S. Truman was well aware of this grievous and perilous situation and he decided to appoint a man he greatly respected, General George C. Marshall, Supreme Allied Commander in Europe General Dwight D. Eisenhower's top aide and confidant, to be his Secretary of

State. Here is the way the *George C. Marshall Foundation's* website explains what occurred:

> *"From 1945 through 1947, the United States was already assisting European economic recovery with direct financial aid. Military assistance to Greece and Turkey was being given. The newly formed United Nations was providing humanitarian assistance. In January 1947, U. S. President Harry Truman appointed George Marshall, the architect of victory during WWII, to be Secretary of State . . .*
>
> *"In just a few months, State Department leadership under Marshall with expertise provided by George Kennan, William Clayton and others crafted the Marshall Plan concept, which George Marshall shared with the world in a speech on June 5, 1947 at Harvard. Officially known as the European Recovery Program (ERP), the Marshall Plan was intended to rebuild the economies and spirits of Western Europe, primarily. Marshall was convinced the key to restoration of political stability lay in the revitalization of national economies. Further he saw political stability in Western Europe as a key to blunting the advances of communism in that region.*
>
> *Sixteen nations, including Germany, became part of the program and shaped the assistance they required, state by state, with administrative and technical assistance provided through the Economic Cooperation Administration (ECA) of the United States. European nations received nearly $13 billion in aid, which initially resulted in shipments of food, staples, fuel and machinery from the United States and later resulted in investment in industrial capacity in Europe. Marshall Plan funding ended in 1951.* (The George C. Marshall Foundation website, URL in References).

That *The Marshall Plan* was successful in achieving its goals even beyond its own wildest imagination is an almost universally held view. The prolific and esteemed Harvard and Stanford historian, Dr. Niall Ferguson, has praised its economic performance but added the emotional impact it also had on Europeans for America: "to West Europeans struggling to make ends meet, it was the most visible manifestation of American good will (Author's Note: the same phrase Eleanor Roosevelt used in relation to being a "good will ambassador" to Latin America)—and (was) a mirror image of the Soviet policy of mulcting Eastern Europe. This, more than its macroeconomic impact, explains its endurance in the popular imagination." (Ferguson 2007, emphasis ours)

So what did this finely tuned, thoughtful and humanitarian application of geo-strategic "macroeconomics" cost the United States at the time in actual dollars? Taking the Marshall Foundation's figure as being close to the mark, i.e., $13 Billion, what would that be in U.S. dollars in 2015 figures? According to Dr. Ferguson's calculations: "A Marshall Plan announced today would therefore be $740 Billion." (Ferguson 2007). Wow! That's sure a mother lode of money, but let's compare that to the size of the economy of the United States in post-World War II times and at present. Keep in mind, also, that in both of these time periods, the United States had run up quite a large war debt. So an analogy remains valid.

The way Professor Ferguson arranges the numbers, the $13 Billion that *The Marshall Plan* cost the U.S.A. was, get this: 5.4% of America's Gross National Product (GNP) at that time (1948-50). Gasp. That is quite a significant donation. How many people actually tithe 5% of their gross income to charities these days? But at the national level, in the United States of today, the real amount of ALL foreign aid is so negligible as to border on the despicable. And what is that paltry sum?

The amount America gave to foreign countries during the George W. Bush administration from 2001-2006—including the entire Middle East with most of that going to Israel and Egypt as mandated by the Camp David Peace Agreement—was—are you ready for this: 0.2% of the GNP of the USA, which is approximately where it stagnates today (Ferguson 2007). We call that a Jesus Slump. Jesus and the early American Christians would hang their heads in shame if they found out that almost all of their donations to Israel and Egypt that was a "gift", was in the form of military equipment they got directly or had to return these "grants" in deals to purchase big ticket items from the American military industrial complex.

So, for example, the U.S. gives about $1.5 billion a year to Egypt. For what? Here's what the *Congressional Research Service* reported about that: "The biggest chunk is military aid, averaging about $1.3 billion per year since 1987, with much of that military equipment. For instance, Egypt plans to acquire 1,200 M1A1 Abrams Battle tanks from the United States." (Plumer 2013). But that is miniscule to the amount of war equipment that the U.S. sends and has pledged to send as "foreign aid" to Israel over the years and into the future. Again, here is another, more recent *Congressional Research Office's* report:

> "In 2007, the Bush Administration and the Israeli government agreed to a 10-year, $30 billion military aid package for the period from FY2009 to FY2018. During his March 2013 visit to Israel, President Obama pledged that the United States would continue

> to provide Israel with multi-year commitments of military aid
> subject to the approval of Congress.

For FY2016, the following legislation addresses U.S. foreign assistance to Israel:

- *A draft House FY2016 Department of State, Foreign Operations, and Related Programs bill would provide Israel $3.1 billion in FMF as requested.*

- *H.R. 1735, the House version of the National Defense Authorization bill for FY2016, authorizes up to $371.2 million for various U.S.-Israeli joint missile defense systems including: $41.4 million for Iron Dome, $249.8 million for David's Sling; $34.5 million for Arrow 3, and $45.5 million for Arrow 2.*

- *S. 1376, the Senate version of the National Defense Authorization bill for FY2016, authorizes up to $372.4 million for various U.S.-Israeli joint missile defense systems.*

- *A draft House FY2016 Defense Appropriations bill would provide $487.595 million for U.S.-Israeli joint missile defense programs, of which $55 million is for Iron Dome, $286.526 million is for David's Sling, $89.550 million is for Arrow 3, and $56.519 million is for Arrow 2."* (Sharp 2015)

Doesn't sound much like *"The Good Neighbor Policy"* and *"The Marshall Plan,"* does it? People can't eat an Abrams tank and although we don't mind watching a football game under a dome, we'd hate to live under one with armed missiles bouncing off it. So, America is going to have to face up to the Devil-in-the-Wilderness on this one.

Does the United States of America continue to feed the Dogs of War in the Middle East (and call itself "exceptional" for doing so), or does America revert back to a more spiritual and truly Christian part of its history and become a far more righteous nation by applying some past successful practices of its national spiritual heritage like *The Good Neighbor Policy* and *The Marshall Plan*, to the new Middle East community it would be joining?

We don't think America and Israel have much of a choice here. And with this new political entity in their midst acting in a positive, pacific, and constructive way, we don't think their neighbors will be doing much complaining, much less any fighting, to keep this from happening.

Actually, someone has beaten us to the idea of applying *The Marshall Plan* correctly to the Middle East and environs and created a website, complete with a well-researched and carefully considered book called *Reawakening: The New, Broader Middle East* (2007). His name is Dr. Jerry Rosenberg, a New York University Ph.D. who is a Professor of International Business at Rutgers University. Dr. Rosenberg seems to agree with us that *The Marshall Plan*, though obviously fraught with economic, political ideological, and geo-political motives, was also—to a remarkable degree—the consequence of the more beneficent American spirituality.

For example, in his book, Dr. Rosenberg notes that: "Increasingly, Marshall warned that the choice was between good and evil, and that the U.S. had to lead the forces of good." (Rosenberg 2007, Ch.3, p.5, emphasis ours) The professor goes on to observe that President Truman, himself, was a man of deep moral convictions both in his own life and about the nation of his birth and success.

Recalling that Truman was from Missouri, Mark Twain's youthful stomping grounds, Dr. Rosenberg tells us in no uncertain terms that "Truman repeatedly argued that any country that had avoided physical damage to its land during the war was obligated to come to the assistance of needy countries. Relief was attractive, moreover the answer was that outright funding was required for reconstruction. Europe was to be remade by American power at its most intelligent and benevolent best." (Rosenberg 2007, p.86. All emphases ours)

So, given Professor Ferguson's estimate of a new Marshall Plan in 2007 dollars being in the $700-$800 billion dollar range, and that the amount of "bail out" money that was given to "The-too-big-to-fail-banks" in 2007-2008 was about the same, it wouldn't be too much of a leap of positive, peaceful, progressive "strategic planning" to suggest that the United States could spend about $1 Trillion in today's money on such a magnanimous venture. By the way, in contemporary fiscal terms, this would amount to approximately 5% of America's 2015 GNP, roughly the same percentage as the original Marshall Plan.

That is surely enough direct capital investment and capital reserve for borrowing to build an entirely new future-friendly infrastructure for the economies of South Lebanon, Southern Syria, and New Palestine that would simultaneously develop new technologies—available to the entire world—to deal with the inevitable rampages of Climate Change. Like what?

Without going into detail, since this is well outside our expertise, we can easily think of three major areas of futuristic, environmentally friendly, and Middle East-friendly manufacturing and commercial enterprises that would work wonders for that little corner of the Middle East with that new Marshall Plan money. It could put millions of people into productive, creative, ecologically friendly work and generate products, services and markets good for the future of the planet that as of now seems unattainable. Here they are:

The first of these would involve the manufacture, storage and distribution of Mr. Sunshine's infinite amount of blazing, searing and eternal flows of energy.

The second would be the invention, development and miniaturization of water desalinization, i.e., turning a dollop of the globe's seawater into bottomless reservoirs of fresh water that can be used for drinking, irrigation, industrial and residential sanitation.

The third is to turn the Gaza Strip in the Mediterranean's duplicate of Dubai.

The Middle East is Perfect for Gigi-factories Galore

Our preliminary research on solar generation, storage and distribution systems has shown us that the same issues and naysaying are being used to denigrate the value, efficiency, and economies of scale for solar photovoltaic systems and batteries as have been used for decades to deny even the existence of the looming threats of Climate Change now being felt strongly throughout the world. In much the same way and for the exact same selfish reasons, the oil-coal industry in the U.S. and elsewhere, and its well-paid, in-house scientific community, generate data to deny, or at least question, the need and viability of this carbon-free and ubiquitous energy source.

One of the hurdles they cite as being extremely hard to overcome is that in order to create vast arrays of solar "farms", enormous rows of sun reflection systems constructed on huge amounts of land with great and steady streams of sunlight, are needed. For the continental United States, this could be a great problem unless the federal government dedicates large parts of Arizona, Nevada, and Texas (by the legal process of "eminent domain") to bolster the new 21st century American solar power grid for the 'public interest.' This is a most politically unlikely event to occur in 2016, if not into the distant future.

In the Middle East, this is not a problem at all. In fact, in the Middle East, vast tracts of desert land are bathed most of the time in glorious sunlight and are available for just this kind of massive energy project.

Some studies show that in 2012, Germany and Italy alone produced over 50% of solar energy in the world with the U.S.A. and China only slightly above 12%. Nowhere is any Middle Eastern country shown to be producing more than 2%. It doesn't take a string theorist in physics to recognize that the solar-power industry is the wave of the future in green energy and that places like Jordan and the Sinai Desert alone could become the Saudi Arabia and Iran of non-carbon based electric power as quickly as the infrastructure can be built. This would leave the present oil deposits where they belong: under the sand.

Elon Musk, the brainy South African inventor and entrepreneur, is currently developing his first "Giga-factory" in Reno, Nevada, which will be producing electric batteries for his Tesla automobile, but also home solar-power packs that can be attached anywhere on a house or garage at very affordable prices, at least by American standards. But that price will decrease drastically as demand for it explodes. People everywhere want to "get off the grid" and be power self-sufficient.

By using *The Marshall Plan: Middle East Edition* for developing this essential industry in the contiguous area around the new American state of Israel, these new and present countries could become economic-energy powerhouses that will provide great educational opportunities and good jobs for countless Islamic youth. Additionally, this huge industrial base will provide inexpensive energy for all kinds of commercial, cultural and educational enterprises in that area.

Altogether, this collection of opportunities would offer a bright future on Earth to this teeming mass of alienated Islamic youth, instead of with Allah as Islamist martyrs.

In geo-strategic terms: this would be an ideal way to counter Iran's plan to "destroy" Israel and America, particularly their long-range presence in the Middle East, by wearing them down. Iran is presently putting all of its economic eggs into an obsolete energy basket, with oil and nuclear power being the foundation of Iran's domestic and export energy plans. One of these (oil) continues to fuel climate change and the other (nuclear) is fraught with unimaginable dangers (think Three Mile Island, Chernobyl, and Fukushima).

Germany is rapidly switching from nuclear to solar. China is also planning on a tidal shift towards solar leadership funded, of course, by its government. The New Marshall Plan for Solar Energy in the Middle East would put the United States in an excellent location to help the world reverse or end carbonization of our atmosphere and make the future look, pardon our pun, sunny.

Turning Oceans into Reservoirs and Deserts into Hydroponic Farms

There is another major infrastructure investment that this plan could finance that would inject a healthy dose of economic hope serum into the Middle East environs where the United States would be moving. One of the major problems facing the people who live there is their rapidly rising population with greatly dwindling water supplies . . . plus the generally arid nature of the topography there.

Thus, if a good part of America's New Marshall Plan investment into the Middle East was to construct ways to turn seawater into large reservoirs of potable fresh water, water to turn desert into arable land and to devise and build widespread distribution systems, then we could help convert that desert into a tourist and agricultural paradise. We are referring, of course, to the water desalinization industry which is already formidable. There are already thousands of desalinization plants around the world.

We are not going to write an exhaustive survey or analysis on the promise and problems in seawater desalinization around the world in 2016. Suffice it to say the following is a very brief introduction with some pertinent facts:

The current leader in this emergent industry just happens to be in the Middle East, Saudi Arabia. One of the strongest arguments against the desalinization industry at the present time is coming from various segments of the sustainable ecology movement which points out correctly that the amount of energy used—often carbon based—is part of the problem, not the solution. Saudi Arabia, of all places, is the site of the very first solar-powered desalinization facility in the world with it already being the leading nation in the world in producing fresh water from salt water. Desert land is a great place to incubate this kind of research and development for the future. Already 300 million people on Planet Earth use it to survive, subsist, and live a decent life.

Israel is not far behind the Saudis, and in some ways, leads the pack. Although it only has 5 desalinization plants online at present, it is a pioneer in inventiveness in this field. We've seen various estimates as to how much water used by Israelis today has been desalinated and the range varies between 25% and 50%. The modal guesstimate is around 40%. (Dubai gets 98% of its potable water from this process).

Israel's interest in this technology peaked a few years ago during a major drought that was combined with a shrinking of its natural water resources. This should be a wake-up call for the entire United States—with record droughts and wildfires becoming the norm, as they already are in California.

In fact, it is an Israeli company that is helping to build the largest desalinization plant in North America 35 miles north of San Diego that is scheduled to come online in 2016. That will add up to 5 or so for the entire California coastline at present. There are proposals for 15 more, which the continuing drought and disappearing snow pack in the mountains will undoubtedly bring to fruition more quickly.

So, we are not suggesting desalinization as a way America can help Israel, its newest state, get water for its ever-increasing population. No, the reverse is true. Therefore, this aspect of The New Marshall Plan is already based and well developed in Israel and is already available to help the surrounding countries new and old to remake their entire economies through this rapidly evolving technology—particularly the Green-powered varieties. (Cao 2015).

In other words, new ideas and methods have just begun to illustrate how this process can become consumer and ecologically friendly. International co-operative efforts are under way. According to Julie Pyper in *Climate Wire*:

"*While Israel's development of desalination has brought an end to years of living with water shortages, it is also opening doors for more peaceful collaboration with Israel's neighbors.*

"In my opinion, it's a big future also for our neighbors," Shlomo Wald, chief scientist at the Ministry of Energy and Water Resources, said of the desalination boom in an interview. "I think Israel is willing to assist Jordan, Egypt and even the Gaza Strip ... and hopefully in the future Syria and Lebanon. Water is a crucial commodity in this area. I think all our neighbors should look to this huge technological effort to make water more available to the region," he added.

In December, Israel, Jordan and the Palestinian government in the West Bank signed a major agreement to share water resources through desalination. Water produced from a new desalination plant in Aqaba will be divided between Israel and Jordan. The brine waste product will be piped north to the highly saline Dead Sea, where water levels are dropping at a record pace. Mekorot, Israel's water utility, will also sell up to 30 million cubic meters of desalinated water each year to the West Bank.

It's in Israel's interest to work with the Palestinians, 'because morally it's not healthy to have a thirsty neighbor and politically it's not healthy to have a thirsty neighbor,' said Eilon Adar, director of water research at Ben-Gurion University.

The Gaza Strip, home to roughly 1.7 million Palestinians, is also in need of new water supplies. Today, 90 to 95 percent of Gaza's sole water source is polluted, according to UNICEF. In addition, overuse and a drastic drop in rainfall have caused wells to dry out.

"The United Nations has cautioned against withdrawing too much groundwater in Gaza and called for the use of seawater desalination as an alternate source of drinking water. Yousef Abu

> Mayla, water expert at Al Azhar University in Gaza, said the only way to end the water crisis and realize a desalination plant in Gaza would be to set aside political differences and focus on exchanging expertise.
>
> We need more water, we need clean water," he said. "Climate change in the area affects our water resources and their quality as well. We have a growing population, increasing demand for water for agricultural purposes, industrial drinking, for domestic use for drinking purposes. We have to meet all these requirements with a regional approach, with cooperation and coordination."
>
> He added, "If we start to work together on water issues . . . we can improve the situation between us, between the Palestinians and Israelis. We cannot wait for the political problems to be solved." (Pyper 2014)

The efficiencies of scale provided via a monster stimulus by the American government's New Marshall Plan would provide momentum for a quantum leap in cheap, sustainable economic growth for that region and for the entire world, particularly for the hundreds of millions people today who have zero access to clean drinking water. With Israel already a cutting edge research dynamo in this technology, it will be able to help the rest of the United States itself, which has just begun to see what climate change is doing to California and the Southwest in terms of epic droughts.

As a new state, Israel would quickly be paying material dividends on its new shareholding in the United States of America as a partner with a lot to bring to the table, in terms of new sustainable energy and water enterprises.

Such a development in the Middle East, midwifed by the U.S. and its new state, would also be of intense interest and use for China, which is currently in the throes of an immense potable water deficiency and which could use all the help it can get from other countries and regions. After all, at this writing in 2016, China has already embarked upon a humongous desalinization program through which it plans to quadruple its desalinization plants by 2020.

New fresh water technologies, distribution systems and applications in inhospitable terrain could be an important avenue by which the United States can collaborate with China on "The World Island"—which as mentioned above— will be a gigantic power throughout Central Asia via its New Silk and Belt Roads. As the U.S. moves out of the central region of the World Island and settles into this small—but potentially powerful and useful—corner of the Middle East, China may well find the United States and its 51st state to be a major supplier of some of its most pressing needs, even greater than its present day insatiable appetite for oil.

Creating the Gaza Miracle

As Professor Adar of Ben-Gurion University said about the moral (and material) conundrums of having a "thirsty neighbor" in Gaza, it is probably at least equally true about having a hungry, desperate, and perpetually raging neighbor there as well. Add to this the fact that Iran—in particular—steams with rancor about the Israeli treatment of Muslims there and is pledged to do all it can to make Israelis feel as uncomfortable as possible for an infinite period of time (See Grand Ayatollah Khameini's website).

So what might be a good model for Israel to use to help develop (rather than deconstruct) the Gaza Strip which would diminish some of Iran's hostility towards Israel as the 51st state? How about Dubai and Doha? If the reader hasn't seen what they look like, just Google them and click on "Images".

Keep in mind (or Google) what Dubai in the United Arab Emirates and Doha in Qatar looked like only 20-25 years ago. Actually, they appeared to look pretty much what Gaza looked like before it was much more heavily damaged by the Israeli attacks in 2014. There was plenty of ocean, many decrepit apartment house blocs, over-crowded slums, and not much of a waterfront along the edge of the sea. The beaches were run down and the places for fishing boats looked rather seedy.

Today, Dubai and Doha are showcases of glittering, original, creative Islamic style high-rise architecture as well as various visually eye-boggling, aesthetically pleasing cultural and entertainment venues, including the only indoor ski run in the Middle East. The marinas are some of the most astonishing in the entire world.

No private investor or entrepreneur or any major entertainment or hotel company is going to plow capital into premier architectural gems on the Gaza Strip today . . . or tomorrow. With Israeli jets as likely as not to reduce them to dirt with Hellfire missiles, it would not be a wise wager. Equally certain today is that no European tourists are going to risk their lives to surf in the Mediterranean off of Gaza rather than take a few more hours to splash around in Red Sea resorts in complete safety.

But Gaza, as a major part of The New Palestine, is potentially an equally beautiful shoreline playground as Beirut or Tel Aviv, two Mediterranean cities that have thrived as ocean-side locales. As matters stand today, Gaza is mired in its post-World War II state of being, a consequence of geo-strategic conditions, not geographical or geological ones.

Once Israel becomes the 51st state and the New Marshall Plan is put into effect with New Palestine getting a huge part of that windfall, the Gaza Strip can easily become competitive with Dubai and Doha. In other words,

Gaza, which is much closer to Europe and the evolving Eurasian Economic Union, could be transformed into a dazzling jewel by the seaside. It has real potential to become a major economic profit center, as well as cultural and educational attraction for the New Palestine.

It does not take a genius to figure out that such a merger between Israel and the United States of America can produce entirely different prospects for all the people in that part of the Middle East. Constant fighting and haggling and military interventions, crossfires, and insurrections are making the lives of people in that region of the world increasingly miserable, to say the least.

With Israel being free from its nation-state insecurities in that region as the 51st state, it will also be free to help its neighbors grow into wealthy and grateful allies. Please do not confuse our practicality with naiveté. Good deeds are not usually met with a kick in the groin. Bad deeds are more likely to get that reaction.

The vast majority of Arabs, Christians and Jews are decent people who want to live peaceful and gainful lives. As we have said before, those are among the core interests of most of humankind This new arrangement of polities in the Middle East would present the populations of those nations with a much better chance to protect and appreciate them.

Islam, Christianity and Judaism are all religions based on tenets of peace. History has proved through time and in many places that all three can live in close proximity without there being constant war and harsh oppression of one against the other. (For a current example in Tunisia, see Hanley 2003, with link in References). What exists in Palestine/Israel now is a modern example of the downside of those religions fighting with one another, also with a good deal of historical precedent. But it is not written in scriptures or unprecedented in history that all can live together amicably and collaboratively as helpful neighbors to the advantage of all.

Israel becoming the 51st state, with America living up to some of the greatest manifestations of its historical "exceptionality", would be the perfect synergy to turn that tortured part of the world into a God-blessed one. America's 'Manifest Destiny" would have come full circle and become "Manifest Destiny 2.0" thus enshrining Jerusalem, and the entire surrounding area of the Middle East, as that prophesied "City on the Hill"—with its original denizens of Jews, Christians and Muslims joining hands on a shared Holy Land.

With Israel becoming the 51st state, the United States of America would lay claim to a new, admirable leadership status in human history. It would be clear evidence that America is willing to abandon its posture as just another empire, albeit the biggest and most fearsome ever. By casting aside that mantle, and cloaking itself as The First Global Nation, it would also avoid the inevitable fate of all of history's empires, i.e., that of collapse and failure.

By becoming an even more glorious nation in the eyes of the world, the new U.S.A. may well become ever more attractive to, and more willing to embrace, other existing polities (nations, territories, commonwealths) into its fold thereby extending its frontiers or rethinking its polity—yet again—well beyond those presently existing in the early 21st century.

Expanding, incorporating, redrawing new frontiers has always been the greatest challenge and opportunity for the American Spirit. Imperial hubris has always been among the worst enemies of the American people struggling towards liberty, property, happiness, and spiritual fulfillment.

Frederick Jackson Turner was right after all. The American Frontier did not need to stop at any geographic border. The American frontier is indeed a process. The peaceable expansion of America's border into this part of the Middle East would make the U.S.A. "exceptional" in its intended way and would become the next phase of America's truest "manifest destiny."

CHAPTER 7

Further Expansion of the Global Nation for the Global Good.

A S WE HAVE INFERRED throughout the body of this book, even though its title starts with "Israel," it is obviously more about the United States of America and the role America must play in the darkly clouded future of humanity on Planet Earth as the emerging Multi-Polar World Order begins to take shape. We believe we make that clear in the book's subtitle, that is, it is more about avoiding the disastrous fate of all empires and reinventing America's heritage as a truly *"exceptional"* nation, which it was when it was first so dubbed and which it can become again so long as it is true to its original purposes.

How? From what we have written above, clearly, we think a good start would be by becoming the world's first "Global Nation," with Israel as its 21st century linchpin, along with Alaska and Hawai'i as its 20th century predecessors.

In Chapter 3, we hope we left little room for doubt that we do not share Dick and Liz Cheney's re-definition of "American exceptionalism"—specifically as it has come to be widely understood as revolving around military power by many, if not most, Americans today—which they describe in great detail in their new book. (Cheney and Cheney, supra). We are not alone in our viewpoint, even among at least some "conservative Republicans" with unimpeachable academic and governmental credentials.

Dr. Paul Craig Roberts is a prolific author; a former under Secretary of the Treasury under Ronald Reagan; previously held the position of The William E. Simon Chair of Economics at Georgetown University; and is a person who has been affiliated with both the Cato Institute and the Hoover Institute at Stanford. His newest book *The Neoconservative Threat to World Order* (2015) goes into an ultra-fine detailing of all we've said above about the Neo-Cons: their political philosophy, their tactics, and their integration into, if not co-optation of, "establishment foreign policy." A quote from his personal blog exemplifies our agreement about how the misuse and militarization of the word "exceptional" has caused a lot of grieving around this world of ours.

> "If a country is "the exceptional country," . . . it means that all other countries are unexceptional. If a people are "indispensable," it means other peoples are dispensable. We have seen this attitude at work in Washington's 14 years of wars of aggression in the Middle East. These wars have left countries destroyed and millions of people dead, maimed, and displaced. Yet Washington continues to speak of its commitment to protect smaller countries from the aggression of larger countries. The explanation for this hypocrisy is that Washington does not regard Washington's aggression as aggression, but as History's purpose." (Address by Roberts in Moscow, 2015).

We have been in accord with Dr. Roberts on how the words "American exceptionality" can be interpreted by others as being condescending and even insulting to just about all other nations around the world. We also agree that the way it has come to be defined lexically today in America is extraordinarily two-faced and reeks of hypocrisy. This is because it is totally at odds with the man who, as we mentioned earlier, was the very first to claim America as being an "exceptional" nation, Alexis de Tocqueville.

Allow us, then, to elaborate further on the "real" meaning of American exceptionality, according to he who first wrote about it, and how it ties into what we hope becomes a new stage of America's expansion, what we have called Manifest Destiny 2.0, and how that can easily include two other polities eager to join the United States of America in the early 21st century.

Reconstructing "Exceptionality" and "Manifest Destiny 2.0" to Include Two Other New States

In thumbing through de Tocqueville's *Democracy in America* (1840), one is struck repeatedly by his veneration of special features of American life in the early 19th century which he found to be singular in world history up to that point in time.

It was the combination of local democracy—political and communal—plus a deep religious belief, a spirit of forging God's will into the frontier wilderness to make one's fortune, plus the general sense of equality among the citizenry, that were three essential elements of his American "exceptionalism." This was a country like none other before it in history, hence its exceptionalism . . . of wanting to do good for themselves and The Lord, for their community, for their nation, for the world to see and perhaps learn, i.e., an important spiritual and secular lesson to improve the lives of all humankind.

These were not just ideals, but common practices he witnessed personally. He saw what was missing and the flaws, but he empathized deeply with something "exceptional" in actual American ways of moving forward that warmly embraced and inventively applied those particular values.

He was particularly impressed by how those Americans who were born here, or those who came from foreign lands and adapted to American values, went into the mountains and forests with not the vaguest idea of the vast array of pitfalls, traps and hardships they would meet and try to overcome. Besides their picks, axes, wagons, guns and animals, they had a staunch belief in God's promise of a better life for them and their offspring in the land they chose to settle. It was a land that was unknown, virgin territory upon which tribes of nomads moved and resisted their advance. This was their divine challenge.

They knew hardship—even death—were ahead, but this did not deter them. Whether they went out from the cities or the less crowded areas, the vast majority of them did not go out to kill Native Americans because they hated them or wanted to "civilize" them. They went to put roots down on the land which they thought God had bestowed upon America. If the natives resisted with violence, they either got killed, killed them off, and either stayed put or trudged on. Give them a break. They were incredibly brave, "God fearing" people looking for much better life than the ones they left behind.

Thus, American Exceptionalism and Manifest Destiny were both in de Tocqueville's writing about his experience in the United States, although the latter concept was not coined until after he had returned to France. But he witnessed it. He experienced it. He was extremely moved by it. They all go together: rugged individualism collaborating with others; a desire to expand America's federation as God destined; an appreciation of freedom of religion; and a sense of brotherhood and equality. These are the warp and woof of "American Exceptionalism."

It was this unique blend of the Puritan view of Jesus's Sermon on the Mount plus the secular local democracy that accompanied it that were the key components to this totally different society that de Tocqueville spoke of so elegantly. It is this combination of factors that set America apart. It has zero to do with extending American military dominance throughout the world indefinitely at great cost to the lives of millions of people who have done America no harm, and at great cost to the American people psychologically, emotively and financially.

We realize all too well that the other concept that is combined with this view of early American history, i.e., that of "Manifest Destiny," is one that is linked in fact with the eradication of Native American cultures in the United States. That cannot be denied.

However, as stated above, these pioneers were more like refugees than warriors. They were frightened people who feared the future, had no past to which they were rooted or to which they could return, and were held together by their faith that they were doing God's will to find their own personal "promised land" in an unsettled frontier. That is what "Manifest Destiny" was really about, genocide of the widely scattered native tribes was the result, not the motivation.

And now, as times are changing so drastically and swiftly in this world of ours, we see that the positive values held by those who actually practiced "Manifest Destiny" seem to be beckoning to America once again . . . as long as the true spirituality and basic, authentic democratic values are the primary motivation of the expansionism.

It is politically incorrect to state outright that "Manifest Destiny" actually was a spiritually motivated movement. However, it was hardly an early American version of ISIS . . . an organized legion of warrior-invaders bent on conquering already occupied land and vanquishing all the infidels who lived there. Sure there were haters and killers like that invading the American West, but the slaying by most pioneers was mostly in "self-defense" or retaliation for slaughters perpetrated by the native inhabitants against those they perceived as invaders.

We do not advocate that Manifest Destiny 2.0 repeat the blunders, plunders and rationalizations of the past. They were aplenty. The idea here is to welcome various existing nations, territories or whatnot, who want to join the U.S.A. and thus expand its nationhood, its reach, its diversity, its global prominence due to America's most traditional and truly conservative values.

Nothing is carved in granite, or written on parchment, to say that the U.S.A. must be comprised of 50 states and no more. There is no law (international, constitutional, or divine) against more voluntary and positive growth of the margins of the nation—and particularly since there need be no "collateral damage" like there was during Manifest Destiny 1.0. So, why not?

Making Israel into another United State within a federal system is an obvious example of not only how this can be done in terms of better securing America's and Israel's future, but also for the resolution of the unending bitter and bloody conflict in the Middle East and the potential for that to precipitate a world destroying World War III. Israel becoming part of the United States would also be a spiritual re-combination of the original Zion with the New Zion, as the founding Puritans foresaw: Exhibit A of Manifest Destiny 2.0.

It is a historical closure that would bear witness to the power of Destiny. And, as we have described it in Chapter 6, the economic gain that would come from this New Global Nation for the entire Middle East region is not to be discounted as anything other than a major, mutual good for so many of the people living there now in penuriousness and woe. Furthermore, it would diversify our nation at just the right time and extend it from sea to shining sea again, but between much further seas.

There are two other obvious examples of how the United States of America can become an even greater Global Nation in the 21ˢᵗ century in every way via the use of the statehood mechanism to revitalize and improve on its "Manifest Destiny" and "Exceptionality." In this revision of them, there will be no ambushes, burning of villages, atrocities beyond comprehension on both sides, no need for self-defense or retaliation. The inhabitants of each of these new lands and polities must enthusiastically want to become part of The First Global Nation.

So, guess what? As we write, there are already two significant "American Statehood" movements alive and well. Both are bubbling in existing political entities where the native residents need a major economic, political, cultural and psychic boost that actual American statehood could provide them. Moreover, there is a certain amount of "destiny" involved in each of them, as well as the Buddhist concept of "good karma", should either or both come to pass. Neither would be about projecting more "American military power." Each would be gifting the American Dream to American citizens who want to dream the statehood dream too.

Puerto Rico: The U.S.A. of the Caribbean

We are not about to make an elaborate case for Puerto Rican statehood . . . or to dispute the wide variety of economic reasons why this would not be a good deal for the U.S.A. We have sound reasons to believe, though, that given positive economic incentives, Puerto Ricans living there now would rush to get on board The U.S.A Express. Moreover, we think that many Puerto Rican exiles living today on mainland America would gladly return to reconstruct their native islands into a place where they would be able to thrive and be an equal part of a much greater, global America.

We assume the reader knows the basics. The U.S. invaded Puerto Rico to free the natives from the Spanish in 1898. However, since then, Puerto Ricans have at best been second class American citizens who do not have and cannot vote for their own *bona fide* Senators and Representatives in Congress. Worse yet, Puerto Rico has been and remains dominated by large American economic interests to the great disadvantage of the vast majority of its people. This is the principal reason why a huge percentage of native Puerto Ricans have migrated from their sumptuous homeland for mostly low class digs in cities on the U.S. mainland, predominantly in New York and Florida.

This is one gorgeous archipelago, though it is mostly composed of one large fabulously gorgeous tropical island. We keep wondering why so many of the American "elite" salivate over the "business" opportunities in Cuba, but can't somehow see them in Puerto Rico. Cuba will never become a U.S. State (for reasons too numerous to mention) and enhance the American nation. For one thing, it's been controlled by a Communist Party for three generations. Why build it up and run Puerto Rico down?

After all, Puerto Rico is another magnificent island, albeit a somewhat further away from the U.S. mainland than Cuba, but it has unlimited capabilities of becoming the Pearl of the Caribbean and a U.S. state to boot. As such, it would be larger than Florida in land mass and somewhat smaller than Texas. Its present population of about 3.5 million would rank it 29th in the U.S.A.

As we said above, there has been a statehood movement growing there for many years, and there was an elaborate two stage referendum in 2012 where most Puerto Ricans who voted wanted to change their "territorial status" (54%). This majority group then voted on what they wanted instead and overwhelmingly chose U.S. statehood. There was hardly a peep in the U.S. media about it and most Americans know little to nothing of Puerto Rico's history or the majority's ardent desire to join the U.S.A.

To be perfectly frank, Puerto Rico is in huge financial trouble in 2016 (not unlike most American states today). It would be eligible to declare bankruptcy (like Detroit did recently), but is unable to do so by present American federal law. Since the future development of the world into a Multi-Polar framework will occur unless some Cosmic or Earthly catastrophe consumes us all, it makes perfect sense to have the United States extend itself into the crown of the Caribbean and have a majority Spanish speaking American state in Latin America itself. The trade, commercial, and cultural potential to this new U.S.A. would be enormous. And then, including Israel, the U.S.A. would extend from the Central Pacific through the Caribbean to the Eastern Mediterranean Sea.

This would also be a much deserved, ethical move for the United States to make to right past wrongs. It would be a giant step—since it is being initiated by the Puerto Rican people themselves—that is likely to impress people worldwide about genuine American "exceptionality" and come full circle geographically as Manifest Destiny 2.0. It also would place America in an excellent position to help lead all Caribbean nations toward a more stable and prosperous future throughout that region, including Central America and South America: *The Second Good Neighbor Policy* to all our Hispanic neighbors south of the United States.

Latin Americans could no longer say 'Yankee, Go Home" because the newest state would be Latino and Latina and the Yankee's home would be in their midst.

As for Puerto Rico's economy: this, too, would be a much easier investment for the U.S. government than bailing out all the "too-big-to-fail" banks in 2007-08 and a very wise investment for many private enterprises. In other words, it would be a righteous penance to "bail out their economy" and tithe some government stimulus packages.

Puerto Rico is currently about $70+ billion in the red, which would be small change in The New Marshall Plan. Among other things, the U.S. government could grant incentives to Puerto Ricans who fled their homeland for economic reasons to return and help rebuild and reinvent their society as a part of the USA of the Caribbean.

Responding to an article about the sorry situation in Puerto Rico today and how to remedy it, here is what Puerto Rico's sole non-voting "representative in Congress" had to say about its economic prospects and how best to solve them:

> "*Puerto Rico's unemployment rate has been higher than that of every state since at least the nineteen-seventies . . . The average household income in Puerto Rico has been about one-third of the U.S. national average. The root cause of these enduring problems is our political status. My constituents cannot vote for President and, while I represent them in the House, I cannot vote on bills. Each year, Puerto Rico loses out on billions of dollars in federal spending and tax credits that Congress sends to the states. To compensate for the shortfall in federal funding, Puerto Rico's government has borrowed heavily in the bond market, leading to the excessive debt (for which it is criticized). To overcome its economic challenges, Puerto Rico must become a state.*" (Pierluisi 2015, emphasis ours).

While we would favor this happening immediately and Puerto Rico becoming the 51st state as soon as possible, we do not think that will happen unless the whole issue of a multi-state addition—particularly including that of Israel—comes to the forefront of the American political consciousness, as was the case with the combined admission of Alaska and Hawaii in the 1950s. We think Puerto Rico's best chance would come if an Israeli statehood movement arises. America needs to see that the field of white stars against a blue background on Old Glory looks much better as a glowing and growing globe . . . like we have put on the cover of this book.

D.C.: The "New Columbia"

This, too, is a no-brainer. How about "no taxation without representation" for the citizens of America's capital city? They pay taxes but cannot vote for a genuine voting Representative in Congress. The District of Columbia has a population of approximately 700,000 residents, which puts it just ahead of Wyoming and Vermont and just behind North Dakota and Alaska. So, it would not be the least populous state . . . although it would be the smallest in size by a large margin, since it is only about 70 square miles. It would be, then, the only "City-State", sort of like Athens, in the U.S.A. and it is not a territorial expansion as would be Israel and Puerto Rico.

It would be, however, America's first black majority state just as Israel would be the first majority Jewish state and Puerto Rico would be the country's first majority Hispanic state. Thus, together, they make the United States of America a far more ethnically balanced nation in its demographics, more perfectly aligning America into the newly emerging Multi-Polar World as a "more perfect union."

Yes, the appalling fact that 700,000 Americans do not have the power to vote for real Congress-persons is something that needs to be remedied. Thus, there has been a long-standing statehood movement in the nation's capital city. Its starting point was probably in 1980 when D.C. voters called for a "constitutional convention" for "New Columbia". Such was accomplished and its result approved in yet another referendum by the citizens of D.C.

This was the first of a series of failed initiatives for D.C. statehood and there is no need to go into the irritating minutiae here. Unsurprisingly, the people living there are clearly frustrated and some local officials invited President Obama to a "town hall meeting" on the subject. He came and was the first sitting president to endorse D.C. statehood. According to the Associated Press account of his speech, he stated: "Folks in D.C. pay taxes just like everybody else; they contribute to the well-being of the country like everybody else; they should be treated like everybody else." (Associated Press 2014 as reported in *Huffington Post*, July 21, 2014).

There is a fatefully strong argument for including D.C. as a state, since the people who live there are approximately 50% black-Americans. So? Well, guess who built Washington, D.C. by hand, as slaves? Yes, the White House, the first building of Congress and even the original Supreme Court were all erected using black slave labor. So, there is a heritage aspect to this, a justice issue, and, yes . . . here's that word again: Destiny.

The freed slaves never did get that 40 acres and a mule. It might be seen as the right thing to do to give those who make up slightly more than a majority of the population of D.C. the right to run their own government, as a state, with 2 U.S. Senators and 2 Representatives who can actually vote in Congress.

The real reason behind blocking both Puerto Rico and D.C. from statehood is . . . the reader would never guess it . . . .politics. Both lean heavily Democrat in their electoral politics. This would give 4 new seats in the U.S. Senate to the Democrats and is not likely to occur unless Democrats control the presidency and both houses of Congress with substantial majorities.

Would Israel vote Republican? Who knows? But if so, its number of Representatives would far outweigh those of Puerto Rico and D.C. combined, although the Republicans would trail in the Senate through these three state additions by a score of 4-2. Adding these 3 new states should not have anything to do with partisan politics. This is a deal that needs to be done to make America a better, more racially and ethnically mixed, more just and peaceful nation.

From our point of view, once again, we do not think "New Columbia" will occur until the whole notion of the value of incorporating very unconventional states into the union becomes a hot topic. We do not think either Puerto Rico or D.C. will get to that stage unless the Israel-as-the-51st-state comes to some prominence in American politics. We might well be wrong, but if it happens that one of these others becomes the 51st state before Israel, that suits us fine.

As we said or inferred throughout this book, our fondest hope is a modest one, one consistent with the time honored conflict resolution practice of "brainstorming" out-of-the-box options when people get stuck into permanent impasses. We hope this book will at least start a serious discussion about what we consider important peaceful and positive political steps in order to strengthen America's influence for global peace and ecological sustainability in the world presently and unpleasantly unfolding.

In truth, America can no longer ignore the gathering storms coming at it at breakneck speed.

None of these new statehoods would raise national taxes, cause civil unrest, require another aircraft carrier, or be precedent to make Mars a state. All would make America into the largest country in the world geographically (14 time zones), make America the most diverse country in history, in short, to correct Donald Trump's 2016 presidential campaign slogan: they would, without a doubt, "Make America Even Greater Than Ever."

Epilogue

Will the Trump Presidency Alter the
Need for the New State Solution?

M OST OF THIS BOOK was written prior to the election of Donald Trump to the American presidency. A wealthy businessman with a global empire of hotels, resorts and other business ventures, Mr. Trump ran an exceptionally unconventional presidential campaign in the Republican primaries and against his Democratic rival, Hillary Clinton. During both of those campaigns, he made numerous radical promises as to how his presidency would make dramatic departures from past Republican and Democrat "establishment" policies. At the time of this last entry into this book, it is still quite difficult to see how any of his foreign policies and the impact of his domestic policies will impact the United States and its highly diverse population. However, we feel that enough of his White House staff and the composition of the Congress and Supreme Court has been put in place, to hazard a guess as to what ways, if any, the future course of American under a Trump Administration will make matters more favorable for the New State solution we have proposed.

At the end of 2017, we feel it is pretty safe to say that, if anything, the Trump Administration, in conjunction with Israeli political moves, has made it even more imperative that America seriously consider the option we provided in the 7 chapters of this book.

Bibliography

Albright, Secretary of State Madeleine, NBC's *Today Show* (February 19, 1998)

Andelman, David. *A Shattered Peace: The Price We Pay Today*. New York: Wiley and Sons, 2007.

Arango, Tim and Clifford Krauss, "China is Reaping Biggest Benefits of Iraq's Oil Boom," *New York Times*, June 3, 2013. http://www.nytimes.com/2013/06/03/world/middleeast/china-reaps-biggest-benefits-of-iraq-oil-boom.html?_r=0

Associated Press, "Obama on Statehood for D.C.: "I'm for It," as reported in *Huffington Post*, July 21, 2014. http://www.huffingtonpost.com/2014/07/21/obama-dc-statehood_n_5606737.html

Associated Press, "Former Israeli Spy Chief Rejects Parts of Netanyahu's Speech," *New York Times*, March 6, 2015 http://www.nytimes.com/aponline/2015/03/06/world/middleeast/ap-ml-israel-iran.html?_r=0

ASCE, "The American Society of Civil Engineers Report Card on American Infrastructure," (2013) http://www.infrastructurereportcard.org/grades/

BBC World Service, Global Poll (2013) http://www.worldpublicopinion.org/pipa/2013%20Country%20Rating%20Poll.pdf

Beasley, Maurine H., Holly C. Shulman and Henry R. Beasley. *The Eleanor Roosevelt Encyclopedia*. Westport, CT: The Greenwood Group. 2001.

Becker, Ted. *The Last, Lost Empire*. El Cajon, CA: National Social Science Press, 2nd ed., 2010. www.nsspress.com

Becker, Theodore L. *Comparative Judicial Politics*. Chicago: Rand McNally, 1970.

Bellan, Bernie. "Why Not Make Israel the 51st State?" *The Jewish Post and News (Winnipeg, Canada)*, (17th of Tamuz, 5775) http://www.jewishpostandnews.ca/opinion/920-why-not-just-make-israel-the-51st-state

Berlinski, Claire. "We Are the Children of Versailles," *New York Sun*, (2007). It can be accessed online at: http://www.berlinski.com/node/76

Bennis, Phyllis. "Hezbollah and Israel Call for De-escalation in the Golan Heights," *The Real News.com* January 30, 2015 http://therealnews.com/t2/index.php?option=com_content&task=view&id=31&Itemid=74&jumival=13095

Brown, Andrew. "Bush, Gog and Magog," *The Guardian (UK)*, August 10, 2009 http://www.theguardian.com/commentisfree/andrewbrown/2009/aug/10/religion-george-bush

Brzezinski, Zbigniew. *The Grand Chessboard* (1999)

———. *Strategic Visions*. New York: Basic Books (2013.)

Brown, Eric. "In Gallup Poll, The Biggest Threat to World Peace Is . . . America?" *New York Times,* January 2, 2014 http://www.ibtimes.com/gallup-poll-biggest-threat-world-peace-america-1525008

Bush, George W. Speech to Nation, September 11, 2001. http://georgewbush-whitehouse.archives.gov/news/releases/2001/09/20010911-16.html

Bush, George W. H. Speech to Congress 1990 on The New World Order https://www.youtube.com/watch?v=byxeOG_pZ10

Butler, Smedley. *War is a Racket.* New York: Round Table Press, 1935. For a free copy online in PDF form, go to: http://www.ratical.org/ratville/CAH/warisaracket.pdf

Canada, Mark. "John Winthrop" *Canada's America* (1999) http://www2.uncp.edu/home/canada/work/canam/winthrop.htm

Cao, Athena. "UNC Charlotte Grads Wave-Based Water Cleaner Make Splash in Paris," Charlotte Observer, July 6, 2015. http://www.charlotteobserver.com/news/business/article26200774.html

Carter, Jimmy. *Palestine: Peace Not Apartheid.* New York: Simon and Schuster, 2006.

Castillo, Mariano. "Puerto Ricans Favor Statehood for the First Time," *CNN,* November 8, 2012. http://www.cnn.com/2012/11/07/politics/election-puerto-rico/

Chomsky, Noam. *Crisis in Gaza.* Chicago: Haymarket Books, updated edition, 2013.

Clemmons, Steve. "Mitt Romney, George Marshall and Israel-Palestine," *The Atlantic,* October 8, 2012.

Cohan, D'Vera, Eileen Patten and Mark Hugo Lopez, "Puerto Rican Decline on the Island, Growth on U.S. Mainland," *Pew Research Center,* August 11, 2014 http://www.pewhispanic.org/2014/08/11/puerto-rican-population-declines-on-island-grows-on-u-s-mainland/

Collins, Sheila D. (ed.) *When Government Helped.* New York: Oxford University Press, 2014.

Congressional Research Service, "U.S.-Mexico Economic Relations," April 20, 2015. https://www.fas.org/sgp/crs/row/RL32934.pdf

Consortium of Defense Analysts, "Iran is a Terror Threat to the Middle East, Latin America and the U.S.A.," March 31, 2015. https://cofda.wordpress.com/2015/03/31/iran-is-a-terror-threat-to-the-middle-east-latin-america-usaere/

Deitch, Ian. "Israel Protests: 270,000 Demonstrate Against Rising Costs of Living," *Huffington Post,* August 6, 2011

De Tocqueville, Alexis. *Democracy in America* (1835). A good print edition is: New York: New American Library, 1956. The entire book is online at: https://www.gutenberg.org/files/815/815-h/815-h.htm

Dickinson, Elizabeth. "How the Multi-Polar World Came to Be," *Foreign Policy,* October 15, 2009. http://foreignpolicy.com/2009/10/15/new-order/

Elliot, Emory. "The Legacy of Puritanism," *TeacherServe, National Humanities Center,* March 14, 2015.

Fanon, Franz. *The Wretched of the Earth.* New York: Grove Press, Translation from the French version of 1961, 1963,

Ferguson, Niall. "Colossus: The Price of American Empire," *New York Times,* July 5, 2004a

———. "Collossus: Intimations of Empire," *New York Times,* July 25, 2004b

———. "Dollar Diplomacy: How Much Did the Marshall Plan Really Matter?" *The New Yorker,* August 27, 2007. http://www.unc.edu/courses/2010spring/hist/140/007/Documents/Hist140Spring2010Reader.pdf

Ford, Peter. "Europe Cringes a Bush 'Crusade' Against Terrorism," *Christian Science Monitor*, September 19, 2001. http://www.csmonitor.com/2001/0919/p12s2-woeu.html

Forenza, Eleanora. "EU-US Free Trade Agreement Risks Undermining Democracy," *The Parliament Magazine*, November 4, 2014. https://www.theparliamentmagazine.eu/articles/opinion/eu-us-free-trade-agreement-risks-undermining-democracy

Francis, Pope. "Encyclical Letter 'Laudato Si' of thre Holy Father on Care for Our Common Home. The Vatican: 2015. Online English version at: http://w2.vatican.va/content/francesco/en/encyclicals/documents/papa-francesco_20150524_enciclica-laudato-si.html

Friends General Conference (FGC), "FAQs About Quakers," (currently online at: http://www.fgcquaker.org/explore/faqs-about-quakers#Sacraments

Fukuyama, Francis. *The End of History and the Last Man*. New York: Basic Books, 1992.

Roger Fisher and William Ury. *Getting to Yes*. (1980.

Frymer, Paul. Building an American Empire: Territorial Expansion in the Ante-Bellum Era," Paper at University of California at Irvine Law School, 2010 http://www.law.uci.edu/lawreview/Vol1No3Articles/frymer.pdf

Garamone, Jim. "Joint Vision 2020 Emphasizes Full Spectrum Dominance," *Department of Defense News*, June 2, 2000 http://www.defense.gov/news/newsarticle.aspx?id=45289artment

Goldberg, Jeffrey, "Look, It's My Name on This: Obama Defends the Iran Nuclear Deal," *The Atlantic*, May 21, 2015. http://www.theatlantic.com/international/archive/2015/05/obama-interview-iran-isis-israel/393782/#Iran

Halberstam, David. *The Best and the Brightest*. New York: Random House, 1972

Hall, John. "The ISIS Map of the World," *The Daily Mail (U.K.)*, June 30, 2014. http://www.dailymail.co.uk/news/article-2674736/ISIS-militants-declare-formation-caliphate-Syria-Iraq-demand-Muslims-world-swear-allegiance.html#ixzz3k81lsQnF

Hanley, Delinda C. "Tunisian Jews Enjoy Religious Tolerance and Peace in Djerba," *Washington Report on Middle East Affairs*, December 2003, pp. 46-49. http://www.wrmea.org/2003-december/tunisian-jews-enjoy-religious-tolerance-and-peace-in-djerba.html

Harris, Dan and Barbara Walters, "Iraq War Raises Suspicions of New 'Crusade'", *ABC News*, 2001. http://abcnews.go.com/International/story?id=79573

Hasan, Mehdi. "The Two State Solution is Dead," *Al Jazeera*, May 27, 2015 http://www.aljazeera.com/indepth/opinion/2015/05/state-palestine-israel-zionist-150527070943455.html

Hatch, Nathan. *The Sacred Clause of Liberty*. New Haven, CN: Yale U Press, 1977)

Holpuch, Amanda. "Utah Judge Strikes Down Part of State's Polygamy Ban in Sister Wives Ruling, *The Guardian* (U.K), September 28, 2014.

Institute for Advanced Strategic and Political Studies. "A Clean Break: A New Strategy for Securing the Realm." 1996. Online at: http://www.informationclearinghouse.info/article1438.htm

Thomas Jefferson, *The Jefferson Bible*. Washington, D.C.: National Museum, 1895. Published online as *The Life and Morals of Jesus of Nazareth*. http://www.beliefnet.com/resourcelib/docs/62/The_Jefferson_Bible_The_Life__Morals_of_Jesus_of_Nazareth_1.html

Jerusalem Post, "BBC Survey Measure Public Opinion in 22 Countries, Places Israel in Company of North Korea, Ahead of Only Iran, Pakistan," May 17, 2012 http://www.jpost.com/National-News/Poll-Israel-viewed-negatively-around-the-world

Kamrava, Mehran. "Mediation and Qatari Foreign Policy," *The Middle East Journal,* Autumn, 2011) http://www18.georgetown.edu/data/people/mk556/publication-61175.pdf

Kasindorf, Martin, "Racial Tensions Simmer in Hawaii's Melting Pot, *USA Today,* March 6, 2007. http://usatoday30.usatoday.com/news/nation/2007-03-06-hawaii-cover_N.htm

Kennan, George F. (as "X"). "The Sources of Soviet Conduct," *Foreign Affairs,* July 1947.

Larson, Christine. "China Turns to the Sea for Fresh Water," *Bloomberg News,* April 9, 2015. http://www.bloomberg.com/news/articles/2015-04-09/china-embraces-desalination-to-ease-water-shortages

Mackinder, Sir Halford. Democratic Ideals and Reality. London: Constable and Co., 1919.

Macmillan, Sarah. "Israel and Palestine: Uneasy Neighbors." *Notre Dame Magazine.* (Autumn 2007) http://magazine.nd.edu/news/9762-israel-and-palestine-uneasy-neighbors/

Maltz, Judy. "Polls Show Israelis Strongly Oppose Iran Nuclear Deal," *Haaretz,* August 12, 2015. http://www.haaretz.com/israel-news/.premium-1.670835

Marx, Karl. *The Communist Manifesto* (1848) This can be found in full online in many places including: http://manybooks.net/titles/marxengelsetext93manif12.html

———. *Das Kapital (Capital)* (Volumes 1-4 from 1867-83). It is all over the web and you can buy copies of Volumes 1-4 on www.amazon.com .

Maurice, Jean-Claude. *Si Vous Le Repetez, Je Dementirai* (Paris: Plon Publishers, 2009)

Mead, Walter Russell. "The New Israel and the Old," Foreign Affairs, July-August 2008.

Mearsheimer, John J and Stephen Walt. *The Israel Lobby and U.S. Foreign Policy.* New York: Farrar, Straus and Giroux, 2008.

Mearsheimer, John J. *The Tragedy of Great Power Politics.* New York: W. W. Norton. (2014)

Megoran, Nick and Sevara Sharpova, "Mackinder's 'Heartland': A Help or Hindrance in Understanding Central Asia's International Relations?" *CA&CC Press,* Sweden (2005) http://www.ca-c.org/journal/2005/journal_eng/cac-04/02.megeng.shtml

Melanchthon, "American Military Occupation: The Rules of the Game, Part I." *European Tribune,* September 7, 2009. http://www.eurotrib.com/story/2009/8/23/114055/036

Middle East Facts website: "What Determined Israel's Borders After the 1948 War of Independence?" http://www.mefacts.com/cached.asp?x_id=10929

Morse, Jedidiah. *The American Geography.* London: John Stockdale, 2nd ed., 1792

Muravchik, Joshua. "A War with Iran Is Probably Our Best Option," *Washington Post,* March 13, 2015 https://www.washingtonpost.com/opinions/war-with-iran-is-probably-our-best-option/2015/03/13/fb112eb0-c725-11e4-a199-6cb5e63819d2_story.html

Nazemroaya, M. D. "Europe and America: Sharing the Spoils," *Global Research Online,* July 26, 2007. http://www.globalresearch.ca/europe-and-america-sharing-the-spoils-of-war/6423

Netanyahu, Benjamin. The 44 Second Deafening Silence by UN General Assembly on YouTube as rebroadcast from Fox News, October 1, 2015. https://www.youtube.com/watch?v=8uSYMHGdkPo

Noble, S. "Ayatollah's New 'Guide' Book on How to Destroy in the Name of God," *Independent Sentinel,* August 3, 2015. http://www.independentsentinel.com/ayatollahs-new-guide-book-calls-for-annihilation-of-israel-ally-of-the-great-satan/

Norton, Ben. "Inside a CUFI Summit: Christian Zionists Dance the Hora and Prepare for End Times in Washington, D.C.," *Mondoweiss,* July 31, 2015 http://mondoweiss.net/2015/07/christian-zionists-washington

Oren, Michael B. *Ally: My Journey Across the American-Israeli Divide.* New York: Random House, 2015.

Osman, Tarek. *Islamism.* New Haven: Yale University Press (2016)

———. "Why Border Lines Drawn with a Ruler in World War I Still Rock the Middle East, BBC (UK), December 14, 2013. http://www.bbc.com/news/world-middle-east-25299553

O'Sullivan, John. "The Great Nation of Futurity," *The United States Democratic Review,* Vol. 6, Issue 23, pp. 426-30 in the *The Making of America* series at Cornell University, https://www.mtholyoke.edu/acad/intrel/osulliva.htm

Parrington, Vernon L. *Main Currents in American Thought.* New York: Harcourt Brace, 1927).

Pederson, William. *The F.D.R. Years.* New York: Infobase Publishing. 2006

Pike, Frederick. *FDR's Good Neighbor Policy.* Austin, TX: University of Texas Press, 1993.

Pierluisi, Pedro R., "Left Unstated," Letter to the Editor, *The New Yorker,* May 4, 2015 http://www.newyorker.com/magazine/2015/05/04/the-mail-from-the-may-4-2015-issue

Plumer, Brad. "The U.S. Gives Egypt $1.5 Billion a Year: Here's What It Does," Washington Post, July 9, 2013 http://www.washingtonpost.com/news/wonkblog/wp/2013/07/09/the-u-s-gives-egypt-1-5-billion-a-year-in-aid-heres-what-it-does/

Postol, Theodore A. "The Evidence That Shows the Iron Dome is not Working," *The Bulletin of Atomic Scientists,* July 19, 2014. http://thebulletin.org/evidence-shows-iron-dome-not-working7318

Pyper, Julia. "Israel is Creating a Water Surplus Using Desalinization," *Climate Wire,* E and E Publishing, February 7, 2014 http://www.eenews.net/stories/1059994202

Rabinovitch, Ari. "Biggest Rally in Israel's History Presses PM," Reuters, September 3, 2011 http://www.reuters.com/article/2011/09/04/us-israel-economy-protests-idUSTRE7821OS20110904

Rai, Manish. "Independent Kurdistan Takes Shape," *Asia Times Online,* July 2, 2015 http://atimes.com/2015/07/independent-kurdistan-taking-shape

Reaboi, David. "Exclusive: First Translation of Khamenei's Book on the Destruction of America and Israel," *Iran Truth,* August 5, 2015 http://irantruth.org/exclusive-first-translation-of-khameinis-new-book-on-the-destruction-of-america-israel

Reeves, Richard. "It's Time to Make Israel the 51st State," *Seattle Times,* September 19, 1991. http://community.seattletimes.nwsource.com/archive/?date=19910919&slug=1306331

Roberts, Paul Craig. *Address to Russian Academy of Sciences and The Moscow State Institute of International Relations,* Moscow, February 25, 2015. http://www.paulcraigroberts.org/2015/02/26/neoconservative-threat-world-order-paul-craig-roberts/

———. *The Neoconservative Threat to World Order.* Clarity Press, 2015.

Roosevelt, Theodore. *The Winning of the West.* New York: Putnam, 1893, 1906).

Rosenberg, Jerry. *Reawakening: The Newer, Broader Middle East.* Lanham, MD: Rowman and Littlefield; University Press of America, 2007)

Philip Roth, *The Plot Against America.* New York: Houghton Mifflin, 2004.

Rudolf, Moritz. "China's 'Silk Road' Initiative Is at Risk of Failure," *The Diplomat,* September 24, 2015. http://thediplomat.com/2015/09/chinas-silk-road-initiative-is-at-risk-of-failure/

Rumley, Grant and Amir Tibon, "The Death and Life of the Two-State Solution," *Foreign Affairs,* July/August 2015. https://www.foreignaffairs.com/articles/israel/2015-06-16/death-and-life-two-state-solution

Sage, Henry J. *U.S History 1607-1865.* "The Puritans of New England," Extended Learning Institute, North Virginia Community College, Third Edition (2010) http://sageamericanhistory.net/colonial/topics/puritannewengland.htm

Sampathkumar, Mythili. "Donald Trump to Announce $350 Billion Arms Deal with Saudi Arabia—one of the Biggest in History," Independent (UK), May 17, 2017. http://www.independent.co.uk/news/world/americas/us-politics/trump-saudi-arabia-arms-deal-sale-arab-nato-gulf-states-a7741836.html

Savir, Uri. "Could Jordan-Palestine Confederation Be in the Cards?" *Al-Monitor, Israel Pulse,* May 2015. http://www.al-monitor.com/pulse/originals/2015/05/israel-palestine-jordan-confederation-diplomatic-solution.html

Schiff, Stacy. "The Witches of Salem," *The New Yorker,* September 7, 2015.

Sharp, Jeremy M. "U.S. Aid to Israel," June 10, 2015. *Congressional Research Service,* CRS 7-5700 http://fas.org/sgp/crs/mideast/RL33222.pdf

Shishtreet, Shimon. "Human Rights in Israel: Freedom of Religion" *Jewishvirtualhistory.org* (current)

Sizer, Stephen. "The Theology of the Land", *The Balfour Project,* online at: http://www.balfourproject.org/the-theology-of-the-land/

Lee Smith. "Friend or Foe in Syria?" The Weekly Standard, March 2, 2015. http://www.weeklystandard.com/articles/friend-and-foe-syria_859648.html

Smith, Richard. "China's Communist Capitalist Ecological Apocalypse," *Truthout,* June 21, 2015 http://www.truth-out.org/news/item/31478-china-s-communist-capitalist-ecological-apocalypse

Smith-Spark, Laura and Youssuf Basil, "Iran's Supreme Leader Vows No Change in Relations with 'Arrogant' US," *CNN,* July 19,2015. http://www.cnn.com/2015/07/18/middleeast/iran-us-relations-khamenei/

Speckhard, Anne. *Talking to Terrorists.* McLean, Va. Advances Press, 2012

———. "End Times Brewing," *Huffington Post,* June 20, 2014. http://www.huffingtonpost.co.uk/anne-speckhard/isis-iraq_b_5541693.html

Spyer, Jonathan. "Behind the Lines: Hezbollah, Iran, Syria Join Forces Near New Golan Heights 'Buffer Zone," Jerusalem Post, February 14, 2015. http://www.jpost.com/Arab-Israeli-Conflict/Behind-the-Lines-Hezbollah-Tehran-Assad-join-forces-against-buffer-zone-near-the-Golan-Heights-390903

Spykman, Nicholas. America's Strategy in World Politics: *The United States and the Balance of Power*. New York: Harcourt, Brace. 1942

———. *Geography of the Peace*. New York: Harcourt, Brace. 1944

Sumner, William Graham. "The Forgotten Man." *Harpers*, 1893. http://www.swarthmore.edu/SocSci/rbannis1/AIH19th/Sumner.Forgotten.html

———. "The Conquest of the United States by Spain," *Yale Law Journal*, 1899. Reprinted online by The Molinari Institute at: http://praxeology.net/WGS-CUS.htm

Taheri, Amir. "Iran Publishes Book on How to Outwit US and Destroy Israel," *New York Post*, August 1, 2015 http://nypost.com/2015/08/01/iran-publishes-book-on-how-to-outwit-us-and-destroy-israel/

Times of Israel Staff and Agence Press France, "Iran Rules Out Diplomatic Ties With 'Illogical' US," *The Times of Israel*, August 24, 2015 http://www.timesofisrael.com/iran-rules-out-diplomatic-ties-with-illogical-us

Times of Israel Staff, "Full Text of UNHRC Resolution on Gaza War Probe," July 3, 2015 http://www.timesofisrael.com/full-text-of-unhrc-resolution/

Totten, Michael J. *The Road to Fatima Gate*. New York: Encounter Books, 2011.

Tretmann, Nina. "Western Firms Bet Big on China's Billion Dollar Infrastructure Project," *Fox Business News*, May 14, 2017. http://www.foxbusiness.com/features/2017/05/14/western-firms-bet-big-on-chinas-billion-dollar-infrastructure-project.html

Trotta, Daniel. "Cost of War at Least $3.7 Trillion and Counting," *Reuters*, June 29, 2011 http://www.reuters.com/article/2011/06/29/us-usa-war-idUSTRE75S25320110629

Turner, Frederick Jackson. *The Frontier in American History*. NY: Henry Holt and Company, 1921)

———. "The Significance of the Frontier in American History," Paper delivered to *American Historical Association*, Chicago, 1893. Here is its online version from the *University of Virginia*: http://xroads.virginia.edu/~Hyper/TURNER/chapter1.html

Twain, Mark. "The War Prayer," in *Europe and Elsewhere*. New York: Harper and Brothers, 1923. To read it online go to www.warprayer.org

United States Energy Information Administration (EIA), "China Brief." May 15, 2015, http://www.eia.gov/countries/analysisbriefs/China/china.pdf.

University of Virginia Crossroads Online Archive, "Penn and the Indians" (current) http://xroads.virginia.edu/~cap/penn/pnind.html

Washinton, George. "Farewell Address" 1796. Full text at Avalon Project, Yale Law School, online at: http://avalon.law.yale.edu/18th_century/washing.asp

Watts, Jonathan. "Argentina Leader Leaves Controversial Legacy with Patagonia Project," *The Guardian (U.K.)*, December 1, 2015 http://www.theguardian.com/world/2015/dec/01/argentina-president-cristina-fernandez-de-kirchner-patagonia-hydroelectric-dam-project

Weber, Max. *The Protestant Ethic and the Spirit of Capitalism*. Germany 1905 and London: Unwin and Hyman, 1930.

Weitz, Gidi. "Nuclear, Iran Is Waiting for the World to be Paralyzed," *Haaretz*, January 16, 2015 http://www.haaretz.com/news/diplomacy-defense/.premium-1.637528

Whittier, John Greeleaf. "Song of the Vermonters 1779" (The complete poem can be found online in *Wikipedia* at https://en.wikipedia.org/wiki/The_Song_of_the_

Vermonters,_1779 It was published anonymously in 1836 but acknowledged by Whttier later in his life.)

Wikipedia. "A Clean Break" (This post presents a large part of the verbatim strategy which is very difficult to find in its complete original form online.) https://en.wikipedia.org/wiki/A_Clean_Break:_A_New_Strategy_for_Securing_the_Realm#Contents

Wilson, Woodrow. *Addresses of President Wilson..* 66th Congress, Senate Document 120, Washington, D.C.: Government Printing Office. For online quotes see: https://en.wikiquote.org/wiki/Woodrow_Wilson

Wise, John. *A Vindication of the Government of New England Churches..* (1717, 1772.)

Wolfe, Tom. *Bonfire of the Vanities* 1984

Wong, Andrea. "A 4 Trillion Force from China that Helps the Euro Now Hurts It," *Bloomberg News*, July 21, 2015. http://www.bloomberg.com/news/articles/2015-07-22/a-4-trillion-force-from-china-that-helped-the-euro-now-hurts-it

Wyatt-Brown, Bertram. "The Ironies of W. E. Lawrence's Relevance and Reputation," Paper given at The Historical Society Meeting, Baltimore, 2008. http://www.cliohistory.org/fileadmin/files/lowell-thomas/legacy-section/B.WyattBrown.pdf

Yinon, Oded. "A Strategy for Israel in the 1980s" as translated and edited by Israel Shahak online as "The Zionist Plan for the Middle East" at http://www.informationclearinghouse.info/pdf/The%20Zionist%20Plan%20for%20the%20Middle%20East.pdf

Zahran, Mudar. "Jordan is Palestinian," *The Middle East Quarterly*, Winter 2012, pp. 3-12 http://www.meforum.org/3121/jordan-is-palestinian

Zartman, William. *Ripe for Resolution.* New York: Oxford University Press, 1885, 1989).

Index